MURDER
AT THE MET

Books by David Black

MURDER AT THE MET

David Black

Based on the exclusive accounts of
Detectives Mike Struk and Jerry Giorgio
of how they solved the Phantom
of the Opera Case

THE DIAL PRESS
Doubleday & Company, Inc.
GARDEN CITY, NEW YORK
1984

Library of Congress Cataloging in Publication Data
Black, David, 1945–
  Murder at the Met.
  1. Murder—New York (N.Y.)—Case studies. 2. Mintes,
Helen Hagnes, d. 1980. 3. Victims of crimes—New York
(N.Y.)—Case studies. 4. Crimmins, Craig. 5. Crime and
criminals—New York (N.Y.) 6. Metropolitan Opera
(New York, N.Y.) I. Title.
HV6534.N5B56 1984   364.1'523'097471   84-7079
ISBN 0-385-27852-7

Published by The Dial Press

For *Deborah* and *Susannah*

ACKNOWLEDGMENTS

In some cases, especially involving suspects, I have changed names and identifying descriptions of people to protect their privacy. All direct quotes come from official records, newspaper accounts, or interviews with the people being quoted. With a few exceptions, if I was not able to verify a quote with the person who allegedly said the words, I have dropped the quotation marks. I have edited some transcripts for grammar, continuity, and dramatic effect; but in doing so I have been careful not to change the meaning. In a few instances, where there was a self-evident mistranscription, I have corrected the language.

I would like to thank the Met investigation team, particularly Leo Rosenthal, Brian Connell, Juan Medina, Pat Heaney, James McVeety, Wiley Bergan, and Roger Hayes. I also would like to thank Richard Dienst for his part in putting this project in motion. I owe a great debt to Jay Acton, who first brought the case to my attention, to Harry Stein and Priscilla Turner, Meg Blackstone, Naomi Black, William O'Rourke, Lewis Cole, and Bob Ward for their good advice, and to Joyce Johnson, who once more has done a sensitive and thorough job of editing.

Mike Struk and Jerry Giorgio spent hours answering questions and going over details of the case. Often these sessions were held after work when they normally would have been on their way home. Despite what must have been a great inconvenience, neither of them ever betrayed any impatience. I must thank them for their patience, generosity, candor, and trust.

D.B.

Moosbrugger was a carpenter, a big broad-shouldered man . . . with hair like brown lamb's-skin and harmless-looking great fists. His face also expressed goodhearted strength and the wish to do right. . . . One stopped as though rooted to the spot, when for the first time one encountered this face so blessed by God with all the signs of goodness. . . . For Moosbrugger had killed a . . . woman . . . in a horrifying manner. Even when the facts had scarcely become publicly known Moosbrugger's . . . excesses had been felt to be "something interesting, for once" by thousands of people. . . . Although indeed one sighed over such a monstrosity, one was inwardly more preoccupied with it than with one's own affairs. Indeed, it was quite likely to happen that some staid assistant under-secretary or bank-manager would say to his sleepy wife as they were going to bed: "What would you do now if I were a Moosbrugger?"

Robert Musil
The Man Without Qualities

PART ONE

1

HELEN HAGNES MINTIKS'S NAKED and bound body was not found until eleven hours after she left the orchestra pit at the Metropolitan Opera to take a break. The performance that night, Wednesday, July 23, 1980, was the Berlin Ballet with guest stars Valery Panov, his wife Galina Panova, and Rudolf Nureyev, all Russian defectors who had become celebrities. The second ballet on the evening's bill, the pas de deux from *Don Quixote*, danced by Panov and Panova, ended at nine twenty-nine. Helen put her violin under her chair. The orchestra was not needed for the next act, *"Five Tangos,"* which was performed to taped music.

Helen, a free-lance violinist, was thirty years old. She had grown up on a dairy and poultry farm in Aldergrove, British Columbia, about half an hour's drive east of Vancouver. At two, she could play the piano by ear. By three, she was winning prizes. Her parents drove her forty-four miles to her first violin lessons.

Music must have been an escape, the magic that could rescue her from the dull routine of chores: haying or cleaning out the chicken coop. Sometimes, she'd go right from the fields to an elegant home in Vancouver to perform. Her father would drop her a block from the driveway, so he wouldn't embarrass her with their old pickup truck. To hide the smell of manure, she'd pour her mother's perfume over her hands.

She won a scholarship to Western Washington University and went to New York City to study at the Juilliard School of Music from which she received her Bachelor's and Master's degrees. The Chigiana Academy in Siena, Italy. The Institute for Advanced Musical Training in Montreux, Switzerland. Scholarships were her passport into the world of art. She worked with the best teachers: Zino Francescatti, Nathan Milstein. . . . At a summer arts camp in Montreal, she met an American sculptor, Janis Mintiks, whom she married in the autumn of 1976.

Like many child prodigies, Helen seemed trapped by her youth, as though her body were unwilling to give up the advantage of seeming precocious. Her cheeks and chin kept a suggestion of baby fat. In photographs, when she posed with her violin, she often looked childlike: a bubbly kid trying hard to appear serious, betrayed by the crimp of a smile.

She was cute rather than beautiful, but her cuteness was relieved by ambition, which sharpened her features. In the center of her face, the lines of her eyebrows and nose formed a perfect Y as hard-edged as the cutout in an old New York City subway token. If there was a hint that her face might be quick to narrow into anger—a tightness to her forehead and a stubborn set to her jaw—it was nevertheless likable, generous in its proportions.

What might shock someone into staring at her, however, was her hair: a Goldilocks mass, blond, long, curly, which seemed incandescent, as though it were about to burst into flames.

Helen had planned to duck out during her break to get a quick drink with another violinist, Alice Montoya; but in the women's locker room she told Alice she wasn't feeling well. And she had to talk to Panov. She went up one flight to stage level, looking for Panov's dressing room.

About a quarter of an hour after she'd left the pit—at nine forty-five—Helen was walking away from the area where the stars' dressing rooms were, down a corridor that passed behind the stage. She was accompanied by a man, who seemed to be discussing something with her. They turned a corner and saw a ballerina, dressed in practice leotards, who was waiting for an elevator.

Helen stopped next to the ballerina and chattered away, animated, almost frenzied. She didn't know her way around that part of the building, she said. Was the ballerina performing that night? Was Panov busy? Would it be a good time to talk to him?

The man stood slightly behind Helen, saying nothing, but somehow part of the conversation. The elevator came. The ballerina pushed the button for C level, the third basement.

"Now which floor do I have to go to?" Helen said.

The man said either "Second" or "Third floor." He may even have pressed the button. Helen looked at him.

When the elevator door closed, Helen began chattering to the ballerina again. She didn't want to bother Panov. She knew how busy he must be. Did he speak English?

The elevator stopped at C level. The ballerina got off and went to a rehearsal hall. Helen moved to the back of the elevator. The door closed. She was alone with the man.

The elevator rose. The man said something rude to Helen. She slapped him.

Once, when she was in Italy, Helen had escaped being raped by convincing the rapist that she had VD. Another time, when someone grabbed her pocketbook, she ran after the man, caught him, and fought until she got it back. She was tough and resourceful, not someone who would give up or go along with an attacker easily.

In the elevator, the man must have done something that scared Helen enough to make her do what he said. At the second floor, he took her off the elevator and led her from one side of the building to the other down a dark corridor. The right-hand wall was lined with racks of costumes, which were shrouded with pale dust covers. The floor was silent except for the distant hum of the huge air-conditioner fans on the roof. At the end of the corridor, they turned right, passed another elevator, and went through a door into a stairwell.

The stairs were wide, twice the width of stairs in a house, which made them seem queer, something out of *The Cabinet of Dr. Caligari* or one of Piranesi's dizzying dungeons. They must have been hard to walk down. Given the width of the treads, Helen must have expected the risers to be taller. But the proportions were peculiar. Each step must have come as a shock.

The man walked Helen down five flights—from the second floor to the first floor to A level, where the stairs narrowed and the walls seemed to close in. Down to B level and finally C level. They stopped in the small landing on the bottom, a space about eight feet by five feet, the size of a cell. It was dark, dirty. There was a scrawl—"Fat Louie Sucks"—on one wall. Against another wall leaned a folding chair, which like everything else must have seemed vaguely threatening, its possible uses obscene and brutal. There was a shut door and around its knob, some rope.

Helen screamed. She tried to slug the man. He grabbed her hands and when he couldn't silence her pulled out his hammer. He threatened to hit her. She stopped screaming. He told her to strip. She did—probably unable to drag her eyes away from the hammer. She was tan except where she'd been covered by a two-piece bathing suit. Her legs were shaved up to her thighs, where there were long downy hairs. She was in the last days of her period. Terrified, she took out her tampon.

The man told her to lie down. She did. Even in the summer, the floors were cold. And on the C level, they were gritty. Looking up, Helen would have seen a pipe passing through the ceiling to the level above and the ceiling itself with smudges on it like scuff marks from shoes, as though it were the floor and the floor were the ceiling, a dizzying perspective.

The man, who was probably dressed, only his fly unzipped or at most his pants pulled down to his knees, lay on top of her. He tried to enter her, but couldn't. So he rubbed against her, between her legs, until he came. He stood, told her to dress. She gathered up the things strewn around the floor—blue panties, pink bra, black slip, black jersey, and black skirt—and put them on.

What happens after a rape or attempted rape? The rapist runs. But what if he doesn't run? What does he do next? What else could he do to her? Panic hollows out the heart and, when you're forced to admit the incredible is happening, can make you laugh as easily as cry—or shock you silent. The mind skitters around, looking for an out, a loophole. This can't be happening. Not to me. You try to make bargains: all right, rudeness but not pain; pain but not rape; rape or attempted rape but that's all. It wasn't even a rape. He didn't enter. Just that, and I won't complain. I'll be grateful if it is just that.

The man told Helen to walk upstairs. She did. He followed. They retraced their steps: C level to B level to A level to the first floor. Through the door and down a hall was the stage. Beyond the stage was the audience. Hundreds of people—who could help her if she could only reach them.

Second floor. Third floor. The stairs can seem endless, like stairs in a dream.

On the third-floor landing, on the other side of a door, a

radio was broadcasting a baseball game. How wonderful the ordinary drone of the announcer must have sounded—life going on as usual, nothing tragic, only the dull routine of a typical evening—and how terrible it must have been to be shut off from it. Helen ran to the door and pulled. It was locked. She must have kept pulling and pulling, hoping that it would open. Pleading, praying that it would open.

The man grabbed her. They struggled. A flower and some bobby pins fell from her hair, a pen spilled from her pocketbook. The man shoved Helen and said, "Keep walking upstairs."

With every flight, the roar of the air-conditioner fans grew louder. On the sixth floor, the man made Helen go through a door, past an air-shaft that plunged down floor after floor, where the sound of the fans was like an approaching subway train, through another door and onto the fan roof, where the noise was deafening.

The roof smelled wet, moldy. The floor was gravelly. They walked down a short hall, past a crate stuffed with rags, past a metal ladder set into the wall, which seemed to go nowhere—one more escape cut off—around a corner onto the main part of the fan room, which looked like a penitentiary yard, an enclosure formed on one side by the wall of the building and on the other three sides by a two-story rampart with a metal walk running along the top. Through narrow dirty windows in the ramparts, Helen could have seen the lights of the city: to the south, Times Square, lower Manhattan, the World Trade Towers; to the north, the Upper West Side. The city stretching out below—which could be seen but which couldn't see in—gave the roof a secret feeling, like a child's tree house.

Along the base of each rampart was a rectangular pit the size of a mass grave; in each pit, set below the level of the roof, were the air-conditioner fans: two smaller ones on each side and four larger ones along the back. The fans looked like great concrete cakes. Inside were propellers with blades the size of a man. Unmoored, one of the propellers once spun into the sky, crashing to the street below.

Along the wall of the building, running half the length of the roof, was a pipe as thick around as Helen. Another pipe, perpendicular to the first, came out of the wall and ran the width of the roof, dividing it into two roughly equal-size spaces. A third pipe, parallel to the second, ran along the far end of the roof. In the dark, they looked like gigantic snakes, slithering from holes in the floor across the roof into holes in the wall.

The man sat Helen against the wall of the building, next to one of the pipes. Stalling for time, ready to try any angle to save herself, Helen—probably shouting over the roar of the fans—asked if the man worked at the Met and if he was afraid he wouldn't be able to get away without being caught.

The man—who also must have been shouting, his raised voice shattering the intimacy of violence—said he didn't work there.

Was he lying? Telling the truth? Helen must have been calculating frantically. What could save her? Should she accept his answer? Challenge it? He looked like a member of the backstage crew.

The man tied her hands behind her back and bound her feet together. He told her he was going to leave her on the roof. He promised to call someone and tell where she was.

He left the main part of the fan roof, went down the short hall toward the door, and stopped.

What if she got free? he wondered—just as she did get free. He heard some rattling, rushed back onto the fan roof, and saw Helen run to the pipe that divided the roof, sit on it, swing her legs over it, and head toward another door, escape.

The man chased her, vaulted the pipe, caught her, and carried her back to the wall where she had been sitting. He tied her up again, using some rags he'd found in the crate, and took off her shoes so she'd have trouble running. The gravelly surface would hurt her feet. He carried her to the biggest fan pit, lifted her over the edge, down into the recessed area, and leaned her against one of the fans. The noise and, worse, the vibration, must have been terrifying—the massive blades whipping around right next to her.

Helen was still talking to him—shouting; it must have been like screaming into the opening mouth of Hell—trying to be nice, to soothe, pacify. She rattled on as though her voice were the thread connecting her to life. The more she talked, the more she would become for him a particular person, someone who liked to fish and hike and ski and play basketball and cook, who grew up speaking Swedish at home, learned English at school, picked up French, Italian, and Spanish, had a sister named Delcie; anything that would make her more than a body, more than an aid to masturbation to be used and discarded, more than a scapegoat on which he could revenge every slap he'd ever received from a haughty woman, every rejection, every petty humiliation he'd suffered—if he were, as he seemed to be, a member of the Met backstage crew—at the hands of musicians and dancers who, since he stood outside the magic circle of art, would have had contempt for him or, worse, ignored him, annihilated him with their snubs.

Helen's slap in the elevator may have brought to a boil years of simmering lust for every woman seen backstage in leotards, the fabric stretched pale over breasts and crotch, who passed him as though it didn't matter if he saw the outline of a nipple or not, as though he weren't even there. It may have triggered a sexual panic suppressed every time he saw a man in tights whose bulging genitalia demanded comparison, mocked, insinuated intolerable erotic fantasies. To escape, Helen had to remind him of her uniqueness. She was only herself. She was not those others. She talked and talked, Scheherazade delaying her execution with speech. Her only hope was to create herself in

his imagination—to make herself real enough for him so he
would pity her and let her go.

He gagged her.

He may have also blindfolded her, as though he could not
bear to have her witness what he would do to her. If she didn't
see, she wouldn't know. What pitiless gaze had he experienced
in the past to make him so fear her gaze?

He was afraid she would run away again. Figuring that, if she
were naked, she would be too embarrassed to go for help, he
cut off her clothes. His faith in the power of humiliation had to
be great for him to believe she would risk death rather than
embarrassment.

He slit her skirt and slip up the side. As he was cutting off
her jersey, she must have felt the knife at her neck. When he
cut off her bra, she must have felt it between her breasts.
When he cut off her panties, she must have felt it on her
thighs, on her hips. Blindfolded, she would not know where the
blade would cut next.

Around the sides of each pit was a space about two feet wide
that opened onto a shaft twenty-nine feet deep, a three-story
drop. He threw the clothes and pocketbook down the shaft.

With Helen beside him, bound, gagged, blindfolded, he sat
and wondered what he should do. Minutes passed. He climbed
out of the fan pit, started to walk away, and, over the roar of
the fans, heard her bouncing up and down. To make such a
noise, she must have been slamming herself around in an effort
to get free. Why wouldn't she stay still? Why wouldn't she let
him leave? He may have felt that she was forcing him to do
what he did not want to do, making him be bad, like a child
who feels that the world is conspiring to wrong him.

He climbed back into the fan pit and kicked Helen down the
shaft.

2

AT 3 A.M. ON THURSDAY, July 24, 1980, Detective Jerry Giorgio got a phone call from the 20th Precinct. There was a missing person at the Met. A violinist. The 20th was not asking for help. This was just a *scratch*—a notification for the Manhattan Area Nightwatch. The Nightwatch is a unit organized to investigate major felonies, which is on duty from midnight to nine o'clock in the morning. It is made up of eight detectives drawn from all over the borough, local precincts as well as the Task Force.

The Task Force is an elite division that is brought in on the most sensitive cases. Between it and the precincts is an interdepartmental rivalry. Detectives from the precincts call the Task Force detectives "the stars"—not a compliment.

That night, Jerry was the representative from the Task Force. He was troubled by the call. The 20th Precinct had mentioned something about an abandoned violin. Jerry had a friend who played the violin. He knew how unlikely it was that any musician would leave behind an instrument.

Fifteen minutes after the first call, the 20th Precinct phoned again. Jerry, Patrick Egan, the sergeant in charge that night, and Patrick Heaney, a detective with the 28th Precinct in Central Harlem, drove up to the Met. It was a warm night, in the seventies. The buildings at Lincoln Center, their marble facades pale in the streetlamp light, looked like mausoleums. They went around the complex to Sixty-fifth Street, through a tunnel under the plaza, and parked near the stage door. In the entrance hall, standing around the switchboard or sitting on chairs patched with colored tape, were half a dozen Met employees, security guards and administrators, and some uniformed cops from the 20th Precinct. They told the detectives what they knew about the missing person: Helen Hagnes Mintiks.

After her break, Helen had never returned to the orchestra pit. When the final act of the evening started, someone moved her violin to a back row and sat in her chair. The curtain came down. The dancers took their bows. The musicians filed out of the pit. Helen's violin lay, unclaimed.

Donald MacCourt, a bassoon player and the subcontractor for the orchestra, the man in charge of the orchestra's day-to-day summer operations, noticed that Helen was missing and alerted Antonia Sunderland, the assistant house manager, who was on duty that night. Sunderland organized a search of the most obvious areas backstage. But Helen wasn't found.

MacCourt telephoned Helen's apartment on West Seventy-fifth Street and left a message on the answering machine for Helen or her husband, Janis—who, calling home at the same moment, got a busy signal and assumed his wife had returned from the Met. Janis had waited for Helen in their beat-up van around the corner from the opera house, a block away—just as Helen's father used to when Helen performed at elegant houses in Vancouver. When she didn't appear, he called, then drove the few blocks back to their apartment. Three of Helen's co-workers arrived, looking for her. By one o'clock on what was now Thursday morning, Janis realized something was wrong.

The 20th Precinct, which had been contacted a little after midnight, checked out neighborhood restaurants and bars and the nearest hospital without success. Three cops made a second search backstage at the Met, which, like Sunderland's, was limited to two of the nine levels and to areas around the stage and dressing rooms.

Jerry suggested that they do a thorough canvass, a room by room sweep of the entire building.

Impossible, said the security guards. Even they didn't know their way around the whole place. The Met was a maze. Corridors on corridors. Flights of stairs vanishing up into the six top floors and down into three basements.

But Jerry wanted to make a start, so the guards led him, Egan, and Heaney to the stage. The curtains were closed. The cables for opening them ran diagonally across the cloth like sutures. Above them, the huge vault of the flies disappeared in shadows. On either side of the stage were wagons, as large as the stage itself, which could roll back and forth. Behind the stage was another rolling wagon, also as large as the stage. The stage itself was divided into a series of long, narrow elevators, which that night were in their normal position, tops level with the stage floor. Scattered around in the darkness were glowing blue exit signs. There was a smell of stored wood. Black curtains hung everywhere like funeral crape.

Jerry walked upstage to the freight elevator, which carried scenery into the bowels of the building. He turned. The proscenium was lined top and bottom with bulbs white as teeth.

They descended the stairs to A level, passed double-bass cases the size and shape of sarcophagi, crates of costumes, canvas bags the size of refrigerators—all large enough to hide a body. Around a corner of the dark corridor, vending machines hummed. Their panels, casting a pale light, reminded Jerry of locked gas stations in the middle of the night.

Corridors forked and forked again or ran parallel, leading to halls that seemed not adjacent as they should have been but in different parts of the theater. The floor plan of the building appeared to defy logic, as though in designing the Met the architect had thrown in the fourth and fifth dimensions, making Möbius-strip hallways and Klein-bottle closets. Jerry had the impression of entering a room on one side, walking to a door on the other side, exiting, and finding himself where he began.

In the crossover behind the orchestra pit, they couldn't find the light switch. The walkway skirted a three-story drop into a darkness so total it hurt the eyes. They scraped their feet forward inch by inch so they wouldn't step into empty space.

To enter the orchestra pit, Jerry had to duck through a low door. Beyond the kettle drums, folding chairs, and music stands was the auditorium. Lit by emergency lights red as torches, it seemed a vast crypt.

In front of the orchestra pit was another crossover: a corridor as dismal as a subway station underpass. It was walled with exposed cinder blocks and curved. When you stood at one end you could not see anyone at the other. You could tell someone was there only by the shadows cast along the wall.

They looked in the locker rooms, the artists' dressing rooms, which had a faint new car smell, and storerooms for scenery and props. Their flashlights swept across papier-mâché mountains, painted forests, towering columns, minarets, a Romeo and Juliet balcony, a ship's mast with rigging that looked like the work of a giant spider, gladiator shields, a stagecoach, a World War I army truck.

Jerry thought of *The Phantom of the Opera*. In his imagination shadows trembled like bat-winged capes. The echo of their footsteps threatened to become the sound of Claude Rains scuttling through a secret passageway on the other side of the theater.

The guards warned them not to wander off. They could walk into a hall, proceed to the end, find the exit locked, retrace their steps, and discover the door by which they had entered also locked. You could pound on the door for hours, the guards said, before someone heard you and let you out.

There were so many out-of-the-way places in which Helen could have gotten trapped or been hidden, such a vast and confusing area to cover, that Jerry figured they would need a hundred men, each escorted by someone on the Met staff who knew the way, to make an adequate canvass.

At 5 A.M., Jerry, Egan, and Heaney went to talk to Alice Montoya, the last person who had seen Helen alive—at least as far as they knew. Her apartment was on West Seventieth Street, near Helen's. She was so upset she hadn't been able to sleep. She told them what little she knew of Helen and Panov and how Helen had said she wasn't feeling well. Maybe Helen had gotten sick, Jerry thought; maybe she'd lain down to sleep or passed out somewhere.

The early morning was already muggy. It would be another hot, humid day. After checking back at the Met—no news— Jerry, Egan, and Heaney went to Janis's apartment. Janis had a high forehead, a trim beard, and extraordinary eyes. His face was a disconcerting combination of expressionlessness and intensity. He spoke in a monotone. Jerry thought he was odd. But artists, he'd found, were often strange. They seemed to follow different rules from those Jerry was used to. The world of the street and the world of the arts. The only thing that could connect them, Jerry thought, was a crime.

The morning before Helen disappeared, Janis said, she had received a letter from her mother, who had recently broken her hip. Her parents still lived on the farm in British Columbia.

Although in pain, her mother was hobbling around on a walker, doing chores. This had upset Helen.

"Could she have just taken off to go home?" Jerry asked. "Gotten on a bus or plane without telling you?"

Janis shook his head. No. Their relationship was close. She wouldn't have left without letting him know.

"Could she have gone off to a hotel by herself to think?" Jerry asked.

Janis said no—for the same reason.

"I'm sorry to have to ask you this," Jerry said, "but could she have a boyfriend?"

Janis again shook his head. No.

As the detectives left the apartment, Jerry said, "You watch, we'll find out she's on her way to Canada to see her folks."

Heaney turned thumbs down.

"Nope," he said. "She's dead somewhere."

They got back to the Met at 7 A.M. and were told that the door to the dressing room for the female musicians was locked. None of the passkeys worked. The security guards couldn't understand it. Jerry telephoned the Police Department Emergency Service, who arrived with crowbars and pinch bars and pried and hammered without success. A Met engineer, afraid they were going to destroy the door, stopped them. Carefully, he tried to force the lock. Jerry, growing impatient, grabbed a hammer and screwdriver. He banged away, listening every so often, hoping to hear Helen stirring. When the door at last opened, they found the room just as it should have been. An uncomfortable-looking couch. A dirty red carpet. A speaker on the wall, which during performances functioned like a clock: You could hear how far the show had progressed. No bodies. But in Helen's locker, number 4, they found something that was not as it should have been. Helen's street clothes were still there. She had never changed out of her orchestra blacks after leaving the pit.

The workday began. While waiting for police reinforcements who would help in a full-scale search, Jerry watched Met employees drift in through the stage door. Mostly rough-and-tumble guys, Jerry thought. Not the kind of men who'd be happy to see cops hanging around. That could be a problem. They were asked to report anything unusual they might see—and to keep Helen's disappearance to themselves. Jerry didn't want the press underfoot, not until they'd had a chance to secure the area.

A little after 8 A.M., a maintenance man, Lawrence Lennon, came up to Jerry. He was pale and looked scared. He'd been on the roof to turn on a fan, his usual morning job, and had seen a pair of women's shoes.

"Oh shit," Jerry said. Helen, feeling depressed about her mother, must have taken a header: jumped. "Okay," Jerry told Lennon. "Show us where."

Lennon led Jerry, Egan, Heaney, and two Emergency Service officers to the sixth-floor fan roof. Jerry glanced at the parapet, which was virtually impossible to climb, and thought: She didn't jump.

While Lennon waited, the cops spread out. Jerry hadn't gone too far, when he heard one of the Emergency Service officers say, "Oh, my God!" Jerry ran to where he stood by one of the fans. He looked down through the narrow opening into the shaft and saw at the bottom, twenty-nine feet—three stories—below, Helen's body: naked, hands apparently tied behind her back, legs draped over the sluiceway on which she lay.

Jerry had seen hundreds of corpses and worked on three- to four hundred homicides—so many, he'd lost count; but this was one of the most pitiful sights he'd ever come across. The whole lower part of her face and her neck were bloody. He thought her throat had been slit.

A fan roared on. Jerry jumped. Mist sprayed them.

Not only was the murder horrible, Jerry thought; it had happened at the Met, sacred ground. The victim had been on her way to talk to a superstar who was a Russian defector. Publicity —and it would be national—could make the case a carnival. Pressure on the department would be intense. And they would need the cooperation of the backstage crew, one of the most tightly knit father-son unions in the city.

"This is going to be a bad one," Jerry said.

He left the Emergency Service cops to safeguard the roof and went with Egan and Heaney to the third floor, where Helen had landed. On the way down in the elevator, Jerry thought: My God, the husband's at home, waiting for a call from us. He was certain Janis was not involved and was sick at the idea of his being told.

On the third floor, they went through the electrical shop to the bottom of the shaft: an area with exposed pipes raised on blocks about a foot off a damp floor; valves with handles the size of steering wheels; exposed girders crisscrossing the ceiling. Lying in a puddle of water was a pink bra. Behind a pipe next to a brick wall was a straw pocketbook and what looked like its spilled contents: a comb, keys, a wallet, sunglasses.

Jerry stood right under the sluiceway on which Helen lay. From that angle, her torso was hidden. All he could see were her legs, which looked strange. They were bent, not at the knees, but halfway up the thighs where there is no joint. The bones had snapped. One foot was turned so its toes touched the other foot's arch, a parody of coyness. The parts of the body that seemed most exposed, most vulnerable were the dirty soles.

Jerry climbed up to the sluiceway for a closer look. The spray from the fans rained on him.

"Jesus," he said.

Her throat wasn't cut. A rag was stuffed in her mouth. She had hemorrhaged. Blood had soaked the gag and spilled over her jaw and neck. A tuft of hair, and possibly scalp, ripped off in the fall, was caught along the edge of a trapdoor in the sluiceway.

"Call the Twentieth," Jerry said. "Tell everybody who's working to get their tails up here."

3

THAT MORNING Detective Mike Struk of the 20th Precinct was jogging around the Central Park reservoir. The day before, he'd worked the 4 P.M. to 1 A.M. shift. As usual, something had come up and kept him on the job another couple of hours. Although exhausted, he had dragged himself out of his bunk at the precinct dormitory after three hours of sleep. No matter how tired he was, he never missed his daily workout.

He came out of Central Park at Eighty-fifth Street, three blocks north of the station house. From a pay phone he called to see if he should pick up anything for the other cops. Orange juice? Doughnuts? Wiley Bergan, another detective with the 20th, answered the phone. His voice, usually slow, was urgent.

"Get right in," Bergan said. "There's a missing person."

"We've had them before," Mike said. "Do you want any milk or coffee?"

"I think you better hurry up," Bergan said. "The body's down some shaft at the Met."

The body? Mike thought.

"It doesn't sound like a missing person," he said. "It sounds like someone found someone that's very dead."

When Mike got to the Met, the place was swarming with employees who were trying to find out what had happened by eavesdropping on the cops. It reminded Mike of the advertisement, "When E. F. Hutton speaks, everyone listens."

On the third floor, he went into the electrical shop, where the cops who had already arrived had set up temporary headquarters. Spotlights two feet high stood in a group like R2D2's family reunion. In the middle of the floor was a chandelier the size of a wrecking ball. A cluster of upright metal poles; drill presses; circular saws; colored wires spaghetti-ing out of their gray sheathing; orange, red, blue, and purple gels; skeletal lamp arms; transformers that looked like fat black beetles; rows of switches; rolls of electrical tape; bins of screws, nuts, washers . . . One wall of boxes had labels that read like the inventory of a sex shop: 3-wire Hubbell male, mate 7974-C; 3-wire female; chain pulls and shackles; 3-wire 15A twist, male and female; tormentor track covers; sliding collars; turnbuckles; AC-DC converters.

Heaney came over to Mike and asked with a grin, "Are you the lucky one?"

"I think I'm in the jackpot," Mike said.

Mike wanted the case. He'd been on the force for fourteen years, half of the time as a detective. He'd had his share of good cases, but this promised to be a great one, a chance to distinguish himself. He'd be recognized as one of the best detectives on the force, used in the most complex and interesting cases for the rest of his career. It was normal for someone from the local precinct to take over in the morning from whoever had been handling the case on Nightwatch. If they followed typical procedure, Mike was the guy.

"Who's dead?" he asked. Mike had worked with Heaney in

narcotics and trusted his judgment. "Is she the palace blow-job? A nun? What?"

"She checks out okay," Heaney said. "A decent gal. Happy marriage. Nothing shady in her background."

"Anybody touched the body?" Mike asked Egan.

"Far as I know," Egan said, "you got a cherry scene."

Trailed by cops who would be helping on the case, Mike rattled off what had to be done.

"We'll need more manpower," he said.

"Giorgio took care of that," he was told.

"The borough office has to be notified."

"Giorgio called."

"What about the Chief?"

"Giorgio let him know."

"The medical examiner?"

"Giorgio phoned."

"Crime Scene Unit? Press Office?"

Giorgio. Giorgio. Giorgio.

At last, Mike asked, "What the fuck's a Giorgio?"

Mike went to his boss, Arthur O'Connor, a lieutenant at the 20th Precinct, to find out if he was catching the case or if it was being given to the Task Force—to this guy Giorgio.

O'Connor assured Mike it was his case. The Task Force was assisting.

"Who from the Task Force?" Mike wanted to know. He didn't want to work with Giorgio. He didn't like the guy's style. It was Mike's case, and Giorgio hadn't even had the courtesy to come over and introduce himself.

One of the other Task Force detectives was assigned to help, Mike was told. Benny Leotta.

Leotta was a nice guy. Mike figured he could work with him.

By now the press had heard about the murder. Reporters were demanding information. Cops were pouring in from all over the city. People were throwing facts at Mike, everything from Helen's movements the night before to possible suspects: the guy downstairs with the broken tooth, pervs, psychos, weenie-waggers, weirdos who hung around the opera, groupies —important stuff, trivial stuff. Mike got an instant headache.

Leotta came over to Mike and said he wasn't going to work the case after all.

"Who is?" Mike asked.

"Jerry Giorgio," Leotta said.

Giorgio again. Mike was pissed.

Across the room, Jerry was holding court, surrounded by cops who—Mike thought—seemed too respectful. After all, Mike told himself, Giorgio's just another grunt. But he wasn't. Mike watched as Jerry gestured expansively, the *padrone* stopping in the field to chat with the workers. He tried to figure out what it was that gave Jerry such a commanding presence. He was big, but not so large he could use his size to impress. Although he was ten years older than Mike, he kept himself in good shape; he didn't let himself slide like some guys did. But that wasn't unusual. Lots of detectives took pride in their appearance. They exercised not so they'd look tough, as some of the uniformed cops did, but so they'd look professional, like bankers or stockbrokers who had the leisure to work out regularly at their clubs. He dressed well, conservatively, but no more expensively than anyone else.

He got his power from a quality that was hard to pin down, a confidence that came from feeling like the hero of some private drama. He thinks he's Kojak, Mike thought; and this case is a two-hour special. But I ain't no bit player. This is my show.

Mike went to Heaney and told him, "Look, when your friend Giorgio gets caught up with his bullshit, have him come over and tell me what he's doing."

Mike climbed up to the sluiceway to look at the body. Planks had been balanced precariously across some beams fifteen feet above the electrical shop floor to make a catwalk next to the crime scene, so investigators could examine the body without stepping over it. The planks sagged as Mike walked across them. The fan on the roof was still blowing mist. Mike looked at Helen.

Blond hair. Blue eyes. About 5 feet 5 inches. Maybe 150 pounds. Well developed. Her hair was in either a ponytail or two pigtails, it was hard to tell which. Her face was turned to the right. Her left eye had hemorrhaged. Blood had oozed from her ears. There was a crust of blood over her upper lip and chin. A piece of sleeve, which had been ripped or cut from her black jersey, was still around one arm.

Pathetic, Mike thought.

He had worked on 150 to 200 homicides. He didn't like to make judgments about the relative value of the victims' lives. But a lot of people killed in the cases he'd handled had been scum. Here was a talented young woman who apparently had been killed for no reason except for the classic one: being in the wrong place at the wrong time.

Mike took a few Polaroids for the files.

Heavies were arriving. The Manhattan chief of detectives, Richard Nicastro. The chief medical examiner, Elliot Gross, who rarely did field work.

Mike and Gross hunkered down side by side on the shaky planks and examined the body. In 80 percent of the sex murders Mike had worked, the victim was tied—as Helen had been. But this didn't seem to be the typical sex crime. Except for her nakedness, it had none of the usual sex-crime signs: no bite marks on the nipples, nothing shoved inside her.

Two hairs—fiber, the cautious medical examiner called them —were found: one in the gag, the other stuck to her chest with what appeared to be sweat or blood. By the end of an hour and a half, Mike admitted that the ME had given the job the hundred-dollar treatment. First-class all the way. Which was one of the advantages of pulling such a big case. When he climbed down from the sluiceway, Mike was told that the Crime Scene Unit's photographs, which could often take two or three weeks to be processed, would be in his hands by the end of the day.

On the way up to the roof, Mike learned that in the stairwell outside the electrical shop they'd found a pen, bobby pins, a cigarette butt, and a blue flower. When Helen was last seen, she'd been wearing a flower in her hair. Evidence of a struggle.

The roof was swarming with cops: some from the Crime Scene Unit, working up the scene, others just milling about.

"How many Met employees were here last night?" Mike asked.

"About two hundred," he was told.

Great, he thought. Two hundred possible interviews just to start with.

"How many people worked here since January first?" he asked.

"Two thousand six hundred."

Mike cast his eyes up to the sky, turned in place as though the number made him dizzy, and saw the low-rent housing projects across the street from the Met. Hair prickled along his neck. If the killer worked at the Met, he had a shot at finding him. If someone left a back door open at the Met and one of those turkeys from the projects had slipped into the building, Mike figured those 2,600 Met employees would be only the first of the people he'd have to interview.

"This is one case I'm going to eat," he said.

Fingerprint experts were dusting the roof. But Mike was cynical about the possibility of finding prints. You rarely found anything. When you did, it was only a fragment that appeared after painstaking work. But one of the cops slapped a duster against a low horizontal pipe and up popped not just a fingerprint but a whole palm! It was too good to be true.

A technician did a Groucho Marx cigar-tapping routine and pantomimed jerking off.

"Obviously one of the heroes leaned against the pipe," Mike said. A sloppy cop must have contaminated the scene. Mike ordered everybody off the roof except the few cops doing specific jobs.

Their first strategy session was held in the temporary headquarters set up in the electrical-shop office, a cubicle off the work area that was just large enough for two desks, three filing cabinets, and a small bookcase, empty of books. On the floor were telephone directories for every borough in the city and most of the suburbs. On one wall was a medicine cabinet containing a few loose Band-aids and a small bottle of antiseptic. Scattered around the room were solid-state circuit panels.

Usually in public, detectives keep their coats on to hide their guns. But the room was so hot, they were all in their shirt sleeves, holsters visible at their sides, at the small of their backs, and on their chests.

Chief Nicastro told them that they were going to pull men from all over the borough. By the time the investigation was over, it would involve the largest force ever assembled to work on a single murder in New York City's history. Nicastro said that anybody anticipating a vacation, anybody who would not be able to stay with the case all the way through, should let him know.

It's going to take a while, he said. He confirmed it was Mike Struk's case and introduced Mike.

As the Chief talked, Jerry studied Mike. Tall, rangy, a Clint Eastwood type, Jerry thought. His mustache was trim, more Douglas Fairbanks than the droopy cowboy kind then in fashion. That shows a hidden romantic streak, Jerry thought. Obviously, he doesn't just keep in shape; he's a serious weight lifter. That shows he's vain, not the kind of guy to take a back seat to anyone else. His suit and shirt were immaculate; the creases in the trousers perfect; his tie knot well formed. He must have taken care getting dressed; he wants to look presentable, a sign of ambition. But what was most noticeable was Mike's look of barely controlled rage. Okay, Jerry thought, maybe I stepped on his toes this morning, but he's overboard. He's a hothead. It's going to be hard to keep him from going off half-cocked and screwing up the investigation.

At the elevator, Jerry came up to Mike and said, "Let's get together for a minute."

Mike, trying to needle Jerry about the difference in their ages, said, "Gee, after working all night, you must be very tired."

"Fresh as a daisy," Jerry said, his grin widening.

With fake innocence, Mike asked, "You a third-grader?"

"No," Jerry said. "Detective second-grade."

"You must be high up on the list for first-grade," Mike said. "This case won't hurt you."

"Let's cut the crap," Jerry said. "What's your plan?"

"I'm going to talk to the husband," Mike said.

"I talked to him already," Jerry said.

"Are you forgetting what the man said?" Mike said. "It's Mike Struk's case."

They were silent in the elevator on the way down to the Atrium, the heart of the Met where the offices are, which had been offered to the police department as a headquarters for their investigation. Compared to the hell of backstage, this was heaven. Or rather, if heaven were a business, this would be its corporate headquarters. All red plush and gold and silver. The teak-colored doors were so tall they seemed designed for super-human creatures. White draperies covered the glass walls of the offices.

Outside the door to one room, Mike and Jerry stopped. Mike peeked in to check out Janis, who sat at a table inside. In front of Janis was a bottle of Jack Daniels. Mike looked at Janis's beard and asked Jerry, "What is he? A beatnik?"

"He's okay," Jerry said.

Look, Fucko, Mike thought. I know I'm probably wasting my time talking to him. I still got to do it. You know I got to do it. If I don't do it, I'll look like a country asshole. So don't give me that shit. I'm going to eliminate him or make him a suspect real quick.

Out loud, Mike told Jerry, "We got two thousand six hundred people to talk to. I'm not going to waste time. I'm going right for the jugular."

The fastest way to tell if a guy is guilty, Mike figured, is if you go in and say, "Hi, how you doing? Who was your wife fucking?" If the guy comes at you—that's normal. If he shifts his eyes and hems and haws, you look at him a little harder. Something's got to be there.

When Mike entered the room, Janis swung his head up. Grief made Janis's face radiant. It was obvious to Mike that Janis was not implicated in his wife's death.

Mike ran through his questions. The only answer that seemed at all noteworthy was when Janis said he'd spent the night working on their new loft with a friend, Clifford Enright.

Maybe he's seen too many cop movies, Mike thought; but when someone offers a name, it sounds like a fabricated alibi. Still, Jerry's right. The poor guy's been through it.

"Go home," Mike told Janis. "Get some sleep."

After Janis left, Mike turned to Jerry.

"Let's get some ground rules around here," he said.

They each chose a partner. Mike's second would be Pat Heaney. Jerry's second would be Leo Rosenthal, a soft-spoken Task Force detective, who taught at a local college. Mike told Jerry, "You scratch this way. I'll scratch that way. At the end of the day, we'll get together. Just let me know what you're doing.

I don't want no surprises. Like, 'Hey, Mike. I just closed the case.' I don't mind your stealing my thunder. Just don't make me look stupid. If you do, I gotta go at you." As they separated, Mike said, "Remember, we're not going to have any secrets."

4

START WITH the obvious. Start with the husband. If he's not involved, look for a lover. If there's no lover, find someone who was where he shouldn't have been.

Helen's stand-partner in the orchestra, Clay Reude, had seen a balding white man in some kind of uniform with a red-and-white patch lurking around the Met about midnight—just after Helen must have been killed. The uniform made sense to Mike. The murder had to be an inside job. The murderer had to know the layout of the Met well enough to get Helen from wherever they met to the roof. And the employees of the Met who would be most likely to know the layout of the Met well were also the ones most likely to wear uniforms or something resembling a uniform like coveralls. Security guards, engineers, porters . . .

Mike asked for a list of guards, engineers, and porters. He wanted to know who didn't show up for work that morning, the morning after Helen was killed, or who showed up with a fresh black eye or scratch marks on the face, possible defense wounds.

One porter, Jarett Kipp, had been wandering around in a suspicious manner—at least according to Panov, who was also a suspect. There were dozens of rumors about Panov, everything from his having an assignation with Helen, who after all had been on her way to see him when she'd disappeared, to CIA-KGB involvement. But Helen apparently was going to see Panov only to help Janis get work as a set designer. Panov was rapidly eliminated as a suspect. And so was the limping porter he'd seen, Kipp, whose bad foot was so swollen, half of his shoe had to be cut off before it would fit. He could barely walk, let alone struggle with a strong woman like Helen.

But Kipp said there was a porter who hadn't shown up for work that morning. A supervisor. Perry Rooney.

"Tell me about Perry," Mike said.

Kipp said he was okay.

"Is he a drinker?" Mike asked. "He use drugs? Is he a lover?"

Kipp said he was a good guy.

"Is it common for him to miss work?" Mike asked.

Kipp said no. He almost never missed work.

"Let's visit Mr. Rooney," Mike said to Brian Connell, another detective from the 20th Precinct.

Rooney lived in Harlem. When Mike and Connell arrived outside his apartment, it was 7 P.M. The street was busy: kids played in spray from the hydrants, adults cooled themselves on stoops, or strolled up and down the block, drinking wine or beer, their heads tipped back. The paper bags hiding the bottles and cans protruded from their mouths like speech balloons in a cartoon. It was so humid, Mike hated to get out of the air-conditioned car.

In Rooney's apartment building, Mike knocked on the door.

"Who is it?" asked a Papa Bear voice in the apartment.

If this guy is as big as his voice, Mike thought, we could be in trouble.

The apartment was dark. Shades drawn. No lights on. Rooney kept in the shadows. Mike was suspicious. If Rooney had scratches on his face, it would be hard to see them. As Connell talked, keeping Rooney busy, Mike tried to get a good look at him. He changed chairs, leaned over to fix a cuff on his pants, ducked closer and closer to Rooney, until Rooney began giving him strange looks.

It turned out that Rooney was a workhorse: He held down three or four different jobs. Mike figured he probably came home the night before dragging his ass and just wanted to take the day off to catch up on sleep. But Rooney was worried that Mike and Connell were going to report him for goofing off. He told them what Mike thought was a cock-and-bull story about getting sand in his eye, so he had to take a sick day. A speck of sand in his eye would stop this guy the way a dandelion puff would stop a charging bull, Mike thought; but I can columbo as good as anybody. So Mike told Rooney, "Thank God, you saved your eye; but frankly it looks okay to me."

Mike wanted to leave, to get on with the investigation. He was satisfied Rooney was not involved. But Rooney wouldn't let them go until Mike believed him. He dragged Mike to a floor lamp, which he switched on. Leaning back in a chair, he pulled Mike on top of him so Mike could see how irritated his eye was.

When they got to the car, Connell hooted with laughter.

"I can't believe it," he said. "You were practically sitting on the guy's lap."

Back at the Met, Mike learned that Joe Brady, a detective with the Task Force, one of the fifty cops who had been canvassing the Met, had found a witness: a dancer who had been on the elevator the night before with Helen and an unknown man.

The witness, Laura Cutler, had a face as oval as the back of a spoon. She seemed mousy to Mike, too innocent for an adult, but the innocence seemed hard work, a shield she struggled to maintain. It was the kind of behavior Mike associated with people who were rich or in the arts, an attitude that made him impatient. This innocence was a luxury they could afford, but he couldn't.

Laura spoke in such a low voice Mike kept asking her to repeat things.

"Show us which elevator," he said.

Laura led Mike and Heaney through corridors on the stage level. A matinee was in progress. Mike heard the hum of music. Dancers and stagehands rushed back and forth. It was like being in a submarine on battle alert.

At the elevator—elevator number 12 near the women's dressing room—Mike, Heaney, and Laura acted out what had happened, with Laura playing herself and Mike and Heaney playing Helen and the unknown man. This is where Laura was standing. Here's how Helen and the man approached her. There's where Helen stood. There's where the man stood, slightly behind her.

Jerry, not wanting to miss out on the report of a key witness, joined them. Mike was annoyed. He felt that Jerry immediately assumed the role of director of their little play.

They went over and over what had happened. What in the way Helen and the man were acting had given Laura the impression they were together? Just from their talking together? From the way he'd followed Helen and Laura into the elevator? From the way he'd answered Helen's question about which floor Panov's dressing room was on? He'd said it was two—or three—quickly and confidently—although Laura admitted that if she'd thought about it she would have found it odd, since the stars all had their dressing rooms on stage level.

In the elevator, Jerry, Mike, Heaney, and Laura kept shuffling around, trying to reconstruct exactly how Laura, Helen, and the unknown man had been standing. Laura said she had been surprised because the elevator had gone not up, as the directional arrow was pointing, but down—to C level, where she'd gotten off.

"Let's go to C level," Jerry said.

Down and up they went, occasionally surprising performers who were waiting to use the elevator and, when the door opened, did not expect to see three cops and a dancer milling around as though they were choreographing a ballet for cramped spaces. Mike felt conspicuous.

"What about this guy, this unknown male?" he asked.

Laura hadn't gotten a good look at him. He was white. Maybe five foot ten inches. Dark hair. Not very long, not terribly short. Sort of fly-away, she would later describe it.

Fly-away? What's that? Mike wondered.

Laura thought the man was a little overweight. Not freshly shaven. Maybe he had a New York accent. And he was dressed in work clothes. Laura assumed he was on the Met crew.

If he wasn't the killer, he might lead them to the killer.

After Laura left, Mike said, "We got to find that guy."

5

MIKE HATED the morgue. Years before, he'd gone there to take some Polaroid pictures for identification. He'd pulled out a drawer in the refrigerator, a huge unit with bodies on rollers stacked tier on tier. At the same moment, someone had opened a door diagonally across from him on the other side of the refrigerator. The light had shone across two rows of corpses lying head to head.

In his years on the force, Mike had seen people cut in half, sawed in pieces, run over by trains, slammed to the street from fifteen stories high, burned, dragged, gouged, kicked, stabbed, punched, shot, blown up, strangled, drowned, bashed, smashed, and squashed. Normally, he could eat a ham sandwich while watching an autopsy.

But when he saw those cadavers in the morgue lit by the dull light from the open door on the other side of the refrigerator, it felt as if someone had touched the back of his neck with bared teeth. It was the creepiest, most depressing thing he had ever seen—like something out of the comics he'd read as a kid, *Tales from the Crypt.*

In the autopsy room was a typical scene: people in bloody aprons working at the half dozen tables, which had wire-mesh tops like stalls in a fish market so they could wash the body parts as they worked. Some of the bodies had bullet holes, which looked like the puncture a skewer makes in shisk-kebab meat. Or stab wounds. A few bodies had been lying on their backs long enough for the blood to settle. They were ringed: reddish-purple below, yellow-white above. Others were already dismembered. One had its scalp cut and pulled down over its face, so the exposed skull looked, Mike thought, like a yarmulke.

While Gross worked on Helen's body, an assistant took notes. The corpse had already been exposed to fluorescent light to check for traces of semen. None were found. Swabs were taken of her vagina, rectum, and mouth, also for semen traces. None were found. If there had been a rape attempt, it had not been successful. Or, if successful, it had not left any evidence. The body had been washed and X-rayed. No foreign objects were found jammed inside her.

Gross removed the two fasteners, one red and one white, from her pigtails—and six bobby pins. A contact lens was still in her left eye, but the one for her right eye was missing. He photographed the body. There were vertical scratch marks on her right side: breast, thigh, knee, made—Mike assumed—when she scraped through the opening of the fan shaft. There was a faint scratch on her neck—where the killer may have held a knife. Her fingernails were not broken, which meant she might not have fought back. Or at least not scratched the killer in fighting. Possibly she hit him, since her left knuckles were bruised. The ropes had been removed. The knots had been examined and videotaped. Her wrists were blistered.

"How long does it take a blister to rise?" Mike asked.

Since a blister wouldn't form after death, Mike was trying to figure out how long Helen's hands had been tied before she'd been murdered.

Gross said about fifteen minutes of chafing produced a blister.

The blisters were not broken, so Mike figured she hadn't been tied very long. Long enough to get a blister, but not long enough for the rubbing to pop it. Fifteen minutes to half an hour.

Gross removed the black jersey cuff from her wrist.

Her upper thighs and right collarbone were broken. Probably from the fall, since there were no signs of any brutal beating.

The gag was still in her mouth. She would have suffocated on the gag, Gross said, if she hadn't gone off the roof.

Gross took out her esophagus and put it on colored paper to examine it. It reminded Mike of a chicken neck. The esophagus hemorrhages easily, so if the killer had strangled her, it would be obvious. But there had been only minor bleeding. She'd probably been grabbed around the neck, not throttled.

Gross used a hacksaw to cut out her crotch, which he lifted from her body. He opened up her stomach. Mike had been dreading this part of the autopsy. Gross emptied her intestines onto a tray. Mike wanted to go to Hawaii. Gross washed away the stomach juices. Mike saw potato peel, string beans, cucumber, tomato skins, onions . . . Janis had told him that the last time he'd talked with Helen, about seven o'clock the night she was murdered, she'd said she'd bolted a quick supper of leftover salad. She was worried that her breath would stink of onions. From the condition of the stomach contents, her full bladder, and other evidence, Gross estimated the time of death to be between eleven and eleven-thirty—about the time the last ballet of the evening, *Miss Julie,* was ending.

Miss Julie, Mike found out, was adapted from a play by the nineteenth-century Swedish writer August Strindberg. It was about an aristocratic girl who has a fatal erotic encounter with her father's servant—about violent sex and death, humiliation and revenge, the conflict between men and women and between the upper and lower classes. At the same time Miss Julie died on stage, Helen was being murdered.

When Mike returned to the Met from the autopsy about two o'clock in the afternoon, Jerry asked what he'd learned.

"We'll hold a conference," Mike said. "Why should I have to say it twice."

Jerry backed off, but it galled him. He was second in command of the case. He wanted to be privy to the information before it was made general.

The meeting was in the Atrium conference room. Because the glass wall made them feel exposed, the cops closed the curtains—which then made the room claustrophobic, narrower-seeming than it really was, an elegant subway car stalled on a dead-end track.

During the day, there was clutter, but temporary clutter—charts taped to walls, cigarette butts, manila file folders, husks from the sunflower seeds one of the detectives, Juan Medina, ate, pens, pencils, suit jackets hanging humpbacked over chairs, forgotten coffee cups containing penny-sized spots of drying coffee. Nothing personal or permanent. No cartoons tacked to the walls, no fortune-cookie fortunes, no photographs of families. Every night, the cops took down the charts and lugged the files to the 20th Precinct. Every morning, when they returned, the Atrium was spotless, wastepaper baskets emptied, ashtrays wiped out, the chairs arranged neatly around the conference table. The attention the Met gave them made some of the cops feel like guests and therefore at a disadvantage, especially when interviewing employees who might feel too secure, too cocky on their own turf to be cooperative. And the luxuriousness of the setting seemed as inappropriate for the investigation of such a grisly crime as using a velvet-lined jewelry box to store coffee grounds. But Jerry thought the setting worked for, not against them. Whenever they interviewed a Met employee, the employee felt secure, less on guard, more open with the cops. Psychological judo.

During the conference, Mike explained how Gross had determined that Helen had been alive when she'd gone off the roof. After he cut off the top of her skull with the rotary blade, he found there had been a lot of bleeding in the brain, which meant that the heart was still beating when she landed on the sluiceway.

My God, Jerry thought. What did this poor woman go through? She was abducted about nine forty-five and killed around eleven to eleven-thirty. An hour, an hour and a half of hell.

During the meeting, they also discussed how to handle the sketch made from the description given by Laura Cutler, who had repeated her impressions under hypnosis. It showed a man anywhere from twenty to thirty-five with medium-long hair that half covered his ears. A sparse beard. Average-sized mouth. Common nose. Nothing unusual about the eyes or eyebrows.

Medium. Average. Common. Nothing unusual.

Everyman. Except he may have been a killer.

They decided to keep the sketch limited, show it only to supervisors at the Met, and above all not let the press get hold of it. But within a day or so a reporter called, saying, "We hear you've got a composite. We demand—the public demands—the right to see the sketch."

Somewhere in the department, possibly on the team investigating the murder, was a leak.

The opera buff in the ratty swallowtail coat who haunted the Met. The stranger who was once on the Grand Staircase, gazing at the chandelier and getting an erection that was obvious even through his baggy pants. Somebody's brother-in-law. Somebody's mother-in-law. The woman who, after the first act the night Helen was killed, wanted to throw flowers onto the stage and got into a fight with some musicians. The cab driver who picked up Helen on Tuesday. Vibrato the Great—whoever that was—who wrote a letter saying, "To solve the opera murder case, go no further than the evil bass." The breather who phoned one of the Met dressing rooms, asked a twelve-year-old dancer, "Are there any girls there?" and started to croon obscenities.

By that night, the madness had started: the anonymous callers, the freaks, the cranks, each with a theory, each with a suspect. Each had to be logged into the record book, the bible of the case, checked out, filed away.

Jerry was doing field work, everything from interviewing suspects to reassuring the parents of a female musician that the Met was safe, their daughter had no reason to quit her job. Mike imagined him beaming at some grip as he wheedled information from him, chuckling with a stage carpenter to gain his confidence. Jerry's belief in the significance of his own life was so strong that it drew in others, people who didn't find their lives important and who merely lived from moment to moment, who, unlike Jerry, had no internal narrative linking their days. Jerry could open them up by recruiting them as bit players in his story. They were happy to go along because Jerry's sense of his own life gave their lives a reflected shape and intensity. Mike pictured Jerry strutting through the backstage corridors trailing an entourage of stagehands, Met security guards, and uniformed cops.

Mike seethed with resentment. Jerry could selectively entertain what he thought were promising leads. But, since Mike was in charge of the case, he had to coordinate the efforts of all the other detectives like Jerry, who were doing the canvassing. He was stuck with paperwork in the Atrium, playing ringmaster to the circus. Employees were stopping by with tips. Cops were feeding him bits of information, most of it random facts that wouldn't match up with anything in the investigation. It was clear he would be caught at the desk until two or three o'clock in the morning. Someone had even stolen his sandwich.

When Vinnie Jenkins came up, Mike was in a bad mood. Mike liked Jenkins, who was a detective with the Task Force. He thought he was capable, a real pro. But Jenkins had been Jerry's partner for seven years on Homicide, and some of Mike's anger at Jerry spilled over on him.

"Mike," Jenkins said. "On C deck. We were down there searching the back of the building. And we found some napkins and this tampon."

"What about it, Vinnie?" Mike said impatiently.

"Well," Vinnie said. "It looks like it's got a little blood on it."

Just great, Mike thought. Blood on a tampon. What's unusual about that?"

"Where is this again?" Mike asked.

"In the back of the building and way down in the sub-basement," Vinnie said. "C deck."

There were three sub-basements. C level was the lowest. The murder happened nine flights up and, from what Jenkins said, on the opposite side of the building. To Mike, the tampon could have been on Mars. And Mike had no memory of the medical examiner's mentioning that Helen was having her period. The tampon seemed like one more random fact. One out of hundreds.

"Thanks, Vinnie," Mike said. "Anything else? You want coffee or something?"

"What do you want to do with the tampon?" Jenkins asked.

"What do *you* want to do with it?" Mike asked.

When Vinnie said nothing, Mike said, "Hey, Vinnie. Why don't you take the fucking thing home and suck on it."

The next day, in a strategy session, Mike reported on the phone calls he had gotten.

"Nothing real hot," he said. As an afterthought, he added that, while he was handling the calls, "Jenkins comes up and tells me this way-out thing about a tampon being found on C deck."

"What?" Jerry said. "Vinnie Jenkins told you that?"

After being Jenkins's partner for so many years, Jerry trusted Jenkins's instincts. If Jenkins mentioned something, no matter how far out, it was worth checking.

"Well," Jerry asked, "where's the tampon?"

"Probably where he found it," Mike said.

Jerry and Captain Frank Ward of the 5th Detective Zone left the conference and descended into the recesses of the building. The bright colors gave way to gray. The music from the show got softer and softer until they could no longer hear it. They passed dressing rooms, rehearsal halls, storage rooms, until they came onto the landing at the bottom of the stairs on C level.

The graffiti—"Fat Louie Sucks"—looked less like something spray-painted on the wall than like some message from the building itself that had seeped from the inside and had finally reached the wall's surface. An ordinary folding chair. A red rug. A piece of rope. Stuffed into a hole around a pipe going up through the ceiling were some paper towels. And on the floor, the wicklike string making it look like a firecracker, was the tampon.

This is it, Jerry thought. A classic setting for a rape. But, if Helen had been taken there, it meant the crime scene was spread over the whole building, bottom to top. Very unusual. Laura Cutler saw Helen waiting for the elevator on stage level and then riding the elevator apparently headed for the second or third floor at about nine forty-five. Helen was killed about eleven to eleven-thirty. Which meant that sometime between nine forty-five and eleven to eleven-thirty the murderer had to get Helen from the second or third floor to C level to the roof through a maze of corridors in a busy building without being seen. Improbable. But Jerry was positive the tampon was Helen's. He was annoyed at Mike for having ignored it.

When Jerry returned to the Atrium conference room, triumphantly claiming the tampon was a crucial bit of evidence, Mike was furious at what seemed to be Jerry's grandstanding.

As they left the meeting, Connell told Mike, "Take it easy."

"Certain stars give me a royal pain," Mike said.

"I can't see Jerry upstaging anyone," Connell said. "Not intentionally."

But by this time Mike was sure Jerry was going to let him do all the paperwork and grab the glory for himself.

6

SUSPECTS on parade!

Together, Mike and Jerry interviewed Francis Foat, who was nicknamed Soapy. A real creep, his co-workers agreed. He stuttered, showered twice a day, kept half a dozen uniforms of different colors always ironed, lived with his mother, and read the *Wall Street Journal.*

Mike thought the obsession with uniforms promising. The lurker Helen's stand-partner had seen was wearing a uniform. Also, Foat's hair was full—maybe even "fly-away," which is how Laura Cutler had described the hair of the man in the elevator with Helen. And Foat was odd, a loner, which always is suspicious.

They don't talk to me, Foat said about his co-workers.

While the other stagehands were drinking, blowing dope, snorting coke, screwing whores, Foat was saving his salary, investing in the stock market. Even though he had just lost $30,000 in municipal bonds, he claimed he was still worth about a quarter of a million dollars.

"Soapy," Mike said, "people say you got some strange habits."

That, Soapy said, is because I'm cheap.

They watched and listened to Soapy, threw him casual questions that seemed significant and significant questions that seemed casual; and, having probed, dismissed him. He was too candid, too calm. His story had no gaps or contradictions. His idiosyncrasies seemed benign.

Mike and Jerry didn't agree on much, but they agreed that Soapy was an unlikely suspect.

Among the crew, Jerry's favorite suspect was an electrician, Cosmo Fallarino, who was on duty the night of the murder—who, in fact, was in the third-floor electrical shop listening to the Yankee game on the radio, while outside the shop, about twenty feet away, Helen apparently was struggling with her killer, losing a bobby pin, a pen, and her flower.

Fallarino—who struck Jerry as a Robert Blake type—was nervous. As Jerry talked to him, he squinted and blinked and babbled and asked too many questions. He was strong enough to have subdued Helen; his arms were big. And Jerry found it hard to believe that with all the racket Helen and her killer must have been making, he hadn't heard anything.

You mean, Fallarino asked, if I'd heard her, maybe I could have helped?

What is this? Jerry thought. Pangs of conscience?

Fallarino was acting like someone with something to hide. Crimes like this were usually solved in the first forty-eight hours—or not at all. Jerry thought he'd gotten lucky.

Fallarino kept throwing out names of people he'd seen that night.

Keep talking, Jerry thought. The more you say, the more stuff I've got to check your story.

Guys are always wandering around up here, Fallarino said. You can even go right out on the grid. Here, I'll show you.

He led Jerry onto a metal lattice about fifty feet above the stage. Below, small as puppets, dancers performed. Music drifted up softly. Jerry thought of detective movies, falling sandbags, fights on the edge of catwalks.

Fallarino asked about the investigation. What had they found? Who were the suspects? Any clues?

Too many questions, Jerry thought.

When they got back on solid floor, Jerry was relieved.

It turned out that Fallarino was hiding not a guilty conscience but a case of mistaken identity. Someone had used his name while committing a crime in New Jersey. The police had contacted him. The mix-up had been straightened out. But Fallarino was uneasy. He didn't want any more confusion.

The questions he asked about the case were not defensive, but the curiosity of a detective-story buff—or, at least, the husband of a detective-story buff. His wife loved mysteries and evidently pressed him to get all the details of Helen's murder.

Jerry gave up the idea that Fallarino was the killer.

Mike—for his first prime suspect—liked a porter named Bill Willingham. He hadn't shown up for work the morning after the murder and came in the following day with a cut on his hand. Possibly a defense wound. Willingham kept changing his story about how he had hurt his hand. He'd been mugged. Not likely, Mike thought. Not this guy. He cut his hand when a box he'd been sitting on collapsed. Better, Mike thought. He'd been shooting up when the box collapsed. Still not good enough to convince Mike that Willingham was innocent of Helen's murder. Too many things fit. Willingham had a long arrest record. He had access to napkins; Helen had been gagged with a napkin. He lied about where he was the night of the murder at nine forty-five—just when Laura Cutler saw Helen at the elevator with an unknown man. Best of all, he placed himself on the sixth floor near the fan roof from which Helen fell, at ten o'clock, close enough to the time she was killed to be suspicious.

Willingham was outraged that Mike suspected him—not of killing Helen—but of raping her.

I don't have to buy no pussy, he told Mike. I don't have to take no pussy. I got all kinds of women who want to give me pussy.

At the Police Academy on East Twentieth Street, Willingham took a lie-detector test, administered by Justin Peters, a bear of a cop, about six feet three inches tall and heavyset— with a cigar impaled in his face.

Mike, you're wasting your time with him, Peters said, when it was over. Go somewhere else.

The next morning, Sunday, July 27, Mike entered the Met through the stage door as usual and saw sitting at the security switchboard a double for the sketch made from Laura Cutler's description. The man even wore a uniform with a patch, which matched him up with Clay Reude's description of the after-the-show lurker. His name was Bobby Anderson.

I'm a genius, Mike thought. Here was a guy in a uniform who looked like the composite, who—Mike learned—had a reputation as a lover, who lied about having a record, and who, according to a phone call Mike got a couple of days later, had molested a dancer. Everything, especially the molestation, fit. This was a gutter case. The killer was some guy with a hard-on down to his ankles who couldn't control himself with two shots of booze in him.

The molested dancer, Linda Allenbach, studied at the Melissa Hayden studio, not far from the Met. As Mike climbed the stairs to the rehearsal hall, he heard music and the teacher saying, "And a one-two-three-four. And a one-two-three-four."

In the room were three dozen dancers arranged in rows of four. Each row tiptoed toward him and just when Mike thought they'd collide with him, swung off to the side as the next row approached. No one paid him the slightest attention.

Mike cleared his throat and stretched up his chin as he adjusted the knot of his tie. He was not comfortable. This was not his scene.

At last, the teacher noticed him and gestured to an assistant to take over the class. He strolled over to Mike and scrutinized him as though he assumed Mike had come to the studio to perve at the dancers in their leotards.

Can I help you? he asked airily.

Mike introduced himself. The teacher ushered him into the hallway. Mike told him he wanted to talk to Linda.

Let me see if she's here, the teacher said.

It was obvious he knew she was there.

"Look," Mike said, "I just want five minutes of her time."

When she finally came out to the hallway, she stared at Mike as though he'd awakened her from a happy dream. Like Laura Cutler and many of the other artists Mike had encountered on this case, Linda seemed to believe her world, the world of art, was the real world and Mike's world, the world of murders and investigations, the world of the street, was unreal.

Mike felt the opposite. He couldn't understand how untouched the artists seemed by the murder, by what to him was a reality that couldn't be ignored. The artists grieved for Helen and were afraid that the killer, their Phantom of the Opera, might strike again. But in some way, Mike thought, all that seemed to them merely bad weather. They escaped from it into their obsession with their art. Their art was a shelter, something that protected them from brutality and ugliness. Mike didn't envy them their naïveté. They seemed as locked up in their innocence as someone jailed for his own protection.

Their different views made the case seem less a contest between right and wrong, cops versus a criminal, than a struggle between two competing versions of reality: one that fought

back against a crime and the other that seemed to enclose and
eject it, the way the body hardens around and finally sloughs off
a splinter. It made the cops' job harder.

It was clear to Mike that under these conditions Linda would
not open up. He made an appointment with her for later that
afternoon—which she missed. The next day, she showed up.

Yes, Anderson had pulled her over and kissed her on the
cheek. Yes, incidents like that happened frequently backstage
at the Met. The fanny patting, the catcalls, the cheap feels in
the crowded halls seemed to be privileges the stagehands felt
they deserved, an equalizer. The artists' refusal to recognize the
world of the street, which irked Mike, seemed to the stagehands to be arrogance. To bring the artists down from their
ivory towers, the stagehands dismissed the men as fags and
reduced the women to sex objects. Linda, obviously furious at
having been treated so crudely, said she would bet a million
dollars that Anderson was the murderer.

But the more Mike checked Anderson out, the less sure he
was that Anderson was the killer. A peck on the cheek isn't
rape. Anderson's two arrests were petty: unlawful assembly,
when he was a kid, and a stolen car, which turned out to be his
father's. Obviously, a family fight that went public. When Anderson was stopped in the car, the cops had found a forged
license and an illegal weapon, a blackjack; but that didn't seem
significant to Mike. A forged license can be a ticket to joy-ride.
The blackjack? It's a rough world out there; if a man is a security guard, he needs an edge.

To get a line on Anderson, Mike went to Dimitri's, a bar a
few blocks from the Met that was a hangout for the Met crew.
Through one of the bartenders, he made contact with a source,
someone from the crew who would tell Mike the backstage
scuttlebutt: Mike's Deep Throat. They met by the docks along
the Hudson River, a scene from a mystery novel, which Mike

chose because the source was a cop buff and would enjoy the cloak-and-dagger arrangement.

Civilians tend to have stylized ideas, drawn from novels, movies, and television, of what detective work is like. In the Met Case, newspapers reinforced such romantic notions. The *Daily News* would run an article that stated,

> If only it were a murder mystery novel, it would be called "The Phantom of the Opera" or perhaps "The Case of the Lady Violinist," and we would be on page 100 or so. The glamorous victim would have been dispatched several chapters back, and our hero . . . would be going over his lengthening list of clues.

Art imitating life . . . Life imitating art . . . The press would exploit this theme. "Violence leading to murder is a common facet of ballet and opera plots. . . ," a piece would state. The latest edition of the Met's *Opera News* coincidentally ran an article titled "Murder at the Met" about mystery novels that used opera for a setting.

Mike had often found that if he didn't go along with a civilian's overly dramatic vision of his job, the civilian might balk, as if he felt betrayed by the humdrum truth. So Mike sometimes had to play a role, which is what he did that night. The setting was perfect. Mist rose from the water. Shadowy figures approached, passed a few words, separated. Corny stuff that made Mike's Deep Throat believe in the scene he was living.

Nothing Mike heard about Anderson damned him. Over the next couple of days Mike checked out Anderson's alibi: When Helen first disappeared, Anderson claimed he was having dinner at Pat's, a bar and grill on Amsterdam Avenue, near the Met. Mike knew the place. And he didn't like it. It was a cop hangout, too. A few years earlier, about the time Mike had joined the homicide squad, three cops were drinking beer at Pat's when a guy with a shotgun burst through the door and told everyone to lie on the floor. The guy's partner, also armed, slipped in after him, ready to rob the bar and the customers.

When cops are caught in a robbery, as soon as their badges and guns are found, they are sometimes killed. The three cops had no choice. They jumped the two stick-up men. But a third crook, who had been planted at the bar, pretending to be a customer, stuck a .32 under the armpit of one of the cops. The bullet went through both lungs and the heart. A freak shot. Only cops die that way, Mike thought. One bullet from a little .32. Meanwhile, cops shoot bad guys in bank robberies five, six times, in the head, in the ears, in the dick, in the heart—and those guys live!

Since then, Pat's Bar symbolized for Mike cop-luck. Bad luck. It wasn't a good sign that Anderson claimed to have been there when Helen disappeared. But his story checked out. And three other guards verified that he was back at the Met, working the stage door from the time he left Pat's until midnight.

Anderson probably wasn't Helen's killer.

A former employee who was under psychiatric care because he'd learned that his best friend was the real father of his child was at the Met the night of the murder. So was a supervisor who had ripped a woman's blouse backstage. And a member of the crew who once ground out a cigarette against a woman's breast. Mike had rarely seen in one case such a likely collection of suspects.

The members of the crew who weren't disturbed or violent tended to be remarkable in some other way. One never went anywhere without a Bible. Another, a sound engineer, was an astronaut, working at the Met while he waited for NASA to send him into space.

Mike thought the case was getting stranger and stranger.

An engineer, Matthew Potts, said that an electrician, Tommy Anton, had a room on C level that he kept locked. Anton said he kept the room locked because he brought his girlfriend there. And, Anton added, he'd seen Potts on C level the night of the murder. Potts admitted that he'd been on C level about nine o'clock that night and said he'd heard a moan. The astronaut had heard a door slam. About the time Laura Cutler saw Helen with the unknown man, a dresser with the Berlin Ballet who was on the second floor saw the doors to elevator 12—the elevator Helen and the unknown man were on —flutter as though they were trying to open and couldn't.

The two hairs found at the crime scene, one in the gag and the other stuck to Helen's breast, had tiny knots in them. Who would knot his hair like that? Mike wondered. And how could he do it? Tweezers and a magnifying glass? The paper towels found stuffed around the pipes between B and C levels were stained with semen from three different men at three different times. On the third floor, not far from where Helen's body landed, was a room the crew called the Motel, where more semen stains were found. There was a damp spot—like mucus or semen—in the sound room. What were the stagehands doing? Standing around like firemen at a blaze, spraying their hoses every which way? A tampon tube was found on the grid above the stage. A cleaning lady saw a woman—a prostitute, she said—asleep on the second floor.

Whores in the flies. Porno movies in the basement. It was beginning to seem like there was more vice backstage than at Plato's Retreat.

It turned out the tampon tube from the grid was not connected to the murder. The damp spot in the sound room was not a human fluid. The semen stains in the Motel had nothing to do with the case. The semen-stained paper towels were also red herrings. And the knotted hairs remained a mystery.

Another electrician. Another soundman. Another guard. Mike worked his way through the list of possible suspects. A carpenter who looked like the composite and who now worked at ABC was seen backstage at the Met the night Helen was killed. Mike crossed the street from Lincoln Center to the ABC office and started ascending the television hierarchy, trying to get permission to talk to the carpenter. Jerry thought Mike was wasting his time, which made Mike all the more determined to follow the lead. He wasn't going to stay relegated to paperwork while Jerry was out in the field. When Mike finally interviewed the carpenter, the guy broke down and cried—but it had nothing to do with Helen's murder.

"If you go into a crackerjack box," Jerry sarcastically told Mike, "this is the prize you come up with."

Mike was fed up with Jerry and what he thought were Jerry's cream-puff tactics. A patty-cake approach might work with the musicians, Mike thought; but the stagehands would just laugh at that kind of gentlemanly behavior. The crew was running rings around Jerry, Mike thought.

Mike was so frustrated that even though he believed ESP was nonsense, he was willing to give it a shot. A professional psychic named Gray Wolf sent Mike a tape with information about Helen's killer he claimed to have received in a trance. Mike took the tape to the Chief, who listened politely and then said, Throw the thing in the garbage.

7

ON SATURDAY, Jerry checked in with Potts, caught up on some paperwork, and talked to Leo Rosenthal, who was in Washington, D.C., with some other detectives, reinterviewing members of the Berlin Ballet. Then he headed home. On the front seat beside him in the car, a 1973 Ford sedan, was a yellow legal pad. As he worked his way up Riverside Drive to the Cross Bronx Expressway, he scribbled notes to himself about the case.

He was fascinated with Potts. Every time he talked to him, Potts changed his story; every story was riddled with inconsistencies; and the moan that Potts had heard seemed a little too neat. In Jerry's experience, when suspects began remembering moans, they also began remembering that they caused the moans by killing the victim.

The trouble with that theory was that Fallarino—Jerry's original favorite—confirmed Potts's alibi. But in doing so Fallarino had changed his story and inadvertently put himself back at the top of Jerry's Hit Parade.

Jerry was going in circles.

They had no strong leads and too many suspects, none of them good enough to bank on. The case was stagnating. They'd reached the point of hoping for that little bit of luck, for that next interview containing some forgotten and valuable clue.

What angle had they overlooked? What had they forgotten to do? Or what had they done that they shouldn't have? Were they getting through to the backstage crew? Were they getting their full cooperation? If they stepped on even one person's toes, the whole crew could clam up. Had Mike with his unsubtle methods already alienated everyone?

Mike!

Jerry hit the steering wheel with the heel of his right hand. He imagined Mike bulling his way around backstage, getting into shouting matches with the crew, showing contempt for the musicians and dancers. And if Jerry tried to give him advice, Mike would think he was condescending.

When Jerry reached home, he parked the car in the driveway and sat there thinking about Potts and Fallarino. The outdoor spotlight was on, illuminating the above-ground swimming pool, which in the dusk looked like one of the Met's air-conditioning fans. Jerry's gang was waiting for him.

During the summer, the weekend was party time at Jerry's house. Jerry would pick what was ripe in his garden. Twenty-five to thirty guests would arrive, each bringing something—potato salad, sausages, corn, hamburgers, chicken—for the communal feast. Some guests were new acquaintances, invited on the spur of the moment. Others were friends from the old neighborhood, who reminded him of when he wanted to be a movie actor.

As a kid, growing up in Greenwich Village, he'd spent his days in the Waverly on Greenwich Avenue, the Loew's Sheridan on Eleventh Street, and even the Hudson on Christopher, which his clique called the Dumps. He'd gone from one theater to another, sitting through two double features in an afternoon. Or, when a favorite movie—like *The Maltese Falcon, Gentleman's Agreement,* or *The Gunfighter,* with Gregory Peck—was playing, he'd sit through the same show twice. At the Waverly, where they marked your ticket with the time of each show, this meant playing musical chairs with the usherette who'd come around in the intermission and check your stub.

Movies had seemed exciting, glamorous, not like school: Cardinal Hayes High, which was in the Bronx, a long ride from the Village on the Seventh Avenue IRT. For a while, football made school bearable; but after he made junior varsity, Jerry got into a scrimmage fight with another team and got kicked off the squad.

For something to do after school, he'd joined the Italian Club, where he was a great success. He'd grown up speaking Italian, which as a little kid embarrassed him, made him feel like an outsider even in a neighborhood as Italian as the Village, where he occasionally saw mobsters like Tony Bender and Vito Genovese, who got his hair cut in a local barbershop. On the street, among more assimilated Italians, Jerry would speak English to his mother, who would glare back at him. "Ma," he'd plead, "try to speak English." She'd whack him and say, "When you're with me, speak Italian."

By the time he got to high school, he was proud of his Italian. It proved his roots. In Italian class, when his teacher would say something with a Neapolitan accent, Jerry would correct him and get whacked again. He was good at all languages and math, bad in biology and history. He never took a book home; but, smart and a quick study, would cram just before the end of the school year, so he never had to go to summer school.

In 1951, after graduating from high school, one of Jerry's friends, Tony Lotti, convinced Jerry to hitchhike with him to

Hollywood. They figured that while waiting to break into the movies they'd support themselves as deep-sea divers. They got as far as South Carolina. Between them, they had $31 left, which meant they were risking getting arrested for vagrancy. Jerry had heard stories about Southern chain gangs. So they bummed rides back to Roanoke, Virginia, where they bought two bus tickets to New York City for $15 each, and, with their last dollar, five pounds of apples, cigarette papers, and some roll-your-own tobacco. In the movies, cowboys rolled cigarettes with one hand. With four hands Jerry and Tony couldn't get their cigarettes to stay together. The ride lasted about sixteen hours. By the time they got home, Jerry vowed never to ride another bus, eat another apple, or buy anything but factory-rolled cigarettes.

He got to his parents' apartment at six o'clock in the morning, waited in the street outside the building until six-thirty, and then knocked on the door.

"Why didn't you keep going?" his brother Iggy asked. Hollywood. The movies. He'd been rooting for Jerry.

His mother made Jerry a breakfast of six eggs, which he ate with a loaf of bread.

"Where's Dad?" he asked.

"Fishing," his mother said. "Where else? It's Saturday."

Jerry took the subway out to Sheepshead Bay, where his father went every weekend, and waited on the pier for his father's favorite boat, the *Helen H.*—what omens our lives offer us: Helen Hagnes, who had recently been born, would not cross Jerry's life for twenty-nine more years.

Jerry's family shared a special whistle—a shrill, between-the-teeth hiss, like a teakettle boiling. When Jerry was a kid, his father would give that whistle, leaning out the window. Blocks away Jerry would hear and recognize it, the signal to go home. As soon as Jerry made out the *Helen H.*, when it was still a hundred yards from shore, he gave that whistle. Up came his father's head with a big grin on his face.

"Eh, what happened?" he asked when he docked.

Jerry told him.

"Well," his father said, "you had your taste."

Jerry carried his father's knapsack and bag of fish. They stopped at Lundy's, where they each ate six dozen clams, and then headed home.

Jerry went to work nights in the Coca-Cola bottling plant in Tuckahoe, New Jersey, a two-hour commute from New York City. In the afternoons, he occasionally met with a talent scout. Once he tried out for a role in an Off-Broadway play, starring Ben Gazzara. He wanted to be more than just another guy from the neighborhood. He wanted to be special. He wanted to be a star.

In 1955, hating the suspense of waiting to be drafted, Jerry asked his board to up his number. His fiancée, Doris, wept.

"Look," Jerry told her. "I'll be at Fort Dix. That's only ninety miles away. I'll be home all the time."

When he couldn't get a pass, he sneaked out. Once, while he was AWOL in New York City, he got a phone call from a buddy at the base.

"They know you're gone," the friend said. "They're going to check you out. If you're not in bed tonight, you're going to be in trouble."

"Bullshit," Jerry said. "They're not going to catch me!"

Jerry, Doris, Tony Lotti, and Tony's girlfriend jumped in a car and raced back to camp. Halfway there, they got a blowout. Jerry checked in the trunk. No spare tire. With all the delays, they got to Fort Dix five minutes before bed check.

"Go into the visitors' parking lot, keep your lights off, and wait," Jerry said.

He sauntered into camp through the front gate, waving to the guard on duty. They weren't worried about soldiers sneaking in. He ran to his barracks, jumped into his bed fully clothed, pulled up the covers, and was snoring when the sergeant and corporal flashed a light in his face.

"Son of a bitch," said the sergeant. "He's here!"

Jerry snorted as though the light were disturbing his sleep and turned over in bed.

The moment the sergeant and corporal left the barracks, Jerry flung back the covers, sneaked out of the barracks and over to the visitors' parking lot, jumped into the car, and said, "Let's go back to New York."

He was as lighthearted about the service as Cary Grant would be in *Kiss Them for Me* or Tony Curtis in *Operation Petticoat.*

Late in 1955, Jerry was sent to Korea. The war had been over for two years, and most of his duty was police work: discouraging looters. After nine months overseas, he got a Dear John letter from Doris. She was returning his engagement ring, pearl necklace, and presents he'd sent her from Korea, because she was running off with a married man from Albany who had been teaching her how to drive on her vacation.

Jerry was ready to do anything, forge orders, if necessary, to get home and find out what had happened. He was rescued by another army buddy, who, convinced Jerry would be caught and end up in jail, called some MP's he knew and asked them to stop Jerry. Not arrest him. Just send him back to camp— which they did.

When Jerry finally got back to New York City half a year later, on his first day home he joined his brother Iggy, Tony Lotti, and another old neighborhood pal, Joe Bocassi, for drinks in the Village.

"What's bothering you?" Lotti asked.

"You know," Jerry said.

"You want to go to Albany?" Lotti asked.

The four of them piled into a car and drove the rest of the

night. Jerry was on his first investigation. Find the wife of the guy who ran off with Doris, pump her for information, and track down the two lovers. They arrived before dawn and waited in the car in front of the wife's house until the sun came up. About six-thirty, Jerry rang the doorbell. The wife opened the door, glanced at Jerry's crew cut and new civilian clothes, and said, "I know. You're Jerry."

When her husband ran off with Doris, she told Jerry, he left his family penniless. They couldn't even make the payments on the house. Her son had almost had a breakdown. Her daughter was ill. The woman sobbed. Jerry couldn't finish his coffee. He wished he'd never come. Compared to their problems, his gripe was petty.

"They're somewhere in Florida," the wife said.

It was late in the morning when they left Albany. Jerry was due to be mustered out of the Army that afternoon. If he didn't get back to Fort Dix on time, he'd be held over. He made it under the wire. When an officer asked where he'd been, Jerry said, "I didn't know which building to go to."

Shortly after he was discharged, Jerry sold the returned engagement ring for $700 and used the money to go with his brother Iggy to Florida. Miami. On the streets, at the beach, in restaurants—everywhere he went he searched for Doris. Once, after being out all night, Jerry met his brother at Wolfies' Delicatessen at three-thirty in the morning.

"You'll never guess who I saw," Iggy said when Jerry walked in.

"Who?" Jerry asked as he sank down into the next seat.

"Doris," Iggy said.

"You're full of shit," Jerry said.

"She's over at a corner table with the guy," Iggy said.

"Now?" Jerry asked.

"Now," Iggy said.

"Did you talk to her?" Jerry asked.

"No," Iggy said.

Ever since Korea, Jerry had been tracking her down. He'd risked jail, almost missed being mustered out of the Army, and come all the way to Florida to find her. Now, here she was. All he had to do was walk to the back of Wolfies'. The investigation was over.

Jerry finished his bagel and, without even glancing at where Doris sat, left the restaurant.

He returned to New York and got a job at the Flash Printing Company on Lafayette Street. He was bored, marking time. At night, he, Iggy, Tony Lotti, and Joe Bocassi would carouse. When they stayed out too late, Jerry's mother would chain-lock the apartment door. Jerry and his brother would take the laces from their shoes, tie them together, and slip one end around the chain. They'd pull the door almost closed. Holding the other end of the shoelaces, Jerry would climb on his brother's shoulders and gently tug the chain sideways until it slipped from the latch. Once they were inside, they would re-latch the chain to confound their mother, who in the morning would find them asleep in their beds and the chain still on the door.

"How did you get in?" she'd demand when they woke.

They'd smile.

"Bums," she'd say. But she'd laugh.

Jerry was a Jimmy Valentine of emotion, able to pick almost any locked-up heart.

In November 1957, Joe Bocassi said to Jerry, "Let's go take the police test."

"You got to be kidding," Jerry said.

"Come on," Bocassi said. "Steady work. Good benefits. Retire in twenty years."

"Ah no," Jerry said.

"Come on," Bocassi said. "Give me five bucks for the fee. Fill out the application."

Why not? Jerry thought.

He came out of the test with a high mark and, expecting to be offered a job soon, decided to make one last stab at the movies. At the Sky Top Gym on West Thirty-fourth Street, overlooking the guard dogs on the roof of Macy's, Jerry had met an acrobat named Mo Carson. When Mo went to Hollywood, Jerry and Tony Lotti followed. Mo's father-in-law, who was a film editor at Warner Brothers, arranged a tour of the studio for them. They met Broderick Crawford, who was then playing a cop in *Highway Patrol.* Which would be more interesting: to be an actor pretending to be a cop or to be a cop? They watched Dorothy Malone on the set of *Too Much Too Soon.*

"She's gorgeous," Jerry told Lotti.

Errol Flynn was playing Dorothy Malone's father. Jerry and Lotti were ushered into his trailer. Flynn was sitting at a big bar.

"Mr. Flynn," Mo's father-in-law said, "I'd like you to meet a couple of friends of mine from New York."

"Come on in," Flynn said. "Sit down. Have a drink. What are you drinking? What the hell are you guys doing out here?"

Flynn looked old. Along with the famous ironic eyebrows, mustache, and grin were deep vertical creases on his cheeks.

"We're looking for work," Jerry said.

"Out here?" Flynn said. "Work? New York—that's the only place to be. You kidding? California? This is nowhere."

"We thought we might get a few bit parts or something," Jerry said.

"I may be going on location," Flynn said. Some movie about scuba diving. Did Jerry and Lotti scuba?

Well, they had been thinking about getting work deep-sea diving, they said.

"Leave your names," Flynn said.

"Oh, shit," Jerry said. "We're going to go out on location with Errol Flynn."

They talked and drank, Flynn giving them advice, already planning their careers, a Dutch uncle. Before they left, Lotti, always trying to stir something up, told Flynn, "Yeah, Jerry here really got the hots for Dorothy Malone."

"Really?" Flynn said. "Wait a minute."

He stuck his head out of his trailer and called, "Hey, Dotty, come on over."

She came over. Jerry didn't know whether to thank or slug Lotti.

"I want you to meet a couple of dear friends of mine from New York City," Flynn said. "This is Tony. This is Jerry."

She nodded. Everyone exchanged hellos.

"You busy tonight?" Flynn asked. "Maybe Jerry is free."

"I'm not busy," Malone said. To Jerry, she said, "Call me."

That night, Jerry had a drink, another, and another, nerving himself up for his date. After a while, it was too late to call. Jerry consoled himself by figuring that Dorothy Malone hadn't been serious anyway.

He stayed around Hollywood a few more days, spending the afternoons waddling down to the beach in rented scuba gear with Tony Lotti, getting ready for his acting debut. But in some ways Hollywood seemed as unreal and eerie as the world underwater. Jerry kept remembering the set of *Marjorie Morningstar*, where he saw Natalie Wood shoot and re-shoot a scene thirty or more times.

Holy shit! he thought. This is what movie-making is all about? I can't believe it.

He'd assumed it was just learn your lines and "Roll 'em."

I could never stand it, he decided. And he missed home. Flynn was right. New York was the only place to be. If he was going to be a star, he'd have to be a star not in the movies but in real life.

When Jerry got back to New York, he learned that the Police Department's routine investigation of his application had turned up questions that were delaying his entry onto the force. The questions were about his association with Tony Lotti—who had a police record. Lotti was a few years older than Jerry. During World War II, he'd fought in Italy with the partisans. When the Americans joined the war, he'd joined the Army. But he kept the freewheeling style of his guerrilla days—not only in the service but also when he returned to the States. Out of habit, he always carried two guns. He was caught and charged with illegal possession of weapons. The charge was thrown out of court, but it still showed up on his record. For twenty-two months, Jerry was repeatedly dragged down to department hearings. Getting on the force became a challenge for Jerry. He was not going to knuckle under. To make a point about the ridiculous length of the investigation, Jerry finally decided that he would not go home to wash up and change into clean clothes before meeting the commissioner in charge of his case. Flash Printing, where he was again working, was three blocks from police headquarters. Jerry went directly to the hearing in his greasy clothes, with ink under his fingernails.

"You gotta be kidding," Iggy had said when he heard what Jerry intended to do.

When the commissioner glared at his appearance, Jerry said, "Look, I can't afford to take any more time from work. I lose money every time I take off. I'm here. Ask me whatever you have to ask me."

While waiting to hear the outcome of the investigation, Jerry didn't abandon Lotti—or anyone from his old crowd. After work, as usual, he'd meet his friends for a drink or a stroll. One spring evening, he, Iggy, Joe Bocassi, and another member of their gang, Pete, were crossing the street when a young woman in a new Ford convertible almost ran them down.

They jumped back. The two passengers, also young women, smiled. Jerry smiled back. The car stopped.

"Oh, oh," Jerry said. "Let's go, fellas. This is it!"

Jerry walked up to the driver, whom he thought the loveliest of the three, and said, "Excuse me. Can we help you? Everything all right?"

The driver, whose name was Katherine Corcione, said, "We're looking for Arthur's Tavern."

Arthur's Tavern. Perfect. Not one of the beatnik hangouts with the weird names that had begun opening in the Village, but a neighborhood place. Jerry used to play ball with Vinnie, the son of the owner of Arthur's Tavern. This was his turf. He could guide the girls to the bar with all the offhand graciousness of the insider introducing his guests to a privileged society —like Errol Flynn had introduced him to Hollywood.

"I'll take you there," Jerry said, ready to vault over the closed door into the convertible. "Can we get in?"

Kay looked Jerry over. He wore a DA haircut and pegged pants, the do-wop style of a juvenile delinquent, but it seemed a costume. He seemed respectable.

"Sure," she said.

Jerry, Iggy, and Joe hopped into the car. Pete, who was married, started to climb in, too, but Jerry said, "Hey. There are three of us. Three girls. You go home to your wife."

It was a classic movie meeting.

Iggy paired off with Kay. Jerry paired off with one of Kay's friends, Barbara. They seemed a little highfalutin, Jerry thought; college girls, slumming in the Village. But that was like a movie, too. Cynical down-to-earth Frank Sinatra romancing a classy dame like Grace Kelly in *High Society.*

At Arthur's, they had a few drinks. When Jerry was among friends, he tended to entertain, weaving stories through the conversation, maintaining eye contact with one person, then another, then the first person again, then a third, like a circus performer who was keeping a dozen plates spinning at once. He generated so much intensity that in public his group became the focus of attention. In the restaurant, he presided over his party like a Swing Era star who had joined a ringside table between shows. But his performance wasn't overbearing. It was too generous. He couldn't resist the impulse to play host, making sure everyone was having a good time.

"Gee," Jerry said after a while. "It's getting late. Why don't we go for breakfast?"

With the convertible top down, the lights of the city streaming past them like colored ribbons, they drove to Rattner's on Second Avenue, where they had bagels and coffee.

"My God," Kay said, "we're going to get killed when we get home."

They exchanged telephone numbers. Jerry called Barbara a few times. But, after a while, that romance cooled.

Six months later, Jerry, Iggy, and Joe Bocassi were hanging out on a corner in the Village, feeling as alive to the city as the three sailors in *On the Town,* when Jerry saw Kay and another girl coming down the street.

"Isn't that the blonde we went to Arthur's with that night?" Jerry asked Joe.

A couple of guys—tourists, Jerry thought—were following them, making remarks like, "Hey, baby. How about going out? Having a drink? You look like a million dollars."

"Come on," Jerry said to Iggy and Joe.

He blocked the tourists' way and said, "All right, fellas. Take a walk." The knight rescuing the maiden. But when he took Kay's arm and said, "Hi," she swung her pocketbook at his head. He ducked.

"Wait a minute," he said.

She recognized him and sheepishly smiled.

Jerry and Kay were engaged on her birthday. Within the year, they were married and Jerry became a New York City policeman. He started at the old 20th Precinct on West Sixty-eighth Street, where he spent from 1960 to 1966. The best part of the job was delivering babies.

His first delivery was in a hotel right off Broadway on Seventy-seventh Street. He and his partner, Joe Flynn, walked into the room, which was the size of a big closet, and saw a woman writhing on the floor. She was screaming, "Help me. Help me."

"Okay, Jerry," Flynn said. "I'll go call the ambulance."

Before Jerry had a chance to point out that the room had a phone, Flynn was escaping down the stairs. He was heading for a phone booth on the street, away from the woman, whose water had just broken. The rug was a swamp. Jerry washed his hands and gathered towels. Kneeling beside the woman, he said, "Lady, just relax. Take short breaths." He'd learned about childbearing not only from his police training, but also from his wife, who was in the third trimester of her pregnancy. Jerry took this crisis personally.

"I'm only seven months," the woman screamed.

Shit, Jerry thought.

Flynn burst back into the room.

"It's premature," Jerry told him. "Let them know."

Again, ignoring the phone in the room, Flynn bolted down the stairs. The woman arched and thrashed, grunted and yelped. The crown of the baby's head appeared. And the baby slid out.

Jerry cleaned the mucus from its nose and mouth, made sure it was breathing, wrapped it in a towel, and laid it on the woman's belly. He knew enough not to mess with the umbilical cord, which pulsed with a swallowing motion.

"How's my baby?" the woman cried. She tucked her chin, trying to see the little body on her belly.

Jerry was assuring her it was fine when two doctors arrived.

"You did this all by yourself?" the woman doctor asked.

"Well," Jerry said, "yeah."

"You did an excellent job," she said.

Altogether Jerry delivered five babies. One woman, grateful for his help, asked, "What's your name?"

"Gennaro," Jerry said.

"What?" the woman asked.

"Jerry."

The woman named the baby after him: Geraldine.

The worst part of the job were the floaters, corpses that would sink to the bottom of the rivers in the winter and bob to the surface in the spring. Decomposition inflated the bodies with gas. One, waterlogged and bloated beyond recognition, weighed at least four hundred pounds. The skin was green. The stench was nauseating; worse than putrid cottage cheese. Crabs had plucked at the body. Fish had nibbled ragged holes. Every time they tried to drag it onto the pier, spongy hunks of flesh sloughed off. In the head was a gunshot wound.

Jerry called the detective bureau, a separate branch of the police department, which handled murder cases.

"Don't be so quick to call it homicide," a detective said, lording his experience over Jerry.

"The guy's in the water with a hole in his head," Jerry said.

"Maybe he tripped, cracked his skull on a rock, and drowned," the detective said.

Jerry enjoyed the social work that takes up more than two thirds of a uniformed cop's time: resolving marital squabbles, looking for lost kids, helping the ill, comforting the bereaved— work that, according to a high school aptitude test, he was temperamentally suited for. But detectives were an elite. The pay was better. And the problem-solving involved in investigation fascinated him. He wanted to become a detective.

In 1966, Jerry answered a call and found a woman half-dead, her blouse soaked in blood. A man had taken a plank from an adjacent roof, bridged it across an areaway eight flights up, and crawled through her bathroom window. He robbed and raped her while her five-year-old child watched. The woman tried to escape. The man stabbed her with a pocket knife in the back and chest twenty-six times.

The woman survived. In the hospital, she described the man to a police artist who made a sketch.

"I think I know who this is," Jerry said, looking at the composite. "Don't show it around. If you do, someone is going to warn him, and he'll get away."

"I'll give you a day," said the detective who was handling the case.

Jerry and his partner, Lenny Campanello, cruised through the man's neighborhood until they spotted him. When Jerry brought the man in, the detective in charge thanked him and told him to resume patrol. Jerry was in the police car when he heard that the woman had positively identified the man in a hospital room lineup.

"Come back in," Jerry was told.

When he got to the station house, his boss, a uniformed inspector, said, "That's your arrest."

"Excuse me?" Jerry said.

"You picked the guy up, right?" the inspector said.

"Yes," Jerry said. "I did."

"Why aren't you with your prisoner?" the inspector said.

Jerry couldn't believe he was being given the arrest. It violated all precedents. Officially, a uniformed cop never arrested a suspect in a major case. Only detectives did.

"The detectives were called in," Jerry said. "They did all the work on it."

"But you picked the guy up from the sketch," the inspector said.

"That's correct," Jerry said.

"It's your arrest," the inspector said.

Jerry went upstairs to the detectives' office.

"Listen," he said, "I've been told I've got to make this arrest."

"Who told you that?" the detective in charge asked.

Jerry explained.

"Resume patrol," the detective in charge said.

Jerry went out and climbed into his police car.

Half an hour later, Jerry's boss called the 20th Precinct and said, "I'm keeping on top of that arrest. Is Giorgio doing all the paperwork?"

"He's around here somewhere," the desk sergeant said.

"I want to talk to him," the inspector said.

The sergeant radioed Jerry. "Hey, the inspector just called. You better get your ass in here."

Jerry returned to the station house and went back up to the detectives' office.

"What are you doing here?" the detective in charge asked.

"Hey, let me tell you, your boss better resolve this with my boss," Jerry said. "But my boss is saying I've got to make this arrest."

The next day, after the suspect was arraigned, Jerry got a call from the chief of detectives.

"Would you like to be a detective?" the Chief asked when Jerry got to his office.

Jerry was transferred. Within six months, in the spring of 1967, he got his gold shield. This—he thought—is better than the movies.

Jerry's party weekends were supposed to be an escape from police work. Seymour Kantor, one of his oldest friends, would set up the grill on the patio beneath the deck. Next to the grill was a long table, where a portable television was usually tuned to golf or tennis. Upstairs in the kitchen, the other television would be tuned to baseball. Some of the guests lounged in deck chairs on the lawn. Others played in Jerry's volleyball tournament, which lasted all summer until the finals on Labor Day. Jerry was a volleyball fanatic. Often he'd play for six hours straight.

This evening, by the time he arrived, the game was ending.

"Come on," Jerry said. "Just one more."

He grabbed the ball and popped it over the net. Someone returned it. Teams reformed. Jerry threw his jacket and tie on the sidelines.

Usually, Jerry would be obsessed by the game. But this evening he was preoccupied. In the middle of a volley, he got a phone call.

"Who from?" Jerry called, back-pedalling to get under the ball.

"The office," Kay said.

It was about the case. Some routine details.

Jerry hit the ball and left the field. Someone on the other team caught the ball. The game stopped as they all watched Jerry run to the phone extension under the deck.

No one could remember Jerry leaving a game before.

8

A WEEK AND A HALF after Helen was killed, the best lead they had was the tampon found on C level—if it turned out to be Helen's. If not, they'd be at a dead end. Mike started wandering through the Met, slipping into ladies' rooms and buying tampons from the vending machines. He got strange looks. A few times, when women came into the bathroom and found him—a man hanging around where no man should be—they panicked. Paranoia was so high—people were so sure the Phantom of the Opera would kill again—that Met employees, particularly the women, were easily spooked. Once, not wanting to scare anyone, Mike crouched on a toilet seat inside a stall, hiding while a woman used the bathroom.

Jerry went from drugstore to drugstore buying a box of each kind of tampon. He took all the tampons, his and Mike's, to the medical examiner's lab. One by one, he dipped them in water and compared how they looked when they were swollen with the tampon found on C level, which itself was being tested for blood type.

On August 1, they learned that the C-level tampon was Helen's. They'd finally gotten a break. After reporting this during the daily strategy session, Jerry left to pick up his daughter from ballet class. Fifteen minutes later, a reporter called up the investigating team at the Met to ask if it was true they'd identified the C-level tampon as Helen's.

Only two people outside the conference room at the Met knew the tampon had been identified, the Chief told Jerry the next morning. You, the Chief said, and the lab technician.

"Then we know who's the leak," Jerry said. "The lab technician."

The conference room was swept for bugs. And the following Friday, August 8, while Jerry was talking to Fallarino, the Chief called Mike to a secret meeting. Just disappear, Mike was told. Don't tell people where you're going.

The meeting was limited to about half a dozen people. Jerry was not there. He hadn't been asked to attend, Mike was told. Why? Mike wondered. No one explained. Mike didn't press the point. He figured he'd find out in the course of the meeting.

The Chief got down to business. Using an extraordinary new method, fingertip prints had been lifted from Helen's dress. From the hem—just where they'd be if someone had grabbed the dress to cut or rip it. The prints were not Helen's. They must belong to the killer. All they had to do was get prints from everyone at the Met and find the ones that matched the prints on the dress.

They didn't want to let the killer know what they had, so instead of saying the prints came from her dress, they concocted a story: The tips—they would say—came from a boatswain's whistle they'd found. Since the killer would know he'd never touched a boatswain's whistle, he wouldn't refuse to let the cops take his prints.

One more thing, Mike was told. This plan had to remain secret. No one except the people in the room could know the truth.

"What about Jerry?" Mike asked.

Not even Jerry could know.

Mike thought, They must figure Jerry's the snitch.

Good cops don't hold out on each other. No matter how much you might hate your partner, someday your life may depend on him. You don't hold out.

Mike felt terrible. He was being ordered to betray his partner. That night, at the end of the hour-and-a-half drive home, he passed the spot where there used to be a stand that sold fresh eggs. When he first moved out of the New York City area to this upstate village, he'd been shocked by his neighbors' honesty. The egg-stand owner used to leave the eggs untended, stacked next to a cigar box. People took the eggs and left their money in the box. No one stole the eggs. No one stole the money. This was the world he wanted his kids to grow up in.

If he didn't tell Jerry about the secret plan, he'd be violating his code. It would be as if he smashed his neighbor's eggs and emptied the cigar box into his pocket. But if he disobeyed the order to keep the plan secret, he risked losing his job—losing everything he'd worked so hard to build.

Like Jerry, Mike never expected to become a cop. That's where the similarity between them ended. If Jerry as a boy was obsessed with movies, Mike, ten years younger, was possessed by rock 'n' roll. He could hardly help it. In 1954, the dawn of rock 'n' roll—the year after *Crazy Man Crazy* by Bill Haley and the Comets was the first rock 'n' roll song to make *Billboard's* national chart—Mike's father, George, moved the family (Mike's mother Anne, his older sister Carol, and Mike, who was ten) from one section of Brooklyn to another: from Bushwick to Flatbush.

Flatbush!

By the time Mike was a teenager, you could breathe rock 'n' roll in the air of Flatbush. At night, on street corners in halos of lamp light, do-wop groups sang a cappella. Sha-boom. Sha-boom. If rock 'n' roll were a religion, Philadelphia, home of *American Bandstand*, might have been the Vatican, but Flatbush was the Holy Land.

Mike would wake up at four o'clock in the morning to wait in the snow for tickets at the Fox or the Paramount. When the Dell Vikings came on stage and sang, "Come Go With Me," he'd twirl a girl from her seat and dance, fingerpopping down the aisle, until the cops, shoving through the crowd, sat everyone down again. He wore out his album of *The Paragons and the Jesters*.

These were the years when guys stood in front of mirrors, leaning back, knees slightly bent, as they combed and re-combed their pompadours. When they dry-humped to the Five Satins singing "To the Aisle." Or later learned how to imitate the Big Bopper's dirty laugh in "Chantilly Lace." An insinuating snarl. It was the years when sensitivity was proved by one's level of resentment, and resentment was the one quality a hero could not do without. When guys cultivated an anger as smoldering as Brando's in *The Wild One*. Sha-boom! The sound of a burning fuse and the following blast.

On warm days, Mike played hooky and went to Jamaica Bay. At night, he and his pals would camp in the Canarsie Marshes, conjuring up their own Muscle Beach. Beer, broads, and bikinis. Mike's teenage years arc from Chuck Berry's "Sweet Little

Sixteen" to the Beach Boys' adaptation of the same tune in *Surfin' USA*.

He quit high school just before rock 'n' roll transformed itself into alien rock: English, soul, and psychedelic music. Working-class whites were being replaced by Brits, blacks, and middle-class hippies. Flatbush was being replaced by Liverpool, Detroit, and San Francisco. Mike was seventeen, tough, smart, and restless.

With four friends—Freddy, Kevin, Bobby, and Chucky—he joined the Army under the buddy plan: They'd stay together through basic training. Later, Mike got cushy assignments—Fort Dix, Fort Benjamin Harrison in Indianapolis, Indiana, and Fort Hamilton in Brooklyn—until he started dating the daughter of Fort Hamilton's base commander.

Even though he was just an enlisted man, Mike would be saluted like an officer when he bombed through the gate in his girlfriend's car, which had her father's identification on it. For Mike, camp was as comfortable as a country club—until one day when he was passing post headquarters. The sergeant crooked a finger. Mike swaggered over. He and the sergeant didn't get along, because the sergeant lived in the same barracks as Mike and was infuriated every night by the noise Mike and his cronies made, partying.

"Hey, hot shot," the sergeant said, "you're gonna leave this camp."

"What are you talking about?" Mike said. "You can't make me go nowhere."

"Lover-boy," the sergeant said, "you shouldn't have picked the post commander's daughter."

Five days later, Mike was an MP at Fort Monroe, Virginia.

Jerry may have spent his army years playing Cary Grant; Mike spent his as James Dean.

Six months after Mike was discharged and nine months after he was married—to Marion McPhail—he was back in

Flatbush, working in a Pfizer Pharmaceutical Company warehouse. One Saturday morning, at dawn, Mike was awakened by
the four buddies he'd joined the Army with.

Ready to heave the clock at them, Mike asked, "What the
hell are you doing here?"

"Get dressed," they said. "We're going to take the cop test."

Mike said, "I don't want to be no cop." But he gave in. "I'm
as crazy as you guys," he said. "Let's go."

He joined the force in September 1966. His first assignment
was in Bedford-Stuyvesant, Brooklyn, in the 77th Precinct. The
old Atlantic Avenue station house, built in the 1850s, gave him
the horrors. The floorboards squeaked. The stairs swayed. Bare
bulbs cast bat-wing shadows. It was a perfect spot for *The Mon-
ster Mash.*

The neighborhood was worse. They called the precinct the
Rug, since it covered such a small area: only nine by twelve
blocks. Even though the station house ran nine cars, the streets
were underpatrolled. You'd radio for help and hear nothing but
other cars also calling for help. People, shot or stabbed, stum-
bled out of bars with the regularity of birds popping from
cuckoo clocks.

As a rookie, Mike rarely rode in a patrol car. He walked the
beat, enveloped in the voluminous overcoats cops used to wear.
It was like wearing a tent. It was so heavy, when you ran in it, it
felt as if you were kicking your way through waterlogged
bathmats. The broad expanse of cloth made a good target for
bottles and bricks hurled from rooftops or sniper bullets, all of
which Mike expected every time he went on patrol. The summer before, race riots had made cops patrolling ghettos like
Bedford-Stuyvesant feel like occupying forces, vulnerable to
guerrilla attacks.

One night, when Mike was taking shelter in a doorway at
Fulton Street and Albany Avenue, a gypsy cab roared past. In
the back seat was a man holding a blood-soaked towel to his

face. Blood was trickling down his forearms and dripping from his elbows. Mike stopped a car and followed the cab to the local hospital, St. John's.

The man with the bloody face had pulled a Baretta on a guy in the neighboring 79th Precinct and said, "Give me your money, motherfucker."

The guy being held up reached for his wallet—but too fast. The Baretta, thinking the other guy was going for a weapon, pulled the trigger. The gun didn't go off. The Baretta pulled the trigger a second time. Again, the gun failed to go off.

"Is that right?" Wallet said. He reached into his other pocket and pulled out a straight razor.

The Baretta was slashed worse than anyone Mike had ever seen. His guts were hanging out: red and blue and the yellow of chicken fat. If he'd let go of his face, his cheeks would have slid down to his jaw.

"What the fuck am I doing here?" Mike asked himself.

Cops said that if you spent just one year in a class-A precinct like the 77th, any other precinct would seem like a country club. Mike spent two and a half years at the 77th. In June 1969, he was transferred to the 62nd Precinct, Bath Avenue, Brooklyn, a large Italian section, which included Joe Columbo's home on Eighty-sixth Street. Much safer. If the 77th had ten stabbings in a week, the 62nd had ten stabbings in a year.

In December 1970, Mike went into plain clothes, the Public Morals Squad. Like a hunter in a swamp, he had to wade in hip-deep. To nail someone selling kiddie porn, Mike put on scruffy clothes, dark glasses, and a beret; went into an adult bookstore, scratching his balls; and whispered, "You got anything with really young stuff?" To close bottle clubs, unlicensed gay bars operating mostly in Manhattan's meat-market district, like the Barn and the Anvil, Mike and his partner, Seneca "Tucker" DeGraw, had to pass themselves off as gays. They'd enter the clubs, confirm that liquor was being sold illegally, and get a warrant so the places could be raided.

The first time Mike infiltrated one of the bars, the Barn, he had to prepare himself with a couple of bourbons. Dressed in tight pants, he skipped up to the place holding Tucker's hand. When Tucker complained that Mike's hand was clammy, Mike said, "Look, holding hands with you ain't my idea of mainstream success."

At the door, Mike, in his most ingenuous manner, asked the bouncer, "Hi, is Leslie inside?"

The club was on the third floor of a warehouse. In the elevator, someone pinched Mike's ass.

"That's cute," said Tucker.

"Shut up, or I'll scratch your eyes out," Mike said. He was maintaining his cover.

The elevator door opened. Mike and Tucker stepped into a dark loft that ran the length of the building, a full block. At both ends, jukeboxes blared. Lights flashed. Bodies seethed. The air seemed thick. There was a slight whiff of feces.

"Look at that," Mike said to Tucker. "On top of the bar. One guy giving another guy a mustard shot in the ass."

But Mike thought the sodomy on the bar less astounding than the casual audience of men, who stood around sipping their drinks.

Mike and Tucker made a circuit of the place—from the front door to the back rooms, where the men having sex seemed locked in mortal combat. There were daisy chains like great fleshy engines, grinding away aimlessly, disconnected from the machines they were supposed to run. There were men slumped in corners, as dazed and drained as vampire victims; and other men prowling through the shadows as though seized by blood lust.

Mike and Tucker identified the guy selling admission at the door, the bouncers, the bartenders, the hat-check boys, the principals. They weren't interested in the patrons. Mike jotted brief descriptions on a scrap of paper. Discreetly, so he wouldn't blow his cover, he would slip the descriptions to the raiding party when they arrived, so they would know whom to arrest.

The raiding party was announced by a sledgehammer blow on the door. It was as if someone had set off a firecracker in an aviary. The crowd erupted and surged from wall to wall looking for exits. The bartenders leaped over the bar and, like the other club employees, tried unsuccessfully to lose themselves among the patrons. By the end of the raid, Mike thought the scene had become as silly as *The Three Stooges in Hell.*

At another time, Mike's boss said, "You never made a pros collar."

"I'm game," Mike said.

They gave him the name, phone number, and code word of a hooker who was operating out of an apartment on Lexington Avenue in the low Thirties. On the way there in the squad car with his backup team, Mike wondered, Why is it so easy?

He called from a pay phone at the corner. The prostitute answered.

"Hello, this is Veronica."

"This is Harry," Mike said. "Charlie sent me. You available?"

"Sure," she said. "Come right up. Ring the buzzer twice, and I'll let you in."

The backup team prepped Mike. They reminded him that to make a legal arrest, the woman had to agree to commit a particular sexual act for a fee. Sex act. And fee. Mike needed both. Just a price quoted or an act agreed to wouldn't count. And there could be no physical contact with her.

As he'd been instructed, Mike rang the doorbell twice. Erotic Morse code. Veronica turned out to be in her twenties and pretty. Mike sat on the bed, his heart pounding. He'd never paid for a woman in his life; he felt awkward and nervous.

"What are you looking for?" she asked.

"What do you got?" Mike said.

"Fifty for around-the-world," she said. "Fifteen for French. Twenty-five for a combination: a blow-job and a piece of ass."

Mike stood up, flashed his badge, and repeated the cliché, "Look, baby, the jig is up."

"Oh, really?" she said.

She opened the closet door. Out stepped the biggest German shepherd Mike had ever seen. Mike jumped over a coffee table and backed into a corner, dragging a chair in front of him for a shield. Simultaneously, he was trying to stay behind the chair, keep his eye on the woman and the dog, and lean over to get his gun from his ankle holster. When he bent down, the chair blocked his view. When he moved the chair to see what was going on, the dog lowered its head, ears back flat, and snarled—so Mike would pull back the chair to protect himself, which again blocked his vision, forcing him to straighten up before getting his gun.

"Yo," he yelled to his backup team. "Hey! How about it!"

Finally, he got his gun, told the woman he'd shoot the dog if it attacked, and took her into custody. Outside the apartment, his backup team—who had known about the dog and had set Mike up for the typical hazing due a new recruit to the Morals Squad—were leaning against the hallway walls, weak with laughter.

In a few months, Mike was a veteran. He'd locked up thirty to forty prostitutes and was assigned to check out the massage parlors that were just opening in the city. Norman Vincent Peale had lodged a complaint about one place operating across the street from his church on Fifth Avenue. For $15, you could get a rubdown or rent a Polaroid camera to take photographs of the girls.

When Mike entered, the head jerk asked, "What can I do for you?"

"I'd like to spend some time with one of the ladies," Mike said.

Five women sat along a wall. Four looked as if they had been worked over by their pimps one time too many. Mike chose the fifth woman, who was pretty and vivacious.

She led him into a cubicle, which was bare except for two mattresses on the floor and a night stand, which held a light, a roll of toilet paper, and a bottle of Listerine.

"What do you want to do?" the girl asked.

"I'd like to take pictures," Mike said. "How's that?"

By the time Mike had the camera ready, she was nude. She went from one lewd pose to another: on her back, on her knees, on all fours. Her twists and curves seemed to be shaping letters, as though she were spelling out a lascivious message with her body. Mike snapped away, waiting for her to proposition him—which she finally did. He had the evidence he needed to close the place down: pornographic pictures and prostitution. At the station house, the other cops complimented Mike on his photographic skills.

Nothing surprised Mike any more. Not even the Blood Feast on Wooster Street. A few times a week a satanic cult castrated a goat, slit its throat and drank the blood, while on a stage men and women engaged in ritual sex. People paid $10 to watch.

The night Mike went was low mass: Instead of a goat the satanists sacrificed a chicken. The blood spilling from the neck sounded like juice gurgling from a bottle. Sighs of contentment wafted through the audience.

By a year and a half after Mike had joined Public Morals, he'd seen enough of New York City's Other Life. That's when he moved his family upstate. But, although he wanted to shield his family, he enjoyed plain clothes. The work was not the dull routine of handling typical robberies, stabbings, and shootings.

It was varied, required wit and a dramatic flair. Most of all, he had a chance to investigate. Even though detectives tended to dislike plainclothesmen, Public Morals was as close to detective work as you could get. And Mike's dream was to become a detective.

In March 1972, when Mike got his new assignment—the Narcotics Squad—the odds on becoming a detective did not seem good. The department rarely promoted someone from his new district, the 8th in the Bronx. The area included the 41st Precinct, one of the most dangerous in the city, the notorious Fort Apache. It had been five years since someone from the 8th had been raised to detective. But in November 1973, a little over a year and a half after Mike came to the district, he made the grade.

The streets were busy even in bad weather. Addicts, drunks, curbside con men, penny-ante gamblers, drifters, brown-bag beggars, derelicts, brutes, pimps in pin-striped suits, broad-bottomed whores with cruel pig-eyes, skinny kids cadging coins, rapists, numbers runners, killers, shake-down artists, muggers, high-rollers looking for a game, swindlers, petty cheats, forgers, blackmailers, arsonists, child molesters, hoodlums, kidnappers, pickpockets, psychopaths, embezzlers, necrophiliacs, coprophiliacs, transvestites, transsexuals, political terrorists and free-lance terrorizers, subway rampagers, obscene phone-callers, disturbers of the peace, pornographers, shoplifters, exhibitionists, voyeurs, smugglers, and sadists. Mike thought it was like ancient Baghdad. The only thing missing were fakirs lying on nail beds and snake charmers.

Soon after he became a detective, Mike, still with the Narcotics Squad, went with his partner Lenny Caruso and some other cops to search an apartment on Beck Street off Intervale Avenue, a neighborhood that was the hub of the drug trade. In just one building on that block during the following two years, Mike and Caruso would raid twenty apartments. On this first raid, they parked their van, an unmarked one, on the back block, Fox Street, and climbed over fences, sneaked through back alleys, courtyards, cellars, up stairs, and through corridors carrying a pipe five feet long and four inches in diameter, filled with concrete: their battering ram. Walking at a normal pace, one man might be able to drag it a block. They had to run with it, because from the time they left the van to the moment they broke down the door, they had two minutes before everyone in the neighborhood but the cockroaches knew they were there.

Above them from window to window they heard whistles and warning cries. By the time they were gasping up the stairs of the apartment, behind nearly every door toilets were flushing —evidence literally down the drain. When they got to the fifth floor, they could barely talk, let alone swing the pipe. They drew guns. Mike and Lenny raised the pipe. They charged.

Instead of knocking down the door, the ram penetrated it like a bullet, wedging Mike's finger. It felt like his fingertip had been chopped off. Mike yanked back his hand, just as the door toppled, frame and all.

Inside they found a table piled with forty to fifty glassine bags of heroin; but it was garbage dope—2 1/2 percent, maybe 3 percent purity. Disappointing. They'd been hoping for either quantity—a couple of ounces—or quality—50 percent purity, which would mean that the dope had been stepped on, cut, just once, and the dealer was high up the ladder.

They took photographs, inventoried what was found; arrested the suspects; and headed downstairs, around the block, and back to the van—which had been burned. Nothing was left inside but the handle of Mike's attaché case.

A few weeks later, in the same block, Mike and Caruso raided another dope dealer's apartment. Mike hit the door with the ram and ducked to the side, while Lenny ran in, his shotgun raised. Mike dropped the ram, pulled his revolver, followed

Lenny—and saw over Lenny's shoulder a sixty-year-old woman lying in a bed. The drug dealer's mother-in-law.

Just as Mike started to relax, the old woman reached under her mattress and pulled out an automatic. The room was small. Lenny was blocking Mike, so he couldn't get off a clear shot. The old woman, squinting, waved the gun from side to side, aiming at Mike, who dodged back and forth, shouting to Lenny, "Shoot her. Shoot her."

She's going to kill me, Mike thought; and there's nothing I can do about it.

Lenny hurled himself across the room and whacked the old woman with the shotgun butt. Mike had never been so close to death. Or felt so helpless.

In December 1976, Mike joined the Homicide Squad, which was housed in the 20th Precinct. Three years later, when the specialized units were broken up in a department-wide reorganization, Mike chose to stay at the 20th, which by then felt like home.

Because of the hour-and-a-half commute and the heavy work load of the Metropolitan Opera case, Mike had been home so rarely that when he opened his kitchen door, his huge German shepherd, Kojak, growled at him.

His wife, Marion, offered to introduce him to the kids. She handed him a fistful of notes from customers of the small contracting business he ran on the side. One woman whose yard he'd ripped up for a new septic system was desperate to get it finished; the stench was overpowering. But his bulldozer, an International TD7, had a problem in one of its hydraulic lines.

As Mike worked on the machine, he went over and over what to do about Jerry. Lie to his partner. Or ignore the department's orders. Mike loved his bulldozer so much he carried a picture of it in his wallet. But he was so upset by the dilemma, he threw the wrench at the machine.

"What should I do?" he asked Marion later that night.

They were sitting on the enclosed porch. Spotlights made from Wilson tennis ball cannisters cast pale circles on the floor. Moths bumped against the screens.

"I don't know," Marion said. "What should you do?"

"I don't even want to face the guy," Mike said.

9

THAT SAME WEEKEND, Jerry was feeling discouraged. So many stagehands were so close to the crime scene and, except for a distant moan, a slam, and a fluttering elevator door, nobody saw or heard anything. Mike was concentrating on porters; Jerry was concentrating on engineers and electricians. There was no coordination. The investigation had become a tug of war. A silent tug of war. Mike and Jerry hardly spoke to each other any more. It's a lousy situation, Jerry thought. We got to do something.

By the time Jerry got home, the regular weekend guests had gone. When he entered the kitchen, Lisa, his eighteen-year-old daughter, gave him an uh-oh-you're-in-trouble look and left the room. His son, Marc, who was fifteen and handicapped, sat at the kitchen table, glum. Kay stood at the sink, her back to him. She didn't turn around. Jerry knew he'd forgotten something.

Kay brought him dinner, kept warm in the oven. Jerry ate in silence. At last, Kay said, "We had a nice day at the camp."

Marc's camp. Parents' Day at Marc's camp. Which Marc had been looking forward to for weeks. That's what Jerry had forgotten.

"Oh, shoot," Jerry said. "I'm sorry."

"That's all right, Dad," Marc said.

From his son's expression, Jerry knew it wasn't all right.

"I'm going to be off tomorrow," Jerry said. "I'll take you for an extra treat."

"Promise?" Marc said.

"We'll have breakfast together in town," Jerry said.

"And go by Crazy Eddie's," Marc said, "and pick up a couple of records?"

"It's a date," Jerry said.

As they were getting ready for bed, Kay said, "Birthdays mean nothing. Anniversaries mean nothing. Weddings mean nothing. Christenings mean nothing. Showers, Parents' Day, even your volleyball games. . . . Nothing."

"That's not true," Jerry said.

"You don't even realize it," Kay said. "It's just the job. The job. The job. You don't know what you're doing to your family and friends."

"Things haven't been any different on this case than any other," Jerry said.

"Baloney," Kay said.

Jerry was at retirement age. This case might be his last shot at solving a big one. It would cap his career, get him a promotion, so he'd be able to retire having reached the top ranks of his profession. And, Jerry thought, I'm stuck with a hothead partner who's going to screw it up for me.

On Monday and Tuesday, August 11 and 12, Mike tried to avoid Jerry. During the daily strategy sessions, he couldn't meet Jerry's gaze. During discussions about the boatswain's whistle and the plan to take the tip-prints of all the Met employees, he couldn't even look Medina, Heaney, Rosenthal—any of the other detectives—in the face. Eventually, he knew, everyone would learn he'd held back on his partner.

That evening, Mike worked himself to exhaustion in the gym in the basement of the 20th Precinct station house. Then he ran around the Central Park reservoir until he was ready to drop. By the time he got back to the bunk room at the precinct, he'd decided to tell Jerry the truth about the tip-prints.

"Listen, I got to talk to you," Mike said to Jerry the next morning.

Mike was in such a hurry, he didn't even put down his briefcase.

What is this? Jerry wondered. Does he have a hot lead?

Afraid of bugs in the Atrium office, Mike drew Jerry into a storage room, which was lit by a single sixty-watt bulb. He wanted to study Jerry's reactions. Mike knew that no matter how good an actor you are, your eyes don't lie. When he worked in a gambling squad, Mike always used to walk into a joint and look at the floor, because if the bookmaker saw his eyes he'd know Mike was a cop.

Mike was sure that what he was going to say would upset Jerry. If Jerry's eyes didn't show he was upset, it would prove that Jerry knew about the tip-prints all along and that Mike was being set up, tested to see if he was the leak.

"I know we're not kissing cousins," Mike said, "but there's something I got to say. I don't want to carry it around no more. But you got to promise you won't tell nobody I told you. Not the Chief. Nobody. If you do, I'm dead."

Jerry promised.

Mike told him that the boatswain's-whistle story was a ruse. The tips really came from Helen's dress. He'd been ordered not to tell anyone—not even Jerry.

Jerry never stopped smiling. But his eyes got hard. He puffed out his cheeks.

"I'll be a son of a bitch," he said. "I'll be a son of a bitch."

Mike was satisfied Jerry hadn't known about the plan. But he couldn't tell what Jerry would do next. If it seemed like Jerry was going to storm into the Chief's office and have a showdown, Mike would have to deck him.

"Jerry?" Mike said.

"I can live with it," Jerry said.

"You can't let it show," Mike said.

"All I want you to know," Jerry said, "is whatever went on before—between us—is over. Let's clear the books."

He held out his hand.

Mike clasped it.

For the rest of the day, during the meetings about fingerprinting the Met employees, Mike and Jerry kept exchanging glances. Together, they interviewed some members of the crew to see if they had trichonodosis, a condition that causes hairs to knot as they grow—the condition that knotted the two hairs found with Helen's corpse. This would later turn out to be a blind alley; the hairs came in the dirty napkin that was used to gag Helen. But they didn't know that then. And, in working together—Jerry engaging the suspect in talk while Mike stood behind him and peered down into the guy's hair looking for the bald spots caused by the disease—they discovered that their personalities meshed. Their differences complemented each other. The very qualities—Mike's passion, Jerry's coolness—that had separated them made them an effective team.

That night, Mike and Jerry went for drinks at a police hangout near 1 Police Plaza, the Metropolitan Improvement Company. Jerry razzed Mike about his Heinekens, which Mike called his Greenies. Mike pretended to be appalled that Jerry drank a candy-cane concoction like White Russians.

"Do you have to have manicured nails to drink one of those?" Mike asked.

Both stared into the mirror behind the bar at the reflection of the wall behind them. On that wall were about fifty pictures. A third were historical, copies of old newspaper engravings of New York City. A third were photographs of celebrities: Muhammad Ali, Charles Lindbergh, JFK. . . . And a third—about a dozen and a half—were photographs of cops who had broken famous cases: the hall of fame.

Neither said anything. Both wondered whether or not their pictures would hang on the wall if they solved Helen's murder.

"Do you want to hear a real kick in the head?" Jerry asked Kay when he got home. He was boiling. He told her about the plan to get the fingerprints of the Met employees and the ruse about the boatswain's whistle, about how the Chief had told Mike not to let him in on the secret, and about how Mike had taken a risk and told him. "Here I am," Jerry said. "The assisting officer. And they're keeping this vital piece of information from me."

He dived into the swimming pool and floated on an inflatable chair for a long time, forty minutes. He thought about the Chief and why he would do that. It had to reflect what the Chief felt about Jerry. But—Jerry thought—the Chief was taking a lot of flak. There had to be pressure on him all the way up to the Mayor's office, maybe higher. The Chief had to be a little paranoid and operate on a need-to-know basis. Jerry figured if he'd been in the Chief's place he might have done the same thing.

Still, the Chief's lack of trust hurt. It made Mike's trust all the more valuable. The dynamics of the investigation had changed. Jerry was no longer struggling with Mike. In some ways, he and Mike were together up against the department.

10

THE NEXT DAY, Thursday, August 14, the stagehands came down to the Atrium in twos and threes—so the show would not be interrupted—to fill out questionnaires about their movements around the time Helen was killed. They were photographed there and had their fingerprints printed. Just for the record, their palm prints were also taken—to prove the perfect palm print on the roof pipe was not connected to the investigation, but was a souvenir of some careless cop.

That evening, one of the officers doing the printing told Mike and Jerry that two Met employees had refused to have their prints taken. For various reasons—sex, age, physical description—neither seemed a likely suspect. But a third employee, a stagehand who did let them take his prints, had been very nervous. He'd been hyperventilating.

"Check them out first," Mike said.

He was especially curious about the nervous stagehand, whose name he took note of: Craig Crimmins.

The next day, they were told the fingertip prints on the dress hem were not Craig's.

Mike and Jerry shrugged. So they didn't get lucky.

But the palm print from the pipe on the roof, the print that was so perfect everyone assumed it had to be worthless—that print was Craig's.

Craig Crimmins was twenty-one years old. A stage carpenter. He grew up in the North Bronx, a neighborhood he loved so much he chose to stay there with his father when his parents were divorced and his mother moved. He was a sickly infant who rarely cried. He'd lie in his crib placid and passive. When he was three years old he started to sleepwalk, which he continued to do as he grew older. Sometimes he would go to the refrigerator and, fast asleep, feed himself. Once, dreaming his dog had fallen from the window, he climbed from bed, wandered through the house and out the front door. It was snowing. He walked down the street, looking for the dog. His mother ran after him, took his hand, and led him back to his bed. In the morning, as usual, he had no memory of his night-time walk.

In school, he was a poor and sometimes hostile student. He was left back in the second and fifth grades. In class he lied about his age, so the other kids wouldn't think he was dumb. He believed he was treated unfairly by the teachers and administration. Once, when he was accused of spitting at another student, the principal wouldn't let him explain himself, which left him morose and withdrawn. The more trouble he had at school, the more his mother apparently fretted. The more she fretted, the more attention she lavished on him. He seemed like a bit of a mama's boy, favored more than his older brother Edward or younger sister Donna.

By the time he was thirteen he was staying out late. As he

grew older he began drinking heavily, enough to black out occasionally. And he started smoking grass. After high school, he went to work backstage at the Met along with his father, stepfather, and brother. When his brother left the Met to work at a television studio, he thought about following him. Otherwise, he didn't have much ambition.

He seemed to have liked the Met. The work was physical, which he evidently enjoyed, and there was opportunity to goof off. In the world of opera, the Met was considered a fun job, a reputation that was national. A member of the crew at the Santa Fe Opera recalled hearing stories of how porn movies were shown backstage during a performance of *Aïda*.

Around the time he started to work at the Met, Craig began dating Mary Ann Fennel, who, unlike Craig, went to college, Stonybrook University on Long Island. Craig and Mary Ann were an ill-matched couple not only intellectually but also physically. Mary Ann was a thin, attractive woman who seemed years older than Craig. In some pictures of them together, she looked as if she could be his mother, a chic, youngish mom, more Upper West Side than North Bronx.

Craig had a baby face, plump and round. His beard grew so sparsely that even when it was long it was hard to see from a distance. He had innocent eyes, which, when he was disturbed or distrustful, got sullen—like a grounded teenager's. His mustache, because it looked so inappropriate, made his face seem not older, but younger.

He was husky, slope-shouldered, with powerful-looking hands. A few months before Helen was murdered, Craig saved the life of a girl whose canoe had capsized. The girl's boyfriend had not been strong enough to rescue her. In panic, she'd fought him, dragged him under. Craig jumped into the water, grabbed her, and pulled her to shore. With his baby face and man's physique, Craig seemed like a picture in a kid's mix-and-match book in which you could put the head of one figure on the body of another.

Quiet and well liked by other crew members, he didn't have a reputation as a troublemaker. He was easygoing, content to share whatever six-packs and joints were circulating, apparently ready to go along with the excesses that sometimes made the Met backstage seem like a frontier province, far from civilization, with its own laws and justice.

On his questionnaire, Craig claimed that on the night of Helen's murder, he hadn't missed any of his cues, which, according to his boss and some fellow stagehands, wasn't true. Not only was he missing for the whole second half of the show, a search party had looked for him, unsuccessfully.

On Saturday, August 16, Mike and Jerry sent Pat Heaney to get both Craig and Tommy Gravina, a friend of Craig's who had also been on duty the night of the murder. Gravina was in his twenties. Tall, thin, good-looking. A Sal Mineo type, Jerry thought. Probably in the fast lane with the girls, Mike thought.

Craig waited in another part of the Atrium as Gravina came into the conference room. Gravina looked uneasy, starry-eyed at talking to the police. If this guy is sitting on anything, Jerry thought, and we lean on him even a little, he's going to give it up. Fast.

Gravina glanced from Mike to Jerry and back to Mike. He had worked both shows the day Helen was murdered, he said. Matinee and evening. Between performances, he, Craig, and another stagehand had a few beers, smoked some dope, and drove to New Jersey. An ordinary Wednesday. Nothing unusual.

Mike asked if any of them missed their cues.

No, Gravina said.

Craig? Mike asked.

He didn't miss any cues, Gravina said.

Mike and Jerry looked at each other.

"Excuse me," Jerry said.

He left the room, where Mike and Gravina continued to talk, and went to another office in the Atrium. Gravina was so definite, Jerry wanted to double-check the account they'd heard of how Craig had been missing.

He called Steve Diaz, Jr., who had worked the show with Craig and Gravina. Diaz's mother answered the phone. When Jerry introduced himself, she got hysterical. Jerry tried to calm her, to explain that Steve was not in trouble, that he was just calling to get some information about the violinist who had been murdered at the Met. Murdered! Diaz's mother shrieked. The more Jerry explained, the wilder she got.

By the time Steve Diaz, Sr., took the phone from his wife, he was in a rage. Again, Jerry tried to explain why he had called. But Diaz, Sr., wouldn't listen. What was Jerry trying to do? Why was Jerry upsetting his wife like that? What right did he have to make a call like this?

Diaz, Sr., was one of the backstage bosses. Jerry didn't want to antagonize him.

"Look," Jerry said. "It's very important. Otherwise I wouldn't have bothered you."

Still angry, Diaz, Sr., told Jerry that his son was not there. He was in Brooklyn, fixing up his new home. He was getting married the next day.

Jerry congratulated Diaz, Sr., on the upcoming wedding and once more apologized for disturbing the family, especially on such a happy weekend; but, he explained, he had to talk to Diaz, Jr., that afternoon.

"Could you give me a phone number where I can reach him?" Jerry asked.

Diaz, Sr., finally agreed to call his brother, who lived near the place where Diaz, Jr., was working. The brother ran over to the apartment and told Diaz, Jr., to call Jerry at the Met. While waiting for the call, Jerry glanced in at Mike, who was dancing Gravina around, waiting for Jerry.

When the call came, Jerry grabbed the phone and shut the door of the office he was using to make sure there was no way his conversation with Diaz, Jr., could be overheard by Gravina.

Jerry apologized for bothering him and said, "Steve, this is very important. In your questionnaire, you say people were missing from backstage the night of the murder. Could you have made a mistake?"

Diaz, Jr., said he hadn't made a mistake.

"You sure?" Jerry asked.

Diaz, Jr., was sure. Craig was not there for the second half of the evening show.

"We're talking to some other guys who were working that night," Jerry said. "And I have to tell you Gravina says Craig was there."

That guy's full of shit, Diaz, Jr., said. I don't know what he's telling you. I know Craig wasn't there, 'cause I had to pick up part of that load.

Shortly before "Five Tangos," Craig had disappeared. In detail, Diaz, Jr., described how they had looked for Craig all around backstage.

Jerry felt as happy as if he'd just ended a long volleyball game by acing the ball in front of the strongest player on the opposite team.

Police view lies the way psychoanalysts view Freudian slips. Both lead behind the apparent reality to the truth.

Back in the conference room, Jerry took his time settling himself comfortably in his chair, gave Gravina one of his triple-threat smiles, and said, "Tommy, you've never been in any serious trouble with the police."

No, Gravina said.

"And you certainly don't want to start now," Jerry said.

I didn't do anything wrong, Gravina said.

"Look, Tom," Mike said. "Can you appreciate that this is a serious thing? I'm not calling you a liar, but maybe you better think about it a little better, because we've spoken to many people who were there that night."

"Maybe we should start from the beginning," Jerry said. "You understand this is a murder investigation. A violinist here has been killed. Now, if someone were foolish enough to either lie or cover up for somebody, getting himself involved, it wouldn't be very smart."

What do you mean? Gravina said.

He's doing what they all do, Jerry thought. Trying to pump us, see what we know.

"Tommy," Jerry said, "that's not how it works. Not what we know. What you know. If you don't make anything up, if you don't lie about anything, you'll walk out of here, finish your job, and there'll be no problem. But I tell you now, if you lie to us and we prove it, you're going to jail. And you're going to jail for a long time."

Oh, shit, Gravina said. Now, wait a minute. What are you trying to say? My friend did it?

"What are you talking about?" Jerry said. "What friend?"

Well, Gravina said, Craig missed his cue at one point.

"So what's the big deal?" Jerry said.

I didn't want to get him in trouble, Gravina said. No way Craig did this thing.

"Am I saying Craig did it?" Jerry said. "But if you tell us Craig was there and he wasn't there, that's a lie. That only confuses the issue. Over a bullshit little lie, why do you make yourself look so bad?"

Gravina told them that Craig was drinking and fell asleep backstage on the rear left wagon. He woke Craig up about eleven o'clock. Right after the show.

"Are you prepared to say this in a court of law?" Mike asked.

"Would you take an oath to this effect? Are you aware of what the crime of perjury is?"

I better tell you everything, Gravina said.

"Just tell us the truth," Mike said.

Before I came in here, Gravina said, Craig asked me to tell you the story about falling asleep on the rear left wagon.

"This might be the ball game," Jerry told Mike before Craig came in.

"Should we hit him with everything?" Mike asked. "He's got to know why he's here. Maybe he'll crumble."

"Me," Jerry said, "I like to go slow. Easy. Methodical. Just go on. Rap. Rap. Rap."

"You don't think he'll cave?" Mike asked.

"No," Jerry said. "I don't think so."

Jesus, Jerry was thinking. I hope Mike doesn't press this business about going in and hitting him hard. Because if we do that and it doesn't work, that is our only shot.

Mike knew he could say, "Look, Jerry, be a good boy. If you think of something smart to say, don't be afraid to speak up. But this is my case. I'm going to talk to him." But he didn't want to lock horns with Jerry again. If they went in there fighting, they wouldn't get much from Craig. So he said, "Hey, look. We're not going to play Top-This or Star-of-the-Show, okay? But you got a few years on me. Let's try it your way. We'll go in. We'll discuss his pedigree. We'll have him go through his movements in a general way. And whoever he gravitates to, the other guy takes a back seat."

Jerry thought Mike was saying: If we fall on our faces, it's your way we did it.

At four-thirty in the afternoon Craig came into the conference room. He seemed, Mike thought, very cool.

"Feel free to smoke," Jerry said, immediately taking charge.

"This is Mike Struk. If you want to call him Mike, it's fine. If you want to call me Jerry, it's fine. Can we call you Craig?"

Jerry offered him coffee.

No, Craig said. He usually didn't drink coffee.

"A bun?" Jerry asked. "Soda?"

No, Craig said. He was trying to lose weight.

Mike and Jerry looked at each other. That was interesting. He was trying to change his appearance.

"How about a cough drop?" Jerry asked.

Jerry always carried some Hall's Mentholyptis. Craig took one.

They started with Craig's background. When he was born. Where he grew up. Family. Where he lived. Whom he lived with. When he started at the Met. What jobs he'd had there— which turned out to be significant. Craig had worked in the electrical shop, near where the body was found; as a maintenance man, which would have familiarized him with the layout of the Met's backstage maze; as a prop man, which would have taken him down to C level, where the tampon was found; and finally, the job he had then, as a stage carpenter, which would have placed him around the stage about the time Helen left the orchestra pit for the last time.

Craig talked about his co-workers, buddies, and girlfriend. Something about the girlfriend didn't add up, Mike thought. Craig mentioned that she was studying veterinary medicine, a tough field. The girlfriend had to be smart. While Craig didn't seem like a dummy, he also didn't strike Mike as an intellectual, someone a woman studying to be a veterinarian would find compatible.

Every once in a while, the conference-room door would open a crack and one of the detectives outside would tell Mike he had a phone call. Mike would go out and find everyone from the regular investigating team—McVeety, Boy, his boss, Tom Brady, Ward, O'Connor, Connell, Rosenthal, Medina, about a dozen detectives—waiting, wondering, What's going on in there? What has he said?

Mike would give them a short report and slip back into the conference room, usually with more coffee for Jerry and himself.

"You sure you don't want any coffee?" Jerry would ask Craig. "Soda? Anything?"

Mike would stare at his own cup. He didn't like coffee. It upset his stomach. But it was a good prop. It gave him something to do. It could be used to underline pauses. He had drunk so much, he could feel his heart pounding.

Jerry had drunk even more. Mike was amazed he hadn't started twitching.

After going over Craig's background, they began combing through Craig's questionnaire and his movements on the day Helen was murdered. Where was he at the beginning of each act, during each act, at the end of each act? What was he doing? Who was he with?

Jerry and Mike took Craig over his story three times in detail. Jerry ran out of cough drops and Benson & Hedges. Craig ran out of Marlboro Lights. Jerry asked one of the detectives outside the conference room to get a couple of packs of cigarettes and some Hall's Mentholyptis.

After Craig finished telling his story for the third time, Jerry said, "Now, Craig, we want to make sure we don't misinterpret or misunderstand you." He repeated back to Craig what Craig had told them. His movements act by act. How he hadn't missed any of his cues. "Is that right?" he asked Craig.

Yeah, Craig said.

"The questionnaire is okay?" Jerry asked. That too stated that he hadn't missed a cue. "Correct in every way?" Jerry asked.

Yeah, Craig said.

"Let's take a short break," Jerry said. "Coffee, Craig?"

Craig said no.

"Mike?" Jerry asked. "Coffee?"

Mike almost groaned. But he said yes.

During the break, Mike and Jerry learned that Craig's stepfather, Martin John Higgins, had come down to the Atrium and asked for Craig.

He's been down here since four o'clock, Higgins had said. What the hell's going on?

"He's being interviewed," one of the detectives had said.

I can make do without him, Higgins had said. I can get someone to cover.

That night, Higgins was Craig's backstage boss.

Jerry remembered Higgins as a pleasant guy, a John Mills type with his mustache and perplexed eyes. Jerry had heard he'd gone through a number of cancer operations on his face, which had left his cheeks pockmarked. He was respected by the crew members, who, because of his fight against death, treated him with reverence, the way a veteran is treated by recruits waiting to go into battle.

He had seemed worried that Craig might have used the interview as an excuse to skip work, to get an early start on a two-week vacation that would begin when the show ended that evening. When he found out that Craig was in the Atrium, he seemed mollified and went backstage again.

A two-week vacation.

After the interview, Craig would walk out of the Met with two weeks' advance pay in his pocket. If he was worried about being a suspect, he could jump on a plane to Ireland, which did not have any extradition agreement with the United States. He'd be unreachable.

After Mike and Jerry returned to the conference room, they once more went over Craig's story.

"Gee, Craig," Jerry said when they were through. "Something isn't jelling here. Something's not right. We've talked to hundreds of people. You know how many guys we've had in and out of here. And there seems to be something wrong here. You say you were here for all these portions of the show, and yet somebody missed you."

Craig tried to shrug off the discrepancy.

"Craig," Jerry said, "we went over this very carefully."

"Let's come up front a little," Mike said. "Give us some credit, Craig. We know a bit more than you think we know. This business about you being there for the whole show. We know that's not true."

I was drunk, Craig said. I don't remember everything too clearly.

"We've been very careful in asking you all about your movements that night," Jerry said. "What you did and didn't remember, and you were positive you were there for the whole show. Now that I tell you we know you weren't there, you say you're unclear."

Round and round, they went: Mike calmly telling Craig he knew Craig had lied, Jerry coaxing Craig to tell the truth. They were more comfortable talking to Craig than they were talking to some of the artists at the Met. He seemed a regular guy, who knew his way around, not an arty innocent. They also worked so well together, Mike and Jerry felt they were almost reading each other's mind. Every time Craig began to get too confident, Jerry would look at Mike, and Mike would haul out the heavy ammunition: contradictions between what Craig had said and what his co-workers had said, contradictions within Craig's own story. Craig would slump in his chair and turn to Jerry for help. Jerry, as fatherly as he could be, would urge him to tell what really happened that night. Three days earlier, before Mike had confessed he'd been ordered to keep Jerry in the dark about the fingertip prints, before they'd begun trusting each other, they could not have handled the interview so well.

Finally Craig realized he could no longer claim he made all of his cues. There was too much evidence against him.

I didn't want to tell you I'd missed my cues, Craig said, because I didn't want to get in trouble with the boss. I went to the left rear wagon. I'd been drinking. I laid down and went to sleep.

"Let me get this straight, Craig," Jerry said. "Because you'd been drinking, you went to sleep on the left rear wagon?"

They took Craig over and over this new story, making sure they understood exactly where Craig claimed he'd gone to sleep. The left rear wagon. Not the right rear wagon. The left. Where on the left rear wagon? What time was he there? Was he sure about the time?

They ignored the contradiction in his reason for lying: He said he'd lied so he wouldn't get in trouble with his boss, but his boss already knew he'd missed his cues.

But after they had taken Craig over his new story enough times so he couldn't claim they had misunderstood him, they homed in on a bigger inconsistency.

"There's something else wrong here," Jerry said. "That night, your friends, co-workers, and boss looked for you. And do you know where they looked? They looked on the rear wagon. And not only did they look on the left side, they looked on the right side."

Craig was silent.

"The first statement you gave us, about not missing any cues, we went over that several times," Jerry said. "Each time you said it was absolutely correct. Then, we told you we knew you missed your cue, and you said you were on the rear wagon. And you said that was absolutely correct. Then, we told you they searched for you, looked on the rear wagon, and didn't find you."

Craig was silent for a little while longer.

Jerry, he said at last, can I talk to you alone?

Mike left the room.

"Well," Jerry said, "what is it, Craig?"

There's something about that night I didn't tell you, Craig said.

"Go ahead," Jerry said.

Craig said, I was the guy on the elevator with that lady.

Bingo, Jerry thought.

"Why didn't you tell us this before, Craig?" he asked.

I was afraid, Craig said.

"Gee, Craig," Jerry said. "What the heck were you afraid of?"

Little by little, Craig's story came out, his third account of what had happened the night Helen was murdered.

Not a confession, Jerry thought. But it's more than a crumb. And I would have been happy with just a crumb. This is a nice piece of cake.

Craig said he'd met Helen as they were going to the elevator. Elevator number 12. She told him she was looking for someone, someone with a funny name. (That would be Panov, Jerry thought.) And she asked him for directions to "the studios." (That would be the stars' dressing rooms, Jerry thought.) He told her to go to the second floor. She got off at the second floor. He went to A level, took a six-pack of beer from his locker, and drank it in the locker room.

"Did you ever see her before?" Jerry asked.

Yeah, Craig said, I seen that lady around. In the A level. The tunnel.

So, Jerry figured, Helen leaves the orchestra pit; Craig spots her in the tunnel and follows her to stage level and the elevator.

"Was there anyone else in the elevator with you and Helen?" Jerry asked.

No, Craig said.

Maybe he was so infatuated with Helen, he didn't notice Laura Cutler, Jerry figured. Or maybe he's trying to place himself in the elevator earlier—on another trip, one without Laura —to give himself a better alibi.

Jerry didn't press him about anything. He let him ramble on. The more people talk, the more information they usually give. And Jerry took few notes. He didn't want Craig to get nervous and clam up. Twice, Jerry tried to bluff Craig, implying that the police might have found his fingerprints either on Helen's property or on the second floor outside the elevator, somewhere he said he hadn't gone with Helen.

"Did you pick up something Helen dropped?" Jerry asked. And later: "When she left the elevator on the second floor, did you lean out to point which direction she should go?"

But Craig didn't bite. He answered *no* to both questions.

Jerry still had his ace in the hole: the palm print from the roof. He decided to wait to use that—after Craig had repeated his new story for Mike. It's very hard to tell a story twice in exactly the same way. When Craig repeated it, maybe he'd give them more to work with. Once they'd exhausted every other strategy, they'd use the palm print.

After talking to Craig for a half hour, Jerry suddenly excused himself. He wanted more coffee. Craig could use the bathroom if he wanted. When Jerry walked out of the conference room, Mike saw Jerry hadn't hit the jackpot. If he'd gotten a confession, Mike thought, his asshole would be touching his lower lip. But, after three weeks of working with him, Mike knew Jerry well enough to tell he'd gotten something of value.

Craig waited in the conference room, while Jerry briefed Mike and the other detectives who crowded around. Then, Mike and Jerry withdrew into a corner to talk about how they would proceed. Jerry was the blade of the wedge. Mike was the head.

"If he can tell me about the elevator," Mike said, "if he can open up that much to me, we'll prosper later on."

When Craig retold his story with Mike in the room, he changed it once more—slightly. After he'd gotten the six-pack from his locker, he took it into the electricians' lounge. That's where he drank the beer, not in the locker room.

Mike almost laughed out loud. A bogus story. It was the end of July, he thought. The beer had to be hot as soup.

After finishing the beer, Craig said, he fell asleep on a couch in the electricians' lounge.

Mike and Jerry got out a floor plan of A level and had Craig point out where he got the six-pack, the route he took into the electricians' lounge, where he drank the beer, and where he fell asleep. Was he sure? Was there a possibility he might be making a mistake? Was this the truth?

Craig told them this was just what happened. He was sure.

They couldn't go any further. Not now. How could they test the story of the electricians' lounge? They needed someone who was there at the time, someone who could tell them if he'd seen Craig or not. They'd have to be incredibly lucky to turn up such a witness. And bluffing Craig, claiming they knew he was lying and gauging his reaction, was too risky.

They decided to use their hole card: the palm print on the roof.

"Have you ever been on the sixth-floor fan roof, Craig?" Jerry asked.

Yeah, Craig said.

"Were you there the week Miss Mintiks was killed?" Jerry asked.

Yeah, Craig said.

"Could you tell us exactly when?" Jerry asked.

Again, Craig changed his story slightly. He'd been on the

roof two weeks before the murder, he said; but on the next level up, above the fan roof, the grid level. He'd climbed up the wall ladder with another member of the crew, John Pariente. And they'd sunned themselves up there.

Something about this struck Mike as significant. All evening Craig had been talking in generalities. Suddenly, he got very specific about this ladder. Mike made a note to check the ladder out.

"Craig," Mike said, "your fingerprints were found on the fan roof. In the vicinity of the crime scene."

So, Craig said, don't fingerprints last for five years?

Again, Mike and Jerry looked at each other. Craig's question suggested that he'd been worried enough about something to do a little research on fingerprints.

At one point, Craig leaned forward and with a half-smile said, "Jerry, what do you want me to say? I killed her?"

"No," Jerry said. "Unless that's the truth."

Maybe if I go home for a few days and think about it, Craig said, I'll be able to answer some of the questions I can't answer now.

Jerry's heart sank. If someone feels he is in custody and can't leave, you have to read him his rights, the Miranda warnings. Usually, once someone has heard his rights, he demands a lawyer and shuts up. They didn't want Craig to feel he was being held against his will, so they had to risk losing him.

"Hey, Craig," Mike said, "if you want to go home, if you feel that's what you need, you can leave now. You think you need a lawyer? You want to get yourself a lawyer?"

No, Craig said.

Mike assumed Craig was grandstanding, making a show of strength. Jerry assumed he was afraid of involving his family. If Craig had asked for a lawyer, his family would have started asking questions, questions that he didn't want to answer. From what Jerry knew about Craig's mother, she seemed like a domineering woman. Jerry had the feeling Craig was afraid of her. If she sat him down and worked him over, she would have gotten anything he was hiding out of him. Craig would rather face us than go through that, Jerry thought.

"Maybe we can straighten it out tonight, Craig," Jerry said. Craig agreed. We'll finish up tonight, he said. We'll straighten it out.

After going over the story a little more, Jerry said, "Okay, take it easy. We'll have another break."

When Mike and Jerry left the conference room, they found Craig's stepfather, Marty Higgins, waiting in the Atrium.

Hey, Higgins said, the kid's been down under here since four o'clock. Now, it's ten. What's the beef?

"There are things Craig lied to us about," Jerry said. He told Higgins about the elevator.

What? Higgins said. Are you kidding? I'll tell you what. Can I speak to him? I'm going to go in there, and I'll smack him in his face, and I'll get to the root of it. I'll find out who he's lying for.

"Go ahead in, talk to him," Jerry said. "By all means talk to him. Maybe he'll tell you something he hasn't told us."

After Higgins spoke to Craig, he came out of the conference room and said, Wow. Maybe I should call his mother. Later, he said, I think I should call his father. Higgins and Eddie Crimmins, the stepfather and father, did not get along. If Higgins was considering calling Eddie Crimmins, he must have been upset. But both Mike and Jerry had the impression that Higgins, unable to conceive that Craig was the killer, believed Craig was covering up for a friend.

Jerry told Higgins to call Craig's mother and father if he wanted; but, as usual in such a situation, not knowing if either of them had high blood pressure or heart trouble, he cautioned Higgins not to alarm them unduly.

Higgins left.

Mike and Jerry went back into the conference room. It was time to move on to the next stage. They had a suspect who was missing while the murder was taking place, who'd changed his story a number of times, whose palm print was found at the crime scene, who had asked a friend to lie about his movements the night of the murder, and who was—as far as they could tell —the last person to see the victim alive.

"Craig," Jerry said, "would you mind very much giving your statement to the district attorney?"

Charles Heffernan, the assistant district attorney assigned to the case, was at the Meadowlands in New Jersey watching a Giants game when his beeper went off. He called the Manhattan district attorney's switchboard to find out who was trying to reach him and was told to call the Met, which he did. Captain Ward explained what was happening and said he would contact him again if anything broke.

A minute or two into the second quarter, Heffernan's beeper went off again. Heffernan called Ward, who told him to come to the Met.

A New Jersey State Police car escorted him to the Holland Tunnel. When he came out in Manhattan, he was greeted by a New York City police car, which accompanied him to Lincoln Center.

By the time he arrived, Mike and Jerry, having gone over everything once more, had locked Craig into his new story. They felt proud of the package they had prepared for the district attorney.

Neither of them had ever met Heffernan; but when he walked into the Atrium, they liked his looks. An aging all-American boy. Someone who even in his mid-thirties had a face as candid as a child's. About six feet three inches, Jerry estimated, running down the vital statistics as he usually did whenever he met someone new, a cop's habit; maybe one hundred ninety, one hundred ninety-five pounds. Very erect posture; military bearing. A weekend soldier, officer in the reserve, Jerry correctly guessed. But not a martinet. You could tell that from his hair. While short, it was not a military brush. More a Kennedy cut. A restrained Kennedy cut. When he was young, probably he was very much influenced by JFK, Jerry figured. From the side, he looked like Sonny Tufts.

When Mike and Jerry explained the situation, Heffernan occasionally interrupted with a question. The questions were always to the point and betrayed only a little the natural antagonism between district attorneys and cops. Mike and Jerry had both had their share of district attorneys who assumed every cop was a liar and treated the police with contempt. But Heffernan was a gentleman. If he at times seemed to be playing devil's advocate, it was because he wanted to test where the case was weak in order to find out where they had to strengthen it. Jerry liked his caution. Too often cops bring in good cases only to have district attorneys muff them in court. Heffernan, it seemed, was already looking ahead to the possible trial.

Only once did Heffernan throw them a curve. Did you inform Craig of his rights? he asked.

Did we goof? Jerry wondered. Did we have to give him his rights? Mike thought. They told Heffernan that they hadn't yet given Craig his Miranda warnings because he was not in custody. They had repeatedly made it clear he was free to get a lawyer or go.

Will he videotape his statement? Heffernan asked.

"He said he would," Jerry answered.

Craig was apparently so confident that when his father, Eddie Crimmins, showed up, he didn't want to see him.

Eddie Crimmins had come into the Atrium about eleven o'clock, not long after Heffernan had arrived. He was a nice guy, Mike thought; not a wiseass. In his late forties, Mike estimated, but in ways he seemed older. Mike had the impression that he was beaten down, a little weak. Maybe he was tired or worried. He must have been handsome when he was younger, Jerry thought. He pegged him as a short Arthur Kennedy with a mustache.

What's going on? Eddie Crimmins asked.

Jerry explained that Craig had lied about his movements on the night of the murder and had admitted to being the man on the elevator with Helen they had been looking for.

I'd like to see my boy, he said.

"All right," Jerry said. "Let me go in and tell him." When Jerry entered the office, Craig had his head on the desk. "Your father is here," Jerry said.

Oh yeah? he said. Why?

"I guess Marty called him," Jerry said. "I guess he's concerned. You want to talk to him?"

No, Craig said. I'll do the tape first.

Jerry had the impression that Craig was dismissing his father, that he was in effect saying, He'll sit there and wait till I'm finished. He didn't seem to have much respect for his father; and that irked Jerry, who had a strong sense of family obligations, of a child's proper responsibilities to his elders. "It's going to take some time before we get the equipment," Jerry said.

Okay, Craig said. I'll wait.

As Jerry left the room, Craig put his head back down on the desk. He seemed comfortable, Jerry thought; so comfortable he was almost cocky.

Eddie Crimmins and Higgins had had a brief conversation. When Jerry told Eddie Crimmins that Craig didn't want to see him until he was finished, the father and the stepfather, whose mutual dislike was obvious, chose to wait in separate offices.

The technicians arrived with the wrong videotape equipment. They thought they were going to be taping a crime scene and so had left the audio equipment behind. Someone had to go back to their office to get it.

Mike and Jerry were beginning to get nervous. It was late. The show had ended. The audience had left. The crew and artists were leaving. Craig—who by then had had coffee and soda—had been in the Atrium for eight hours. At any time, Craig could say, "Screw you. I'm going." They'd be forced to arrest him or let him go.

Mike, Jerry, and Heffernan reviewed their game plan: what they would do if Craig decided to leave; what they would do if he stayed; what he had already said; what he should be asked on tape and in what order.

The technicians brought in their sound equipment. Typically for such tapings, the police used a room with a one-way mirror so the person giving the statement wouldn't be face-to-face with the lens, wouldn't get camera shy. In the Atrium, they had to set everything up in the conference room across the table from Craig. It was not an ideal situation. But there was no alternative.

The equipment didn't seem to faze Craig. He's sure of himself, Jerry thought, as if he's thinking, *They're asking me if I want to make a statement; not saying, you have to make a statement. They've already told me I could go home. They've already told me I could get a lawyer. I bullshitted these guys. I sold them a bill of goods, and they bought it. No way the DA can be as sharp as these guys. They know the case. I'll give the DA a line of shit. I'll do my thing.* At least, that was Jerry's impression when the taping began.

"It's twenty-six after twelve on Sunday, August 17, 1980," Heffernan said. "Craig, my name is Charles Heffernan. I'm an assistant district attorney here in Manhattan. Over to your left is Detective Jerry Giorgio. And to your right is Detective Mike

Struk. We're here at the Metropolitan Opera House in Lincoln Center here in Manhattan."

Heffernan spoke quietly, evenly, his face betraying little emotion. He sat, hands in front of him on the conference table, catty-corner from Craig, whose hands were also on the conference table. Heffernan's hands were calm, one resting on the other. Craig's were nervous, fingers twined. Heffernan was in a white turtleneck. Craig was in a black T-shirt. Mike sat a little away from the table. Compared to them, he looked formal in his suit. Jerry, out of range of the camera, sat across from Craig.

"The man who's to your left and behind the camera is photographing our discussion," Heffernan said. "And our discussion is also being tape-recorded. Do you understand that?"

"Yes," Craig said.

"Okay," Heffernan said. "I understand that this afternoon you've been talking to the police officers at Lincoln Center. Is that right?"

"Yes," Craig said.

"And during that time they've offered you—as I understand —a chance to have some food if you wanted to?" Heffernan said.

"Yes," Craig said.

"And did you want any?"

"No."

"They gave you some coffee or some soda?"

"Coffee and a drink."

"Did you have a chance to go to the bathroom?"

"Uh-huh."

"A couple of times, was that?"

"Yeah."

"Do you smoke cigarettes?"

"Uh-huh."

"Did they offer you cigarettes?"

"Yeah."

"I understand you had some cough drops also," Heffernan said. "Is that right?"

"Yeah," Craig said.

Heffernan was trying to establish that Craig had not been ill-treated. But Mike thought that Heffernan was too solicitous, that he was coddling the kid.

"A man named John Higgins would be your stepfather," Heffernan said. "Is that right?"

"Yeah," Craig said.

"Did he come here to Lincoln Center today to talk to you?" Heffernan asked.

"Yeah," Craig said. "He was working here today."

"Did you have a chance to talk to him during the time you were speaking to the police officers?"

"Yeah."

"And your natural father, what's his name?"

"Eddie Crimmins."

"I understand that Detective Giorgio told you that Mr. Crimmins, your father, came down here tonight. Is that right?"

"Yeah."

"I also understand that Detective Giorgio told you that you could have a chance to see your father if you wanted to before you decided to talk to me. Is that right?"

"Yeah."

"And I understand that you said to Detective Giorgio that you would be willing to speak to me without seeing your father. Is that correct?"

"Yeah."

"How old are you, Craig?" Heffernan asked.

"Twenty-one," Craig said.

"You're still willing to speak to me without having a chance to see your father. Is that right?"

What is this? Jerry thought. Heffernan was obviously trying to establish that Craig was not in custody or held incommunicado. But Jerry thought he was going overboard. Craig might think that Heffernan, by asking the question twice, was trying to suggest he should talk to his father first. What if Craig takes the hint? Jerry thought. What if he says he wants to talk to his father right now? And what if his father gets him a lawyer?

But Craig said he was willing to talk to Heffernan without first speaking to his father.

Now, we'll get down to the meat and potatoes, Jerry thought.

"What I'd like to talk to you about tonight," Heffernan said, "is the death of the woman musician Helen Hagnes Mintiks— she went by the name professionally of Helen Hagnes—on Wednesday night, July 23 of 1980. About three weeks ago."

As Heffernan spoke, Craig kept nodding.

Heffernan read Craig the Miranda warnings. "What I'd like you to do," he said, "is listen to me, listen to what I say, and at the end of each right, I'm going to ask you whether or not you understand what I just said. Then, I'd like you to answer either yes or no. At any point during my explanation of these rights, if there's the slightest doubt about what I've said, if you're at all confused, you have the right to ask me. Say: *Stop. Put that another way. I don't quite know what that means.* If there's any confusion, you just let me know. Will you do that?"

"Right," Craig said.

This has got to be the Million Dollar Miranda, thought Jerry, who'd never heard the warnings given with such care, such emphasis on the *are-you-sure-you-understand.*

Craig was being over-Mirandized, Mike thought. Innocent or guilty, he'd be a fool not to clam up. No. Not a fool: arrogant and stubborn.

When Heffernan told Craig he had a right to have a lawyer present, Mike licked his lips and composed his face to betray none of the tension he was feeling. The more Heffernan harped on the question of a lawyer, the more uncomfortable Mike felt.

He stretched his chin up as though his collar were too tight. He looked at the ceiling. He looked at the wall. When Heffernan told Craig, "My question now to you is, having been advised of your rights, are you willing to speak to me at this time without a lawyer?" Jerry thought Mike was about to explode. Is Heffernan the DA or the lawyer for the defense? Mike thought.

Craig said he was willing to talk to Heffernan without a lawyer. After answering some questions about his background and work history, he told the story he'd first given Jerry privately and then had repeated for Mike, his third version of what happened the night of Helen's murder. At the beginning of his statement, Craig put his hand over his mouth, as though unconsciously trying to silence himself. "I went down to my locker room to drink some beers, and on the way down there I met that, uh, lady. . . ." When he first mentioned Helen, just before he said *lady*, he jerked back his head as though flinching from a slap.

When Heffernan asked about Gravina, Craig said, "I just said to him if they ask you tell them I was sleeping on the wagon."

"In fact," Heffernan said, "that wasn't true."

"Right," Craig said.

Now, instead of being too easy on Craig, Heffernan seemed —Mike thought—to be pressing too hard. Jerry had built up a rapport with Craig. Craig wasn't going to tell Heffernan something he hadn't told Jerry. Toward the end of the taping, when Craig asked, "What happens next?" Heffernan said, "This is your chance now. If there's anything you left out you want to correct, any questions you might have, or anything at all you might want to change—if you do, this is the time. This is the chance for you to tell us whatever it is you want to tell us about that night."

Jesus, Jerry thought; that's almost an accusation.

"There's really nothing else," Craig said.

After asking one or two other questions, Heffernan pressed Craig more. "Is there anything that you told us tonight that might not be true?" he asked.

"No, sir," Craig said.

"Craig," Heffernan said. "This is your chance to say whatever it is is true. . . . This is your chance. And I'm just going to point out a couple of things, and the ball is yours." He went over Craig's lies and then asked, "Is there anything you might want to say to me?"

"The reason I told the police that is because I didn't know who that tape today was going to go to," Craig said; "and if it went to my boss, I'd be in trouble. So I lied." When Craig had told the lies, he *hadn't* known he was going to be taped. The response was a dodge.

Heffernan was silent for a while. He gazed at Craig. His lips were compressed in an almost prim line. He nodded. "Okay," he said. "Thank you." Glancing into the camera lens, he added, "That concludes the statement."

While the technician was putting away his videotape equipment in the conference room, Craig waited in another, smaller office. His father went in to talk to him and afterward came out to ask Jerry what was happening. He was obviously upset. Jerry wanted to throw his arm around the guy's shoulders and comfort him.

"Craig just gave his statement to the DA," Jerry said. "We're going to discuss it."

Can we leave? Eddie Crimmins asked.

"Craig is willing to stay," Jerry said.

What time is it? Eddie Crimmins asked.

"Two o'clock," Jerry said. "Have another cup of coffee."

They made fresh coffee, sent out for snacks and beer.

Heffernan told Mike and Jerry, "Let's go in and look at the tape."

All the detectives still hanging around the Atrium trooped into the conference room with them. The technician set up his equipment again and replayed the tape. They scrutinized Craig's expressions, how he held his body, what he did with his hands as he told his story; jotted notes and questions; pointed things out to each other; or simply sat, staring at the videotape, trying to attend to their gut responses, to figure out why they reacted a particular way at a certain point in the statement. They could have been studio executives watching the dailies of a big-budget movie.

Finally, Mike told the videotape technician to go home. Everyone, yawning and stretching, crossed the Atrium lobby to another large office, where they again replayed the statement, this time in their imaginations. They argued over the interpretation of what they had seen, discussed where they should go from there.

As district attorney, it was up to Heffernan to make the final decision about whether to hold Craig or let him go. He inclined toward arresting him, but kept coming back to the palm print on the roof. He wanted to know more about it.

They called Donald Green, the Crime Scene Unit cop who had lifted the palm print.

You guys are fucking crazy, Green said. You got to be out of your fucking minds. Calling me at three, three-thirty in the morning. Asking me about a palm print and how old it is. I got no notes here.

Green hung up.

Jerry called Green's senior partner, Joseph Ferraro.

"He's a friend of mine," Jerry told the other detectives in the Atrium office. "He'll help us out."

"Joe," Jerry said, when he got Ferraro on the telephone, "what's the matter with Don? He's breaking our asses."

That's just his personality, Ferraro said. What can I do for you, Jerry? I'll help in any way I can.

"We're talking about that print that popped up on the roof," Jerry said. "How fresh it is. How old it is." He filled Ferraro in.

Maybe you ought to call Lieutenant Guiney, Ferraro said.

Lieutenant Dan Guiney was the head of the Crime Scene Unit. They tracked him to Rockaway, but couldn't reach him. There had been some family crisis, possibly a death, and Guiney, who was consoling a relative, was unavailable.

Jerry called Ferraro again. The other detectives were getting restless. It was nearing four o'clock. People were hardening their positions either for or against arresting Craig.

Why don't you call the head of the Latent Section? Ferraro told Jerry. He's the expert on prints.

The head of the Latent Section, Lieutenant John Ferrara, told Jerry, Well, you know, Detective Giorgio, there's really no test that can tell you if a print is fresh. It is an individual judgment. There could be various opinions about the same print. You couldn't even begin to decide without having had field experience, without having examined hundreds or thousands of prints.

Ferrara rambled on in detail, explaining how much depended on atmospheric conditions, how perfect fingerprints thousands of years old had been found in Egyptian tombs.

"Enough with the Egyptian tombs," Jerry said. "Tell me about the roof of the Met. I'm talking to a DA here who wants to be satisfied that we got something solid to work on."

Like the other calls, this one was inconclusive.

It's a heavy case, Mike thought. No one wants to be the guy who says, Sure, this is the way it is—arrest Craig.

Heffernan was beginning to think that they should not arrest Craig until they did more work.

Maybe we don't have enough to arrest, Captain Ward said.

"What the hell side are you on?" someone said.

Everyone was talking at once, defending his position, some ticking off on their fingers the evidence they had, others ticking off the evidence they didn't have. Mike and Jerry argued that if they went in now and told Craig he was under arrest, he'd confess. Captain Ward quieted everyone.

I think I'll call Al Sullivan, Heffernan said.

Sullivan, whose nickname was Smokey, was a district attorney with a great deal of trial experience, respected for both his judgment and steadiness. He was methodical and slow. You'd ask him a question and wait twenty, maybe thirty seconds, a long time, for an answer. Sometimes, you'd wait so long, you'd make the mistake of repeating the question. But he always heard the first time. He just took a moment or two to consider the question and formulate a precise answer.

"I'll call him," Jerry said. "I know his number."

"What do you mean, you know his number?" someone asked.

"We're old friends," Jerry said.

As much as Mike was growing to like, trust, and respect Jerry, this habit Jerry had of magically knowing everybody, even happening to have the home telephone numbers, annoyed him.

Jerry telephoned Sullivan. Sullivan's wife, Mary, answered the phone.

"Hi, Mary," Jerry said, grinning as usual, as though she could see him.

Who's this? she asked.

"Jerry Giorgio."

Hi, Jerry, she said. What's going on?

In the background, Jerry heard Sullivan growling as he struggled up from sleep, his grunts becoming more and more human, as though waking were a process of evolution.

Hi, Jerry, Sullivan said, when he finally reached the phone. What are you looking for?

"Now why the hell you have to have that attitude?" Jerry said.

You're calling me at four o'clock in the morning, Sullivan said. Son of a bitch, you're looking for something.

"Well," Jerry admitted, "I'll tell you what. We got a situation here. . . ." For the next half hour, Jerry explained things to Sullivan. For an hour after that, Heffernan talked to Sullivan.

After hanging up the phone, Heffernan said he'd made his decision. There were a few more things they had to do. They would not arrest Craig that day.

"What?" Mike said.

"Jesus Christ," Jerry said. "We come to you with a case. We give you this guy's admission he's with the lady. We have a sketch resembling him. We got his palm print on the roof. He says he knows his way around the building. We have a cigarette butt from the stairs to the roof we think is a Marlboro. This kid smokes Marlboros."

They argued for another two and a half hours, Mike, Jerry, McVeety, and Rosenthal pressing hardest for an immediate arrest. They didn't stop fighting when bagels were brought in. They talked with stuffed mouths and, squinting with discomfort, swallowed half-chewed lumps so they could make their points clearly without mumbling through crumbs.

"How much more do we have to give you guys," Mike said. "What more do you want, for God's sake?"

I want you to check out his story, Heffernan said. Was he or wasn't he in the locker room and the electricians' lounge when he said he was?

"We can arrest him," someone said, "and then check out his story."

"Look," Heffernan said. "The decision has been made."

Afraid the verbal fighting was about to become physical, Jerry said, "Listen, let's cut it out."

"We're all sucking wind," Mike said. "What are we going to do? Fight all night?"

"Let's go back to the office," Jerry said. "Let's knock out our reports. Let's all go home. Let's get a good night's sleep. Let's take Sunday off. Let's get the hell out of here."

Jerry went into the office where Craig waited and said, "Craig, we don't have any more questions."

Oh, really? Craig said. It's all done?

"Yeah," Jerry said. "Sorry we kept you so long. But we appreciate your cooperation."

About sixteen hours after Craig first came to the Atrium, at a quarter to eight on the morning of Sunday, August 17, 1980, the first day of his two-week vacation, Craig walked out of the Met, still a free man.

11

MIKE SANK INTO the chair Craig had been sitting in. Bolt upright, he fell asleep. When he woke fifteen minutes later, most of the other detectives had gone. He telephoned Marion.

"We shot our load," he said. "And it didn't go down."

Mike had bunked at the precinct for the past seven nights. He was furious that Craig hadn't been arrested. He was fed up with New York.

"I got to get out of the city," he said. "I'm coming home."

He drove the hour and a half upstate with the car windows wide open. But it wasn't the rush of air that kept him awake. It was his fury. All around him on the highway were weekenders heading to parks and lakes, picnics and hikes, people for whom murders were merely sensational headlines, news items followed like soap operas. Mike felt resentful that he knew the world in a way they never would.

When he pulled into the development, he took the curves faster than usual and slammed to a stop next to his bulldozer.

Ignoring the family clamor in the kitchen, the boys—Mike, Jr.; Steve; and Tom—appealing to him to settle squabbles, his daughter, Stacy, trying to tell him a story, and Marion with a fistful of telephone messages about his put-off construction jobs, he barged through the house to his bedroom.

He lay on his back on the bed and closed his eyes. Three hours later, when he woke, he was still angry.

In the afternoon, he went to do a quick $50 job he'd promised to finish weeks ago. Halfway through, his back-hoe blew a hydraulic line, spraying Mike head to foot with oil. In the few seconds it took Mike to shut off the machine, $30 worth of oil was lost. The back-hoe's pump would have to be rebuilt. Another $250. The $50 job would end up costing him $280.

Because of the Police Department's limit on overtime, Mike was putting in hours on the investigation for which he'd never get reimbursed. His weekend construction business was shot. His family life was going to hell. And the payoff for all this sacrifice was: They had let Craig go.

He went home, cleaned himself up, drove into the mountains, and jogged. If Craig runs out on us, Mike thought, it'll be the best proof of guilt. I'll just track him down. If he runs somewhere I can't get him, I'll wait. I don't care if it takes thirty years. The minute he comes back in reach, I'll get him.

Jerry didn't think Craig would run. When Craig left the Met, he'd seemed too confident. He hadn't wanted a lawyer. Craig was sure he had them buffaloed, Jerry thought.

Although he was disappointed Craig hadn't been arrested, he figured they could use the time to test the alibi. Two weeks. That would be enough now that they had a direction.

On the way home that Sunday morning he made lists in his mind of what he had to do, whom he had to talk to, and in what order he should talk to them.

Like Mike, he opened all the windows of his car to keep himself awake. He tuned his radio to a rock station he hated, expecting the abrasive music would work if the open windows didn't. But, with his mind on strategy, the car began to weave. That had never before happened to him, even when he'd been awake longer than the thirty hours he'd been up.

By the time Jerry pulled into his driveway, the usual weekend gang was already out on his back deck, eating bagels and drinking coffee. For the next three hours, they wouldn't let Jerry rest, firing questions at him about the case, which he dodged.

At last, Jerry said, "Enough."

He changed into a pair of cut-off jeans, jumped into the pool, and for a half hour floated, eyes closed, on his inflatable seat, sipping a White Russian.

But he couldn't rest. Every time he started to drift to sleep, another angle in the case roused him, and once more he'd go over the whole investigation. On his back, in the floating seat, he slowly circled.

As usual, Seymour handled the barbecue. Jerry let himself be taken care of. Although obsessed with details of the case, on this Sunday, not once did he run inside to take notes. He felt he didn't need to, the case was so vivid in his mind.

All afternoon, he played volleyball. Like a tiger, he thought, prowling back and forth at the net. His team kept losing, which instead of discouraging him goaded him on to even fiercer games. By six o'clock that evening, everyone except Jerry was sick of volleyball. Reluctantly, Jerry left the court and had a bite to eat. With a start, he realized he'd missed a joke and heard only the explosion of laughter, which must have awakened him from a half-minute nap. Or had it been two minutes? Or five? He was so tired, he was disoriented. Physically, he was fine, his body on automatic, doing whatever his body would normally do while sitting on his deck on a Sunday in the midst of his friends. But his mind drifted. He was like a drowsy passenger on a train who, startled into consciousness, isn't sure for a moment whether he's missed his stop or hasn't yet come to it.

Excusing himself, Jerry went inside, showered, and climbed into bed.

The following Monday, August 18, the cops left the Atrium and relocated their headquarters at the 20th Precinct. They were afraid their long interview with Craig had alienated the backstage crew.

During the morning conference at the station house, Mike and Jerry had argued that, despite the tactical move back to the precinct, it would be suicide to drag crew members up there from the Met. Such a change might alarm the backstage workers even more, make them more hostile.

"We want to keep a low profile," Jerry had said.

"Let's not scare our man," Mike had added.

They won their point. The 20th Precinct would be headquarters, which meant the cops would not be so constantly present at the Met, lowering the heat there; but any interviews they had to do would still take place at the Met, so the crew members being questioned would not be spooked by an official-looking setting.

Mike and Jerry went over the things-to-do list that Heffernan had given them. It was excessive, they thought. It included too many minor points, which would slow the investigation if followed up and might tip off Craig that he was their main suspect.

This fight was one that they lost.

After lunch, they went back to the Met to start the new round of interviews. First on their list was Gravina. They wanted to lock him into his story that Craig had asked him to lie about where he was on the night of Helen's murder.

Gravina confirmed what he had said, even recalled that the

beer he and Craig had been drinking was probably Molson or Budweiser. About six cans each in the car from New Jersey back to work and more after they reached the Met.

A few other details. Gravina didn't recall seeing Craig after the show started, although during the first intermission Craig may have been part of a crowd that came into the room where Gravina was working. It was during the second intermission that Steve Diaz, Jr., had asked Gravina, Where's Craig?

Maybe he went home, Gravina said. Or maybe he fell out.

Each fact, no matter how small, was important, because facts were traps, landmines Craig, if he was still lying, would have to negotiate. And some of the facts exploded on contact.

Gravina didn't recall Craig or anyone else keeping beer in a locker.

At the end of the interview, Gravina mentioned that on Saturday, August 16, after Craig had asked him to lie, another stagehand, Vincent Donohue, stopped Gravina and told him he shouldn't cover up anything.

Donohue? Mike wondered. What's he got to do with it? How did he know Craig asked Gravina to lie? He jotted a note to talk to Donohue.

But Gravina had touched on Donohue lightly and was saying he couldn't believe Craig didn't remember where he was that night. Why did Craig ask him to lie? he wondered. It didn't make sense. Craig couldn't be guilty.

It bothered Mike how hard it was for people to believe Craig might be guilty. The more they resisted believing it, the less help they might be and the harder it could make his job. Was Gravina's faith in Craig a friend's trust or a manifestation of backstage sentiment?

John Pariente, their next interview, destroyed Craig's story about sunning himself on the sixth-floor roof, above the fan roof, two weeks before the murder, the story that was supposed to explain any of Craig's fingerprints the cops may have found

in the vicinity of the crime scene. The last time Pariente was
sure Craig had been on the sixth floor was half a year before,
when he went up to the kitchen to get some ice for a party. He
may have been sunning himself on the upper roof in June, but
didn't go up any ladder.

Craig had been very particular about going up a ladder that
was built into the outside wall and that led from the fan roof to
the upper roof on the sixth floor, so particular Mike suspected
that may have been Craig's escape route after the murder: up
the ladder, across the upper roof, through the trapdoor, which
had been found with a broken lock, and down onto the grid,
the network of crisscrossed supports six stories above the stage.

Mike didn't like Pariente. He was a street kid, who tried to
make you think he was being cooperative, but really didn't
want to help. When they pressed him about Craig's sunbathing
story, Pariente gave them such a puzzled look that he helped
them despite himself.

What are you guys talking about? he said. That's a lot of
bullshit.

Trying to pin down who might have been on the second floor
when Craig said Helen got off the elevator, Mike interviewed a
woman who worked in the wig department, which was on the
second floor, and another woman, Stephanie Chereton, a wardrobe supervisor.

The wig woman said her department had been on vacation,
the whole floor was dark, and when she'd been there it had
seemed spooky. Mike was less interested in the spooks that
might have been on the second floor than he was in the hu-
mans.

Stephanie Chereton had more concrete information. When
she'd gone to the second floor soon after the murder, she'd
found right outside the elevator a locker that had been broken
into.

"What was in the locker?" Mike asked.

Sewing equipment, she said.

"Scissors?" Mike asked, thinking about how carefully Helen's clothes had been cut.

Possibly, she said.

"Rags?" Mike asked, thinking of Helen's gags.

Cloth, she said. Possibly.

Often Mike described a detective's job as *weaving a web,* as though he were one of the Fates. As he shuttled from interview to interview, he felt the web grow; he became more confident of their ultimate success.

When he and Jerry talked to Mike Murray, a member of the backstage crew who worked on props, Mike knew this was their best shot at locking the case up. In his questionnaire, Murray had placed himself in the electricians' lounge at the same time Craig claimed he was asleep there. He was the witness they needed. Now, they had to find out if his story ruined Craig's alibi. If he said he'd seen Craig or if Craig could have been in the room without his knowing, their case against Craig would be weakened.

As Murray told what he had done the night of Helen's murder, Mike and Jerry began exchanging glances. He had gone through the locker room, where Craig claimed he had gotten his beer, into the electricians' lounge. He lay down on the couch, the same couch Craig claimed he'd slept on, to take a nap. He'd been alone. No one else was in the locker room. No one else was in the electricians' lounge. No one else was on the couch.

Mike and Jerry, unable to believe their luck, couldn't contain themselves. Their excitement was so obvious that Murray asked them, What's going on?

They took Murray over his story three times. Afterward, Mike said, "Now, show us."

They walked his route, stopping at every point to make sure he was remembering correctly. Finally, Murray got exasperated and said, Look, there was nobody in here. If someone else said he was in that room asleep on the couch, he was full of shit. I'm not a fag. I don't sleep with no guys. *I was the only guy in here.*

Murray was also annoyed at having to repeat everything. Like Craig, he had just started his vacation and had come to the Met to pick up his pay. His wife was waiting outside in the car. He wanted to get going.

When they were through with Murray, Mike said to him, "Don't discuss this with *anyone.* Enjoy your vacation."

I'm going to enjoy your vacation, Mike thought, because you won't be around to tell anyone what you just told us.

After Murray left, Mike and Jerry went into one of the Atrium offices and closed the door. They sat for a moment and grinned at each other. They had just started going over the details of Murray's statement, when the door opened and Murray stalked in. No knock. No apologies for interrupting. He looked bewildered.

Now I know why you guys wanted to talk to me, he said.

"What's the matter?" Mike asked.

What's going on here? he said. What is this that Marty Higgins is telling me that his son—that Craig was down here?

On his way out of the building, Murray had run into Higgins. They had talked. Apparently, Murray told Higgins what he'd just said to Mike and Jerry; and Higgins told Murray that Mike and Jerry had interviewed Craig and that Craig was claiming he'd been asleep on the couch in the electricians' lounge on the night of the murder.

"Take it easy," Jerry said. "You didn't realize what was going on. We didn't tell you. Your being down there is important to us."

That kid's full of shit, Murray said, referring to Craig's story. But you don't think Crimmie did it?

Jerry wanted to calm Murray and downplay their suspicions

about Craig, who—Jerry suggested—hadn't told the truth, that's all.

"Right now we're looking at every possibility," he said. "When somebody lies, they get caught in it."

But Murray wasn't put off. When Mike and Jerry were questioning him he must have felt that he was a suspect. Finding out that they were focusing on Craig seemed to have confused him. He was relieved to be off the hook, but unhappy his story put Craig on the spot.

It was a seesaw. If he was up, Craig was down. If Craig was up, he'd be down. Since they both couldn't be at the same place at the same time, one of them had to be lying. And the one who was lying would obviously be a suspect. He wanted to make sure the cops knew he was telling the truth so he wouldn't be a suspect, but he must also have felt that if only he could get more information he could get both of them, Craig and himself, off the seesaw. So he questioned Mike and Jerry as intensely as they had questioned him.

"We'll get to the bottom of it," Jerry said.

"We just have to be accurate," Mike said. "We don't care who's drinking, who's missed their cues, but we have to know where everybody is. Because some guy, even if he wasn't where he was supposed to be, might have been in an area where he saw something that could help us."

Craig, Mike was implying, was merely being scrutinized as a potential witness.

Murray seemed placated. But before he left, Jerry made sure to tell him to keep what he knew to himself. No sense starting rumors.

Late that afternoon, the Crime Scene Unit came back to the Met to check out the locker on the second floor that had been broken into and the ladder leading from the fan roof to the upper roof. They found no prints.

Before knocking off work for the night, Mike arranged to

meet his informant by the docks to find out how the stage-hands were reacting to Craig's long interview. Were they beginning to line up behind Craig or waiting to see what happened? Or—and this is what Mike hoped—had they bought the story that Craig was not a suspect, just a witness?

Mike's informant understood that the cops had a suspect.

"One of the brothers?" the informant asked.

"Yeah," Mike said. That was as much as he could admit, and he did it only as bait, to draw the informant out.

"Well," the informant said, "fuck him. If he did it to the girl, whoever he is, you guys got to do what you got to do. We'll help you any way we can."

Mike hoped he was right, that the crew would help. If the crew turned on the cops, it could endanger the investigation.

The hostility Mike and Jerry feared from the crew broke out into the open the following day.

Jerry, looking for one of Craig's friends, walked onto the stage and came face to face with Steve Diaz, Sr. He hadn't seen Diaz, Sr., since he'd telephoned him and accidentally upset his wife.

Oh, yeah, Diaz, Sr., said. You're Giorgio, huh?

"I'm Giorgio," Jerry said.

Two dozen stagehands, who'd been hammering, moving props, fixing curtains, stopped work and drifted into a circle around Jerry and Diaz, Sr. The stage became quiet.

You're the guy that likes to call up women and frighten them, Diaz, Sr., said.

Jerry liked Diaz, Sr. He seemed honest and stubborn. An Anthony Quinn type. A stand-up guy. Someone Jerry could respect, even as an opponent. He didn't want to embarrass him.

"You don't have that quite right," Jerry said. "When I called up—and I know what you're talking about—I had no intention of frightening anybody or getting anybody upset. If you recall, on the phone I said if I did that to her, I was sorry."

Jerry was apologizing. Diaz, Sr., could drop his complaint without losing face. But he didn't drop it.

Ah, you cops, he said. You're all alike.

"Hey, look," Jerry said. "That's enough of that bullshit."

The circle of stagehands drew closer.

This isn't just about the wife, Jerry thought.

Diaz, Sr., had been friends with Craig's stepfather, Marty Higgins, for twenty years. And Jerry had the impression that Diaz, Sr., felt protective of him. He probably resented Jerry for putting Craig through a marathon interview and disturbing Higgins.

Some of the stagehands in the circle around him had clenched fists and were breathing hard. Whether they thought Craig was a suspect or a witness, they obviously believed the cops had decided the killer was in their ranks. They resented that.

Jerry waited. If Diaz, Sr., swung at him, every cop in the building would be down on stage. The place would explode. So Jerry wasn't going to provoke him. But Jerry wasn't going to back down. It was a stand-off. Diaz, Sr., had made his point. Jerry had made his point.

The moment when Diaz, Sr., would have swung passed. He shrugged and turned. The circle of stagehands melted, everyone drifting back to his job. Someone started hammering. Someone else scraped something across the floor. People started talking.

Jerry was alone in the middle of the stage.

For the rest of the week, Mike and Jerry continued to punch holes in Craig's alibi. They reinterviewed all the principals in the investigation, some for the fourth and fifth time.

Gravina went over his story in even more detail, describing everything from where he and Craig bought the grass—on 144th Street and Amsterdam Avenue—to how many pretzels they ate. Mike Wexelblatt, who'd been in the car with them, confirmed Gravina's story. An electrician, Robert Rowland, placed Craig on A level about fifteen minutes before Helen left the orchestra pit and went through the A-level crossover. Jimmy Jordan, who was the stage-door guard that night, remembered two guys coming backstage at about ten o'clock, looking for Craig. He had called down to the stage, where Craig should have been and said, Tell Craig two of his friends are here. But Craig couldn't be found. The two guys had left. About eleven-fifteen, after the show had ended and almost everyone had gone for the night, Jordan had seen Craig coming down the hallway that led to the artists' dressing rooms and, beyond the dressing rooms, to a stairwell that went up to the roof. Craig looked grimy, Jordan told Mike and Jerry.

Hey, Crimmie, Jordan had called out, a couple of guys were looking for you.

Yeah, Craig had said, I know.

He'd done an about-face and headed back the way he'd come.

Johnny Maher, a Met old-timer who knew everyone and everything, recalled seeing Craig leaving the stage area long after the show had ended, possibly as he was retreating from Jimmy Jordan.

Henry Schoppe, one of Craig's co-workers, explained how roll call was handled. If someone was present, the roll-call sheet would have a check mark for that day. If he was absent, there would be an S. Mike and Jerry got the roll-call sheets from the office. Under Craig's name, the day the body was found, there was an *S* with an arrow pointing at a check mark. What did that mean? Mike and Jerry had to quiz three or four people before getting a definite answer: Craig had shown up for work, but had gotten sick during the day and gone home.

That fit. The body is found. The Met is flooded with cops. Craig can't deal with it and asks to leave.

They interviewed Tommy Green and Terry Taylor, stage-hands who should have been on stage the night of the murder; Al Ortiz, one of Craig's pals backstage; Susan Winterbottom and Joe Tamosaitas, who saw Helen on stage level when she was looking for Panov, possibly just before she went to elevator 12. They even checked out Mrs. Claude Hill, a woman who'd reported her harp stolen.

During that interview Mike had trouble keeping a straight face. How the hell can someone sneak off with something as big as a harp? he wondered.

They were covering every base. They wanted to make sure that if and when the case went to trial, there would be no surprises, nothing to cloud the issue.

On Friday, August 22, Mike and McVeety drove Heffernan to the Crime Scene Unit to get copies of the photographs taken at the Met. Heffernan wanted all reproduced as 9-by-12 glossies and a few blown up huge.

The sergeant, a cop with great jowls, said he'd have them ready in three weeks. Heffernan said he needed them immediately. The sergeant shrugged. Heffernan insisted. The sergeant said, "What do you think this is? The only case in New York?"

Mike and McVeety had to get in between Heffernan and the sergeant to keep them from slugging it out.

While McVeety calmed the sergeant, Mike explained to Heffernan that every year the Crime Scene Unit had to cover 1,800 homicides, all cases that involved people who were likely to die, all police shootings, all major robberies of businesses, and all burglaries of over $10,000. To do this, they had about thirty people. Not nearly enough. In most cases, they went out once. Sometimes, they went out a second time—on what they designated an A run. Rarely, they went out a third or fourth time—on a B or C run. They almost never went out a fifth time—on a D run. On the Met case, they had made so many runs they had worked their way through a third of the alphabet.

"And we don't even have an arrest yet," Mike told Heffernan. "See why the guy might be short-tempered with us?"

After stopping at the laboratory and spreading all the physical evidence on the table, going over it for possible links to Craig, Mike headed upstate. As usual, he'd spent the week sleeping in the 20th Precinct bunk room. But this weekend, he didn't want to get away. The thought of leaving the city made him antsy. He wanted to wrap up some loose ends, finish Heffernan's to-do list.

But the case was going well. Two days off wouldn't matter. And he probably could use a break.

When he walked in the door, his family exploded around him. The back-hoe pump was still broken. While Marion was cutting the grass, the lawnmower broke. While his daughter, Stacy, was doing the laundry, the washing machine broke. The woman with the half-finished septic field was raising hell. Shedding shirt, shoes, socks, Mike headed downstairs to the gym he'd set up in the basement. His family followed, the dog bounding down the steps, circling Mike, and scrambling back up through the crowd. Mike ducked into the gym and slammed the door.

When Jerry got home that weekend, the house was quiet and tense. His daughter and son looked reproachfully at him, while Kay issued an ultimatum. Jerry had forgotten about a promised vacation upstate in Stevensville on Sunday, Monday, and Tuesday.

"We're going," Kay said. "Either you go with us or pack your bags—and not for a vacation."

Jerry called into the office and arranged to get Monday and Tuesday off.

"Good," Kay said. "Now, enough with the case. For the next four days, no shop talk, no phone calls, nothing. Starting now."

Jerry couldn't resist. Every day, he sneaked off to call the office. Saturday and Sunday: nothing. Monday: nothing unexpected. Tuesday: He was told that Mike and McVeety had gone to the Bronx to talk to Craig's father, Eddie Crimmins.

Why? What happened? What did they find out?

During the rest of the day, until he reached Mike, Jerry called in at least half a dozen times.

Mike and McVeety went to the 52nd Precinct in Craig's neighborhood. Did the cops there know Craig? If they did, what was their line on him? Who did he hang out with? What was the line on his friends?

They didn't get much: only a 1973 bullshit assault case and a 1975 unlawful assembly charge that had been dropped. Craig wasn't the typical suspect with a dozen arrests: petty crimes, dickie-waving.

What about the bars he went to: the Green Isle on Bainbridge at 205th Street? Doc Fiddlers? McQuires?

Nothing special. Bars. That's all.

At the apartment building on Paul Street where Craig lived with his father and sister, Mike and McVeety flimflammed their way through the downstairs door, so they wouldn't have to buzz and alert the family. On the nineteenth floor they knocked on the Crimminses' door.

Who is it? asked a voice. Craig's father's voice?

"Detective Struk," Mike said. "And Sergeant McVeety."

Okay, the voice said. I'll be right there.

During the delay, Mike wondered if Craig was hiding.

When Eddie Crimmins opened the door, the smell of frying sausage wafted from the apartment. Mike realized he was famished.

Crimmins ushered them into the kitchen, where the sausages were sizzling on the stove.

Would you like some? Crimmins asked, gesturing toward the frying pan.

"No, thanks," Mike said. How do you eat at a man's table, he thought, when you know you're going to lock up his son?

While they talked, Crimmins pushed the sausages around the pan. When he spoke, his voice quavered. The cops had never before visited a stagehand at his home. He knew something was up.

To disarm him, Mike used a cover story, based on what Helen's stand-partner had said the day the body was found. He'd work around that to get what he needed: information on the two friends who had been looking for Craig and whether or not Craig went home the night of the murder.

"We're trying to find this big bald guy who was hanging around the stage door that night," Mike said. "Oh—and incidentally—two of Craig's friends were there waiting. Maybe they seen the bald guy. Do you know who those friends might be?"

Crimmins had no idea who they could have been.

Trying to keep the interview low-key, Mike interspersed his questions about the case with general conversation: about the Mets and the Yankees, broads, the weather.

As they talked, Crimmins mentioned that on the day of Helen's murder he went home early, about four o'clock in the afternoon, leaving his car, a 1977 two-door, gray Toyota for Craig, so he wouldn't have to take the subways late at night.

He had a few drinks with some friends who stopped by and went to bed before Craig got home. About two o'clock in the morning, on his way to the toilet, he glanced out the window and saw his car parked in its usual place. He looked in on Craig, who was asleep. The next morning, he and Craig took the subway to work.

Something doesn't add up, Mike thought.

If Craig drove his father's car home on the night of the murder, why did they take the subway to work the next morning? Mike was half-convinced Craig had spent the night at the Met. Maybe his father was covering up. The car story sounded like a memorized speech.

Mike scrutinized Eddie Crimmins. If he is covering up, Mike thought, it's because he believes Craig is guilty only of lying to protect his ass at work, not of murder.

"By the way," Mike asked, "where's Craig now? Maybe we could get together, have a burger or something."

He's at the Jersey shore, Crimmins said.

"Ask him about his friends and the bald-headed guy," Mike said. "Maybe he knows something. If he does, have him give me a call."

When they left the apartment building, Mike, half-crazed from hunger, told McVeety, "I don't give a shit what we're doing. We're going to eat first."

They stopped at a cops' hangout in the Bronx called the Piper's Kilt for some bacon cheeseburgers. McVeety ribbed Mike about the bald-man story: his Mr. Clean routine. Mike didn't respond. He was in a meditative mood.

On the way downtown, Mike asked, "What do you think? The Jersey shore?"

McVeety shrugged.

"Or under the bed?" Mike said.

As Mike and McVeety were walking in the door of the 20th Precinct, Craig called. Mike grabbed the phone. Craig said he hadn't seen the bald man and—this was emphatic—none of his friends had visited him at the Met that night.

He knows those two friends can put him in the jackpot, Mike thought, if they say they were there and Craig never showed up.

They chatted for a few minutes.

Yeah, Craig said, and I even met Jimmy Jordan last night.

Jordan was one of the security guards Mike and Jerry had extensively interviewed. Mike made a note to check out Jordan again the following day.

Craig hung up.

"I don't know if he was under the bed," Mike said. "But he ain't at the Jersey shore."

Craig—it seemed—had telephoned from the Bronx.

Jerry had planned to stay at the Stevensville hotel with his family until Wednesday morning and leave early enough to get to work on time. But, when he learned about the interview with Craig's father, the telephone call from Craig, and how Craig had met Jimmy Jordan in a bar, he canceled the Tuesday night reservations.

"New developments," he told Kay and the kids. "We got to get home." He wanted to be close to the city in case anything broke overnight.

At home, Jerry didn't sleep well. He was restless, eager to get back to work. He was up early Wednesday morning, had a quick breakfast, and drove into the city.

"Loaded for bear, huh?" Mike said when he saw Jerry breeze into the 20th Precinct.

"Four days," Jerry said, "is a long time."

They went to the Met, where they interviewed Jordan in the Atrium.

Jordan had met Craig in one of the Bronx bars Craig frequented, the Green Isle. He was having a drink, when Craig entered with two or three friends. Jordan was at one end of the bar. Craig and his pals stayed at the other. For a while, Jordan thought Craig was avoiding him. Finally, Craig approached and said, Hey, look at my new tattoo. An eagle and flag on his right triceps.

Craig had lost weight, and now he'd gotten a new tattoo. This confirmed Mike and Jerry's suspicion that Craig was trying to change his appearance.

The fucking cops had me in the other day and were breaking my balls, Craig had said to Jordan, doing a tough-guy act, evidently trying to convince himself he'd fooled Mike and Jerry.

Then he'd said something that seemed to Mike and Jerry to be a guilty tic. Although he'd camouflaged himself behind two co-workers who were innocent, Craig fingered himself. He'd said, The cops think the killer's either Gravina, Donohue, or me.

12

THE FOLLOWING DAY, Thursday, August 28, Chief Nicastro called everyone vitally connected with the case into his office. For hours, they discussed everything in detail. They broke for a meal, which was brought in, and then went over the case again just to make sure they weren't forgetting anything.

Craig's alibi wouldn't stand up. Mike and Jerry had covered all the bases. They had good evidence and good witnesses. Their case was solid. There was only one thing more to do: re-interview Craig.

They didn't want to pick him up at his home, because for that they would need a warrant. Craig would get a lawyer. And they would lose their chance to talk to him. They'd wait until Monday morning when he came back to work.

There was nothing to do for the next three days: Friday, Saturday, and Sunday. Labor Day weekend.

After the meeting in Nicastro's office, Mike jumped into his car, the 1976 Pinto, and headed for the Jersey shore, Beach Haven, where he always spent Labor Day. His family had already driven down in their 1973 Cadillac. He arrived in time for a late dinner. It was twilight. Mike, Jr., Steve, and Tom were on the dock fishing. When one of them cast, the unwinding line made the reel sing. Waves slapped against the piles. The air smelled of brine. Mike closed his eyes. He thought, I'm in heaven.

The next day, the weather was perfect. In the sunlight, the water looked like crumpled tinfoil. Mike, wearing cut-off jeans, a T-shirt that said "20th precinct: the land of fruits and nuts," and his cowboy hat, fixed his brother-in-law's broken outboard motor. He'd just gotten the motor in place and the kids in their seats and was shoving off, one foot on shore and one foot in the boat, when Marion came running from the house, shouting that the office was on the phone.

"You got to be kidding," Mike said.

When Mike got on the line, his captain, Frank Ward, said, Don't go anywhere.

"You're lucky you're not standing here, pal," Mike said. "I'm not too happy about this call, but my wife'd kill you. She's not in the Police Department. She's going to tell you a few words."

Look, Ward said, I got to make other calls.

"What's the beef?" Mike said.

The department had gotten word that the *Daily News* was going to run a front-page story, saying a Met stagehand was a suspect in the case.

"When?" Mike asked.

Tonight, Ward said. The paper would hit the stands at seven o'clock, when the story would also be broadcast on the radio on WOR. You know what'll happen when this gets out, Ward said. Crimmins is going to get a lawyer, and we'll lose our opportunity to do a last interview.

"So we got till seven," Mike said. "I'm leaving now."

Stand by the phone, Ward said. We're going to go into a big meeting this afternoon. I'll let you know what's shaking.

Mike hung up the phone. I got to wait *here?* he thought. I got to *wait?* He slammed his fist into the wall. I don't believe they're doing this to me, he thought. I'm not going to be there when this guy is taken into tow. If I get there at all, it'll be just in time to see Giorgio in his television suit marching Craig's ass out of the station house. Fucking Giorgio. Right up front again. I don't know how he did it. But somehow he planned this. He had to. He waited until I was a hundred miles away, and he's going to piss on my parade. He's going to lock Crimmins up behind my back.

That morning, Jerry was at the Latent Section, having his fingerprints taken. Everyone connected with the case had to have his prints taken to find out whose prints had been found on the hem of Helen's skirt. That was the case's one vulnerable spot. Any lawyer Craig got could use those unknown prints on Helen's skirt to plant enough doubt about Craig's guilt to shake a jury. Craig's palm print may have been found on the roof, the lawyer could say; but whose tips are on Helen's skirt? The skirt she was wearing when she was murdered. On the hem. Right where the killer must have held the skirt when he was cutting it off her body. The prints have to belong to the killer. And they don't belong to Craig. Therefore, Craig can't be the killer.

Like most of the people working on the case, Jerry believed the tips on Helen's skirt had been left by someone in the department who had accidentally contaminated the evidence, someone who'd touched the skirt on the day Helen's body was discovered, when the skirt was still on the floor of the shaft outside the electrical shop. The Latent Section had already eliminated stagehands, members of the orchestra, friends, even the people at the dry cleaner's Helen had used. Billy Plifka, the fingerprint expert working on the problem, had spent hundreds of hours examining and comparing prints. The amount of work Plifka had put in was extraordinary. Jerry admired his stamina. He was amazed Plifka hadn't developed a permanent squint.

Pat Heaney was having his prints taken, too. Jerry chatted with him about the case, about how they all were lucky to get a quiet weekend, about how Mike was down at the shore, fishing, crabbing, clamming, having a good time.

When he was through at Latent, Jerry stopped by to talk to a district attorney to discuss another case he was involved in. He hadn't checked into the 20th Precinct since earlier that morning and it was already time for lunch, so he decided to give a call, not because he expected any news, just out of habit.

He reached Frank Ward, who said, Giorgio, where've you been? You better get your ass up here.

When Jerry arrived at the 20th Precinct, Ward was on the telephone, trying to convince the newspaper to hold off breaking the story.

All day, various people from the department and the district attorney's office had been talking to the *Daily News*. As long as there was a chance the newspaper would wait, they wouldn't pick up Craig, since picking up Craig this way probably meant immediately arresting him and losing the chance to talk to him.

"Where's Mike?" Jerry asked.

I already spoke to him, Ward said.

"Is he on his way?" Jerry asked.

I'm waiting for word, Ward said.

"Waiting for word!" Jerry said. "We've got to move."

We have to wait, Ward said.

"I can see what's going to happen," Jerry said.

If we get the go-ahead, Jerry thought; *if* Craig doesn't hear the news on the radio or see it in the paper; *if* we find him; *if*, when we find him, he agrees to come with us to answer some more questions so we don't have to arrest him; *if* his parents don't call the department with a lawyer for Craig; *if* all those unlikely things actually happen, it'll be a long night.

Jerry told Ward he'd be in the bunk room. He'd just stretched out on the bed when Ward came in and said, The decision is made. The *News* is going to go with the story.

Jerry jumped up.

"Someone get on the phone and get Mike in here," he said. He turned to Leo Rosenthal. "Let's go."

Ward said they'd have to wait for the Chief to get there.

"Jesus Christ," Jerry said. "Wait for the Chief! We're going to waste another half hour to forty-five minutes."

Finally Ward said okay. But they had to find Craig as soon as possible. Had to convince him, cajole him, con him, get him in.

Everyone connected with the case paired up and headed out, each team assigned to check a different location.

Jerry and Leo Rosenthal went to Paul Avenue, Craig's home. The evening was warm. Jerry was sweating in his three-piece suit. Craig's father's car, the gray Toyota; Craig's car, a 1970 gold Oldsmobile; and Craig's motorcycle were all parked near the apartment house. Craig had to be in the apartment or nearby. They needed reinforcements to stake out the area, but the radio in Leo's car didn't work. They had to find a telephone, but there were no public phones around. Jerry went running up the street, looking for a store that would let him use its phone, but it was late on the afternoon of Labor Day weekend, and everything was shut.

Jerry saw someone inside a garage. He tapped on the glass door.

We're closed, the man in the garage said.

"Police," Jerry said.

What police? the man said.

Jerry held up his shield.

The man let him in. Jerry called and was told a couple of cars would be there as soon as possible. He ran back to Craig's apartment house, leaned against a tree across from the front door, and lit a cigarette.

At six-fifty, ten minutes before WOR would broadcast the scoop, the apartment door opened and Craig walked out. Jerry didn't move. Craig started to cross the street diagonally, right toward Jerry. He was only a few feet away, when Craig realized who was leaning against the tree.

Hi, Jerry, he said. Is anything wrong?

Jerry flicked away his cigarette.

"Well, no, Craig," he said. "Nothing's wrong other than if you recall the last conversation we had, which was approximately two weeks ago, there were certain areas you said were unclear, that you couldn't remember. In fact, you said if you had some time to think about it you might be able to clear these matters up. Would you mind very much—you know—coming back to the office, and we'll go over these areas."

Is this going to take all night? Craig asked.

"No," Jerry said. "It shouldn't take all night." That was a lie. At some point during the evening, Craig was probably going to be arrested. Either after he talked to Jerry if he came willingly, or immediately if he balked.

Okay, Craig said.

"Fine," Jerry said. "My partner's got his car down the street."

They strolled to where Rosenthal was parked. Jerry opened the door. Craig climbed into the back seat.

On the way back to the city, Rosenthal was the driver. Craig directed him through the neighborhood. The area had the same feeling of a small community within the sprawl of the city that Jerry recalled from the Greenwich Village of his youth. Whatever happens down the road in the trial, Jerry thought, Craig's arrest will change this neighborhood for him forever.

The traffic on the Parkway was so heavy, the trip back to

Manhattan took almost an hour. Before discussing the case Jerry had to read Craig his rights, which he didn't want to do until they reached the office. If he read the rights in the car, he might spook Craig into asking for a lawyer, so he kept up a patter about everything, anything else.

Although Craig never talked about the case, he kept veering toward it. He said he'd heard that the Met management had found out about the drinking and parties going on backstage and was cracking down on the crew.

"Hey, Craig," Jerry said, "you know there's no way we carried those stories back."

Craig was concerned because—he said—the night Helen was killed his father was supposed to have been on the job, was paid for working, but wasn't there. He was afraid that because of the investigation his father was going to be reprimanded or even fired.

"If we have to," Jerry told him, "we'll go to the management and tell them that no one should be hurt because of the cooperation we were given by the stagehands."

Peter Mangecavallo, a Task Force detective, was waiting for them in front of the 20th Precinct. Before Rosenthal turned off the ignition, Mangecavallo called out to Jerry in Italian, Go down to our place.

"We have to go to the Task Force," Jerry said casually. "Mike Struk is going to meet us there."

Okay, Craig said.

Leo understood why they were being told to avoid the 20th Precinct. The news had broken and every paper, wire service, radio and television station was calling the 20th or sending reporters there. If they'd gone in, they would have walked into an impromptu press conference.

At about eight-ten, they arrived at the Task Force office, which was housed in the 13th Precinct. Four or five detectives were sitting around, watching television. Jerry ushered Craig into one of the locker rooms, out of earshot.

"I'm going to try to get us a quiet room," he told him. He went back in the office and told the other detectives, "Look, turn the TV down. I don't want this kid to hear any news flashes."

The Chief, the DA, the captain, and most of the sergeants connected with the case were apprehensive. If Craig's family called the department anywhere in the city—any precinct, any office—whatever he subsequently said would be inadmissible in a trial.

Everyone talked at once.

Okay, Jerry, this is it.

Get the kid.

Let's go.

"Where's Mike?" Jerry said.

He's on his way, someone told him.

Look, the Chief said, you and Leo can start.

"It's not that I don't want Leo to be in there," Jerry said. "He's been in on the case from the beginning. He's got a right. But I really feel, if Mike is on his way, we should wait."

Mike had left the Jersey Shore between four and five o'clock. As he drove through the heavy turnpike traffic, he was seething over what he thought was Jerry's betrayal. When he got to the 20th Precinct and learned that Jerry had taken Craig to the Task Force office, it seemed one more proof that Jerry was trying to upstage him.

It's going to be a Task Force party, he thought. Screwed by the stars.

When he got upstairs to the detective unit, Sergeants Callan and Brady were waiting for him. They looked at Mike's outfit

—his cut-offs, T-shirt, and cowboy hat—and one of them asked if he had any suits in his locker.

When Mike had changed, they grabbed a squad car and, siren on, lights flashing, headed down to the Task Force office.

Before the car had come to a full stop, Mike was out the door and into the building. On C deck, where the Chief's office was, he found Mangecavallo near the elevator.

Jerry's inside, Mangecavallo said. He's waiting on you.

They'd moved Craig from the locker room into the office of the Zone commander, Eugene Burke.

When Mike entered the room, Jerry said, "Where the hell have you been?"

Mike felt like laughing.

"You waited," he said.

"Because you've spoken to the DA before and because you've been advised of your Miranda warnings on a previous occasion, now any time we speak to you, it has to be done again," Jerry told Craig.

The four of them—Jerry, Craig, Mike, and Rosenthal—were sitting around the desk in Burke's office. Mike sat facing Craig. Jerry and Rosenthal flanked them. The room was quiet and comfortable. Small. About ten by fourteen. Simply furnished. The desk, a couch, filing cabinets, a TV for training films. The windows had bars, which worried Jerry. He didn't want Craig to feel he was in custody. But the bars were hidden by shades. The steel buck door, which was closed, had louvers on the bottom half. The walls on either side of the door were metal on the bottom and glass on top. Bamboo shutters covered the glass.

Mike, Jerry, and Rosenthal had decided to handle the interview like the previous one: whomever Craig favored would ask the questions. The others would pull back. They planned to start from the beginning of the day Helen was murdered and take Craig through everything he did, break for a strategy session, and then confront Craig with the discrepancies in his story and his lies.

Mike figured there was only a 40 percent chance that Craig would roll over and blurt out a confession. And he figured there was a 70 percent chance a lawyer would call during the interview. Still, he realized Jerry's slow and methodical method was necessary. If they moved too fast, Craig might freeze and demand a lawyer.

"This is Mike's case," Jerry said, "so he'll do the Miranda warnings." Jerry thought if he gave the warnings himself, he might mar his paternal role and shake Craig's trust in him.

At eight-forty, Mike read Craig his rights from a card. Craig agreed to talk to them without a lawyer and signed the back of the card.

Again, while telling his story, Craig seemed confident. He was definite about what he did, where he did it, and when. Most of the story was the same, although there were a few interesting additions and some significant differences. According to Craig, he'd been on stage during the first intermission on the night Helen was killed, from eight fifty-two to nine-fifteen, changing the set. Just before the curtain had risen, he'd gone upstage, across the rear wagon, and through a door leading to a hallway and elevator 12. At the elevator, Helen had been talking to another woman.

Mike noted that it was the first time Craig had mentioned Laura Cutler.

Craig couldn't remember if Laura had gotten on the elevator with Helen and him. They'd gone up to the second floor. Helen had gotten off. He'd gone down to A level; passed through the crew bathroom on his way to the locker room; taken the cans of beer from his locker; and carried them into the electricians' lounge, where he'd drunk a few and dozed off.

Mike had Craig trace his route on a diagram of the A level.

Craig said he'd awakened after the show had ended and gone to stage level, where he'd seen John Maher shutting off the house lights. He contradicted Jimmy Jordan's story. None of his friends had come to the Met to meet him, and he hadn't been in the hallway where Jordan claimed he'd seen him. Before leaving the Met, Craig had called his father from a pay phone and told him he was late because he'd fallen asleep. He'd found his father's car parked on Sixty-fourth Street, listened to the car radio for a while, gotten a hamburger and a chocolate milk, and driven to the Bronx.

At this point, Craig became less definite. He couldn't recall if his father had awakened when he'd gotten home. He couldn't recall how he'd gotten to work the next morning. He couldn't even recall what time he'd arrived at the Met. He'd been working on the center stage when he heard that a lady had been killed. He'd lunched at the Met and hadn't left the building until the end of the day.

Then he changed his story: Around lunchtime, he'd asked Fred Collay if he could go home. He felt sick, he'd said. Suffer, Collay had said. He was angry at Craig for having missed his cues the night before. Craig had gone over Collay's head to one of the superbosses and gotten permission to leave. As for asking Gravina to lie, this time he said the reason was that he hadn't had time to tell Gravina what had really happened.

That explanation made no sense. If Craig had time to ask Gravina to say he'd been asleep on the rear wagon, why didn't he have time to ask Gravina to say he'd been asleep in the electricians' lounge? But neither Mike, Jerry, nor Rosenthal said anything.

They took a break. Craig asked for a soda. Mike, Jerry, and Rosenthal left the room. The Chief, Ward, Heffernan, all of them outside wanted to know what had happened.

Mike, Jerry, and Rosenthal returned to the room, closed the door, and sat down around the desk again.

This was it.

They listed the inconsistencies in Craig's stories and his lies.

"On your questionnaire, you said you were there all evening and you made all your cues," Jerry said. "That wasn't true.

"Then, you said you were asleep on the rear wagon and were awakened by a friend. That wasn't true.

"Then, you asked Tommy Gravina to lie for you.

"Then, you admitted that you were the man on the elevator with Helen. And you said she got off at the second floor, and you hadn't gotten off with her.

"Then, you told us you went to A level, got beer, and fell asleep in the electricians' lounge. You told us the other stories were lies and this was the truth. Well, something just isn't right here. People were in the locker room when you said you were there, and nobody saw you. People were in the lounge when you said you were there, and nobody saw you. Craig, the story about being in the locker room and lounge. That's not true, either."

Craig's head had been sinking lower and lower until his chin almost touched the top of the desk. For a moment, he sat very still.

Listen, he said at last, would it be all right if I talked to you alone, Jerry?

The last time Craig had asked to talk to Jerry alone, he'd admitted to being on the elevator with Helen.

After Mike and Rosenthal had left the room, Jerry moved around the desk to sit facing Craig.

"What is it, Craig?" he asked.

You know, Craig said.

"How could I possibly know what's bothering you?" Jerry said. "What do you mean?"

You know, Craig said.

"What?" Jerry asked.

That I killed the lady, Craig said. I don't know where to begin.

"Just relax," Jerry said. "Begin where you feel most comfortable."

If you want to ask me about it, Craig said, I'll tell you what happened.

Jerry, being careful not to lead or feed, questioned Craig.

"Did you see Helen Hagnes Mintiks Wednesday night, July 23, 1980, and where?" Jerry said.

"I seen her at the back elevator number 12," Craig said. "I said something to her on the elevator, and she hit me."

"How did she hit you?"

"She smacked me on the right side of my face, on the ear."

"When you got to the second floor, did you get off with her?"

"She kept looking for the studios. We checked all the studios, everything was out. When she smacked me on the elevator, she said something snotty and loud. I said to her, 'Go this way,' and she did. I meant, go to the stairs."

"Was she afraid of you at this time?"

"Yes. She was, and she went with me."

"Where did you go on the stairs, and what happened?"

"We went to either C or B level, and I sort of talked her into fooling around. I said it won't hurt, and she started to get worse. She started freaking out on me. She tried to hit me. I grabbed her hands. That's when I took out the hammer. I just held it and told her to walk up the stairs."

"Before you went up the stairs, what, if anything, happened?"

"When she saw the hammer, she started taking off her clothes. She took them all off, and I saw her take out the rag, but she didn't say anything about it."

"Did you tell her to do anything?"

"I told her to lay down, and I tried to put it in. It wouldn't go in. I tried for about five minutes, and I couldn't get it in. I told her to get dressed and told her to walk up the stairs. On the way upstairs, I don't know which shop it was, she ran and tried to go into a door. I knew the door was locked. And she tried to open the door. I grabbed her and gave her a shove and said, 'Keep walking upstairs.' "

"What happened then?"

"We got to the roof, and I didn't know which of the doors went out. I wasn't sure then. I held her hand and opened the door. It led out to the roof. We went out and sat right by the pipe."

"What happened then?"

"She was trying to make conversation, asking if I worked there and if I was afraid I couldn't get out of there. I said, I didn't work, I didn't work here. I tied her right there because I was going to leave her there. I didn't have anything to do with her sexually after the first time on C deck."

"Did you ever reach a climax that night?"

"I came on C deck. I was just rubbing against her and came on her. I wasn't in her."

"Did you have it between her legs?"

"I guess so."

"Now, after you tied her on the roof, what happened?"

"I tied, I tied her with the rope. I told her I would leave her. I would call somebody and tell them she was there."

"Then what happened?"

"I left her there, walked back toward the door and like standing there thinking, If she gets out of it? As I was thinking, I heard some rattling, and I saw her with her feet undone, and she ran to the pipe, sat on it and went over. I ran after her, jumped over the pipe, caught her, and took her back to the same spot."

"Then what?"

"I think there was a bucket there with a whole shitful of rags in it. I tied her feet."

"Do you remember if she still had her shoes?"

"I remember I took them off and tossed them away so that if she ran it would hurt her feet. I put the rags over the rope so that it wouldn't come loose again. At that point, I picked her up and carried her up in my arms, carried her to the ledge, sat her down, then pulled her down and leaned her against the fan. She wasn't gagged. She was talking to me, trying to be nice. I decided to gag her and laid her flat on her stomach. I know I gagged her, and I think I put one around her eyes."

"How did her clothes get off?"

"I had my knife in the case on my belt. I took it out and cut them off. I figured if she got loose she wouldn't run because she would be embarrassed."

"What did you do with the clothes?"

"I just threw them down on the side of the fan."

"What else did you do?"

"At this point I was just sitting there thinking."

"What were you thinking?"

"What should I do. I sat there for a few minutes."

"What did you decide to do?"

"I decided to leave. As I was walking away I heard her pouncing up and down and that's when it happened. I went back and kicked her off."

Outside the room, Mike, who had been leaning over and listening through the louvers, leaped in joy.

Craig had to go to the bathroom. When Medina escorted him, Craig said, "I was sick that night and the next day."

A little after midnight, Jerry and Craig went over the questions and answers for Mike and Medina. When they were through, Medina jotted, "What happened to the purse?" on a scrap of paper, which he passed to Jerry.

No one but the cops knew that Helen's pocketbook had been thrown off the roof. No one but the cops and the killer.

"Did you throw anything else off the roof?" Jerry asked.

"Her pocketbook," Craig said.

Mike, Jerry, and Heffernan took Craig downstairs and videotaped his confession.

Craig sniffed. He sat with his chin in his fist.

"You can smoke if you want," Jerry said.

Craig nodded.

"All right," he said.

He took a cigarette pack from his T-shirt pocket.

"Menthol?" Jerry asked. "You got that cough. I don't think I have any more cough drops. Yes, I do. Want one?"

"No, thanks," Craig said.

One by one, Heffernan read the questions and answers and asked Craig if they were accurate. Craig barely moved his mouth when he said yes.

When Heffernan read Craig's quote, "I went back and kicked her off," Craig rubbed his mouth so hard he pushed his lower lip out to the side.

The videotape operator noticed some marks on Craig's face. To make sure they could not be construed as the result of any mistreatment, Heffernan asked Craig about them.

"I got two warts burned off my eye," Craig said.

Another way Craig was changing his appearance.

Heffernan got the doctor's name and address.

"Okay," he said. "That concludes the statement. Thank you."

The videotape operator turned off the camera. Everyone stood up, stretched.

Craig asked, Am I under arrest?

"Yeah," Jerry said. "Yeah, Craig."

PART TWO

13

AFTER THE CONFESSION, Jerry asked Craig, "Do you want to speak to your dad?" He'd learned that Eddie Crimmins had come to the station house.

No, Craig said almost inaudibly. He asked if Jerry would tell his father what was happening, that he was being arrested.

"Do you want me to notify your stepfather and your mom?" Jerry asked.

Craig said his mother would be very upset.

"Look," Jerry said, "I won't talk to her. I'll ask to speak to Marty."

Jerry called Marty Higgins at home in New Jersey to say Craig was under arrest. Higgins—Jerry thought—didn't sound surprised. Jerry again had the impression Higgins all along had suspected Craig of being involved in the murder.

You can't blame a father for standing by his son, Jerry thought. Even his step-son. And he wondered if Higgins was shielding Craig for Craig's sake or for the sake of Craig's mother.

By the time Jerry went looking for him, Eddie Crimmins had left the station house. Jerry phoned his apartment. Craig's sister answered.

My father's not home, she said. My mother's been trying to contact him.

"Have him give me a call when he gets home," Jerry said.

There was a lot more they wanted to know. Had Craig ever seen or talked to Helen before the night of the murder? Did he stalk her? What did he cut her clothes off with? When he stripped her on the roof, did he try to pop her again? Why did he do it? Did she remind him of his mother? But they had gotten the essentials; they had gotten enough to arrest Craig.

"You're going to need a lawyer," Jerry told Craig.

Jerry had the feeling that when Craig had confessed he'd wanted to get it off his chest. Now Craig was just beginning to understand the consequences of his confession.

"Do you want anything?" Jerry asked. "Soda?"

Mike was doing the paperwork, taking Craig's pedigree, height, weight. Craig had dropped his cocky manner. He'd withdrawn as if in his mind he'd already put himself in jail and slammed shut the cell door.

"Look," Mike said, "you don't have to love me, but I got to ask you these questions. If you have to go to the bathroom or want any cigarettes, feel free to ask; and we'll try to make this as easy for both of us as possible. It's late. You're tired. I'm tired. If you're going to jerk me off, it's going to take all night. We'll both suffer."

In the cell, Mike took some Polaroid photographs of Craig, front and back, dressed and naked, to show Craig hadn't been mistreated and to show how burly he was, how capable he would have been of picking Helen up and shoving her head-first through the small space at the top of the ventilator shaft—

which is what Mike believed Craig had done. There was no way he could have just kicked her off the roof.

But kicking her off the roof did not seem as brutal as jamming her into the narrow gap, working her through inch by inch, the edge of the shaft raking her body, leaving the scratches Mike had seen during the autopsy. While Craig admitted his guilt, he apparently didn't want to seem cruel. *I sort of talked her into fooling around.*

Mike thought: A guy could say, "Okay, you got me. I had a hard-on I couldn't get rid of, and she was the best thing around." But Craig seemed shy about the sex. He'd offered—from out of left field, Mike thought—that he didn't have sex with Helen on the roof. Why? Mike wondered. Why did he bring that up? Why did he take her to the roof? Why did he undress her there?

Mike didn't believe the cockamamy story about stripping her so she'd be too embarrassed to run. Craig must have been looking to get laid again. He'd failed on C level, and he'd wanted another shot. It didn't work out a second time. Craig got mad. And killed her.

That's one possibility, Mike thought. But who knows? This guy could have been thinking kinky things for years and years, and vented it all on this particular person. Or maybe he was just flirting in the elevator. She whacked him in the mouth. Macho, booze, and ganja took over. And everything just snowballed.

The light in the cell was as pale, flat, and claustrophobic as the light inside a refrigerator. Craig stood naked in front of a wall that looked as if it were built from Lego bricks. His mouth was open. His arms were held out from his body, stiffly at his sides. His muscles were tense enough to make his belly look hard and well-defined, divided into plates like the bottom of a turtle shell.

Mike couldn't help feeling sorry for the guy.

The only thing Craig seemed to care about was that no one tell what happened to his mother.

Mike, Jerry, and McVeety drove Craig downtown to the Criminal Court Building at 100 Centre Street. The surrounding neighborhood was a maze of narrow alleys and open plazas, salvage stores, discount houses, and cut-rate electrical supply shops. The government offices loomed like Roman temples; block-wide stairways and towering columns. But at night it seemed as two-dimensional as the scenery Jerry had seen in the Met storage room, a painted backdrop.

At Central Booking, Craig was processed. His fingerprints were sent to Albany to check against their files; his photograph was taken again. The Legal Aid Society was there in case he needed a lawyer. The Vera Foundation was ready to run a background check on his community roots and to make its recommendation about bail. Craig was entering the System.

After the basic processing was done, Mike, Jerry, and McVeety, expecting the press to be all over the 20th Precinct and the Task Force office, decided to hide Craig uptown in Harlem in the 30th Precinct. Since they wanted Laura Cutler to see if she could pick Craig out of a lineup, they didn't want the newspapers or television to take any pictures of him.

In the car, Jerry and McVeety were in front. Mike and Craig were in back. An hour and a half to sunrise. The Hudson River was the gray of a dead television screen. Trees flashed by, deep green in the streetlamp light. Like Mike, Jerry felt sorry for Craig. He wasn't a typical criminal, not a tough guy or a wiseass. Jerry hooked his elbow over the top of the seat and twisted around to glance back at Craig, who was still expressionless. Jerry thought about what Craig had done to Helen, what must have gone through her head as Craig walked her

around the Met, up and down, having her strip, dress, strip
again. . . .

They passed the Met.

No one mentioned it.

Connell had saved a bottom bunk for Mike at the 20th Precinct dormitory. Mike got sheets from his locker, flapped them
onto the mattress, undressed, and climbed into bed. He felt
exhausted and hyped up at the same time.

The first homicide Mike had gone on—it was another cop's
case—was a guy who'd been hacksawed. His body was found in
Central Park near Eighty-fourth Street in a shopping cart. In
three plastic garbage bags. One bag was stuffed with the shoulders and part of the chest; one, with the rest of the torso and
the legs; one, with the arms and head. Mike thought it was an
illogical way to chop up a body.

The first homicide Mike was in charge of was a double hit, a
drug murder on the carnival stretch of East Eighty-sixth Street
between Second and Third avenues, a block of discos, fast-food
joints, and German restaurants where waitresses wore dirndls
and men in lederhosen played zithers. McVeety had been the
sergeant in charge of Nightwatch. It was mid-winter. Mike's
pen was so cold it wouldn't write. He was trying to get people
to sit in the relatively warm squad car while he interviewed
them, but no one wanted to get involved. There were at least a
hundred and fifty witnesses. Mike was sure some of them knew
who did it. But they were street-wise, not like the crowd across
the Park on the West Side along the strip of Columbus Avenue
near the Museum of Natural History, a neighborhood of young
professionals. There you could cordon off a crime scene, get a
hair-bag sergeant to shout into a bullhorn, "Okay, line up the
witnesses and take their names and addresses," and everyone
would give the information. But this mob on East Eighty-sixth

in front of the disco knew that unless you're the subject of an investigation, you don't have to give your name and address to a cop. Everyone Mike approached said, "I don't have to tell you nothing."

This sucks, Mike had thought. I ain't going nowhere in this business.

That year Mike worked ninety to one hundred homicides. Thirty to forty percent were gay. Typically, the scene would be in a brownstone in the seventies. A uniformed cop would be in the hallway, waiting.

"Hands tied behind his back?" Mike would ask.

The uniformed cop would nod.

"Pants pulled down?"

"Yeah."

"Shit kicked out of him?"

"Yeah."

Gay murders are all the same, Mike had thought.

The surprising murders were committed by teenagers.

On East 105th Street, there was the kid on angel dust whose pals had shoved him into a garbage compactor—alive. The kid dropped down the chute to the basement, where the hydraulic ram crushed him into three small cubes. When Mike dumped the cubes onto the basement floor, each spread apart, like an unbound bale of hay, in pads.

As he was falling asleep, Mike recalled what Connell had said after Craig's arrest, "It's not like TV. We didn't say: 'Book 'em, Dano!' "

Jerry got home at six in the morning. He had called Kay earlier and told her, "We did it!" She was waiting for him in the kitchen.

"Now you can sleep," she said.

"An hour," Jerry said. "I got to go back."

"What do you mean, go back?" she said, but she stayed awake to make sure Jerry got up when he was supposed to.

Jerry dreamed about the case, and woke to the smell of fresh coffee. Kay had put out his blue television shirt. He picked his own suit: an understated, pin-striped three-piece number.

He felt as if he'd won the Super Bowl. The case was solid. They'd done everything by the book. They'd been extra careful in their treatment of Craig.

What could go wrong?

14

JERRY MET MIKE and McVeety at the 30th Precinct. The desk sergeant told them Craig's attorney was in Craig's cell: Robert L. Ellis. He was a thickset man who introduced himself in a booming, operatic voice.

Pavarotti without a beard, Jerry thought. Very impressive. Jerry said they were taking Craig to the Criminal Court Building.

Ellis boomed off.

The case had entered a new stage, Jerry thought. For weeks, all their work had been aimed at making an arrest. Now, their work would be aimed at getting a conviction. This day was the fulcrum of the case. Balanced on either side were the past and the future, the murder and the verdict.

Mike, Jerry, and McVeety brought Craig out to the car. Craig was subdued during the drive.

"This is a well-known case, as you know," Jerry said. "There are probably going to be photographers waiting for you. You don't have to show your face if you don't want to."

Craig didn't want to, which pleased the cops, since they didn't want the lineup compromised. They circled around to the back of the courthouse on Baxter Street. Craig covered his face with a manila envelope. He was handcuffed. Jerry gripped his biceps and guided him into the building past only one photographer. Most of the reporters, assuming Craig was uptown at the 20th Precinct, were waiting there. A few were at the 13th Precinct. Some, thinking Craig had been left in the Criminal Court Building the night before, figured they'd catch up with him later in the day.

After Mike and Jerry handed Craig over to the court, they ran into Ellis in the lobby.

What time did you arrest him? Ellis asked.

"About one o'clock," Mike said.

Is it true you have a videotaped confession?

Mike grinned.

Ellis said Craig's family woke him at seven in the morning to retain him.

Behind Ellis's back, Jerry rolled his eyes. Mike made a mental note to jot that conversation down in his pad. Since Ellis had admitted he wasn't hired until seven o'clock, Craig's confession was guaranteed to be admissible evidence.

At ten-thirty in the morning, in the midst of finishing the necessary paperwork, Mike and Jerry were called uptown to the 13th Precinct for a press conference. The muster room was swarming with reporters—twenty, thirty, from local newspapers, wire services, television, radio, the Spanish press. In most big cases, there usually were no more than half a dozen.

All the key members of the investigating team, even those who had been off for the day, had been called in: Rosenthal,

McVeety, Medina, Bruno, Boy, Connell, Heaney. . . . Plus
the bosses: O'Connor, Ward, Nicastro, and Sullivan.

The cops gathered outside the muster room. Since it was
Mike's case, he stood in front. Jerry fell in line behind him.

"No," Mike told Jerry. "Stand at my side."

At the arraignment, Craig stared straight ahead until the
judge, Bernard J. Fried, said, "His family is present." Craig
glanced back at the courtroom.

He don't want his mother to know, Mike thought.

Craig's father's eyes were red.

Craig pleaded not guilty to the charge that he "intentionally
caused the victim to fall from a high altitude, causing her
death."

Not guilty, Mike thought. *Fall from a high altitude*. He remembered his first look at Helen's corpse, legs bent at the
thighs as though she were a half-deflated blow-up toy, arms
twisted behind her back and tied, the bloody rag covering the
lower third of her face, her cheeks, throat, and breasts blood-
spattered. *Causing her death*.

The judge denied bail and refused to let Craig meet privately
with his father and brother in the courtroom. Craig was re-
manded to Riker's Island.

Outside, Mike and Jerry were on their way to the car when
they saw Craig's father on the other side of the street. Jerry
caught Ed Crimmins's eye and started to cross toward him.

Hey, Ed, Jerry wanted to say. I'm sorry it went down this
way. Is there anything we can do for you? Any questions we can
answer?

Before Jerry was halfway across, Ed Crimmins put his head
down and hurried away.

The next day, Sunday morning, Jerry was up before seven. This was the Big Weekend, the climax of the summer backyard gatherings. Thirty-five to forty people would show up.

Jerry turned on the pool filter, hosed down the patio, and carried half a dozen chaise longues onto the lawn. Seymour and his wife, Edith, always the first, arrived. Seymour's arms were raised over his head in a V, like Sylvester Stallone in *Rocky*. In one fist he held a bag of bagels and cream cheese. In the other, a bottle of champagne.

"It's a party," he shouted. "It's a party."

Edith carried a load of newspapers in her arms, which were straight out in front of her, hands palm up, as though she were a high priestess making an offering.

Jerry found an excuse to putter on the front lawn for twenty minutes. When he came around the house to the backyard, he saw taped to the wall of the patio newspaper headlines and clips from the New York *Times*, the *Daily News*, the weekend *Post, Newsday*, the *Reporter-Dispatch.*

Find Suspect In Met Murder

Hunt For Suspect Marked By Course Of His File Card

Fingerprint, Police Sketch, Alibi Led to Arrest

Stagehand, 21, Seized in Murder of Violinist at the Met On July 23

Stagehand Held In Met Murder

Police Hold Stagehand In Murder Of Violinist

Met Suspect Confessed All: Cops

NY Stagehand Arrested In Violinist's Death

Charge Stagehand In Met Killing

Charge Stagehand, 21, In Sex Slaying Of Violinist At The Met

A Young Stagehand Is Arraigned In The Slaying Of Violinist At The Met On July 23

Suspect, suspect, stagehand, 21, stagehand, stagehand, sus-

pect, stagehand, stagehand, stagehand, 21, young stage-hand. . . .

In the clips on the patio wall, there were three photographs of Jerry and Mike. Helen appeared twice; Craig, five times. He was the news now, not her.

Craig was "gentle and unobtrusive," "well-liked," "a very nice boy," who, according to one neighbor, was "always polite." He was "very quiet," another neighbor said. "He always smiled. . . . He seemed like a good kid."

"I've been alone with him in the laundry room a couple of times, and he was always a gentleman," said a woman who saw Craig waiting for the elevator on Friday just before he left his apartment building and ran into Jerry. "I never felt the slightest bit afraid."

"He's not a greaser," her husband said. "He'd wear T-shirts and jeans, but, you know, always clean and neat-looking. He seemed like a normal guy. I never saw him drunk or spaced-out or anything. He is a good-looking boy. He could have hundreds of girls. If you saw him, you'd say that this kid could never do anything like this murder."

I never saw him drunk or spaced-out or anything.

"He was so bombed when he came back [from his between-shows trip to New Jersey], he couldn't walk ten feet," said Kevin O'Neill, a stagehand.

The case was being tried in the press. Witnesses were not under oath, and there was no cross-examination. Contradictions flourished unchallenged. Anyone with a quote about what a good guy Craig was could become a one-second celebrity. The more extravagant the defense, the bigger play the newspapers would give it.

"He's such a good kid," O'Neill said. "If he did something like this, we would have known. We would have seen it on his face."

"Craig talked to me a week ago at a party on Long Island,"

said one of Craig's cousins who was also a Met stagehand. "He was so nervous. He said the police questioned him for seventeen hours. He said they were thinking he did it. But he didn't know what was going on. I know him, and he wouldn't do something like this."

Craig was the underdog in a city that prided itself in standing up for the underdog. Craig was a regular guy, clean-cut, *very quiet*, a *nice boy* from the boroughs.

"There was nothing weird about him; no problem with girls," said a Met security guard. "He was just a regular guy."

"Everybody's talking about it," said another stagehand. "They can't believe it. He's a great guy. He's the type of guy who wouldn't hurt anybody. In four years, I never saw him get mad at anybody. I know he didn't do it."

"He's a sweetheart," said one more stagehand. "He doesn't have a bad bone in his body. I can't see him committing something like that. It's not in his nature. It's not in his character."

"They must have the wrong guy," said a bartender at Pat's, one of the backstage crew's hangouts. "That kid could never have done it in a million years."

"I don't see how he could have lured her up there," said a stagehand who was drinking beer at Pat's. "The musicians don't associate with us. I couldn't see him telling her any story that would get her to go anywhere with him."

Behind each defense of Craig was distrust of authority; antagonism of the boroughs toward Manhattan; and working-class suspicion of artists and the arts. Class rancor seeped from the interviews. *Life is unfair. There's no justice. The regular Joe always gets it in the neck.*

"This is a frame," said Vincent Donohue, the crew member who had overheard Craig ask Gravina to lie about where he had been the night of the murder. "Crimmins couldn't have done this. I worked side by side with him for two weeks after the murder, and if he did it, he was as cool as a cucumber."

Craig talked to me a week ago at a party on Long Island. He was so nervous.

"This has got to be a frame," Donohue said. "The cops came right to the grips after the murder. They really grilled us."

The crew members were closing ranks, putting up a wall of working-class, union, backstage, and family solidarity.

"The police had to grab somebody and they grabbed him," Ed Crimmins said. "I think the police had a lot of pressure on them and now they're grabbing at straws."

Finally, the comments about Craig reflected anxiety. Since Craig was so typical, if he could crack and do something so horrible, any one of them could.

"Everybody hopes he gets cleared right away," said a stagehand. "We hate to see him going through all this torture."

"If it's true," said Helen's sister, Delcie, about Craig's arrest and the charges against him, "it would be a relief and an end of a nightmare for us."

The sympathetic press Craig was getting didn't dampen Jerry's high spirits. When he climbed to the deck for breakfast, his daughter, Lisa, said, "Here he is. The famous detective."

Seymour and Edith wanted to hear the story.

"Again?" Lisa groaned. She'd already heard it twice.

"You tell it," Jerry told Lisa.

"No." She backed away. "It's your day."

Jerry was in the midst of telling the details that were public, when the telephone rang. Kay stood in the kitchen doorway. "It's the office," she said.

Jerry took the telephone.

McVeety.

"The Chief wants to see us," McVeety said.

On-the-spot promotions? Jerry wondered.

Jerry didn't get back home until six o'clock that evening. He strolled across the lawn from the car, his suit jacket slung over his shoulder, his tie loosened and collar unbuttoned. His forehead was shiny with sweat. He was grinning.

Everybody at the party looked at him. Those reclining in the chaise longues sat up. Those inside the house drifted out. Those paddling in the pool leaned their chins on the pool edge; the lined-up heads looked like targets in a carnival shooting gallery. They all knew Jerry had been called in to see the chief of detectives.

"Well?" Kay asked.

Jerry was beaming too much. He was disappointed.

"Just a debriefing session," he said.

Jauntily, he climbed the stairs to the deck. The people at the rail turned to watch him. He went into the house to change into cut-offs. Someone tossed a volleyball. Someone else crossed the patio to the bar to mix a drink. The party resumed.

Kay continued to stare at the door through which Jerry had passed. This was the first hint of potential trouble. Whether it was because public opinion seemed to be favoring Craig or just because of professional caution, the department seemed to be reserving judgment on Mike and Jerry's arrest of Craig.

15

TWO DAYS LATER, on Wednesday, September 3, the grand jury took up the case. Mike and Jerry drove Robert Rowland and Jimmy Jordan, who were due to testify, from the 20th Precinct to 80 Centre Street. Together, they represented the range of opinion backstage at the Met.

Wow, he confessed, Jordan said. You guys did a hell of a job.

He'll strike again, Rowland said, meaning the killer. You'll see. And you'll find out you got the wrong guy.

The case was being heard by the Special Narcotics Parts, across the street from where the grand jury that normally deals with homicides meets. The DA's office wanted to avoid the press.

There was, as usual, no judge—just the randomly chosen jurors, who would listen to the testimony of the witnesses the DA's office called, consider the evidence, and vote on whether or not to indict Craig. This case was only one of many the grand jury would hear during its term.

Mike testified first.

After asking about the layout of the Met, Heffernan introduced some photographs as evidence. One was so stark it seemed stylized, less like a piece of evidence than a Helmut Newton shot. Helen's body, seen from above, lay at the bottom of the shaft, her nakedness all the more obscene compared to the metal pipes and girders surrounding her. The wedge of pubic hair, the darkest part of the picture, dominated the scene.

Mike shifted his gaze.

After he left the room, he said to no one in particular, "I'd rather be up in a bar in Harlem, fighting with five dudes, than doing this."

Gravina went over his story, adding that after their trip to New Jersey he and Craig had opened up two diet pills and snorted the powdered contents. Poor man's coke.

Rowland testified about seeing Craig just before Helen disappeared. Jordan testified about seeing him soon after Helen must have been killed.

The next day Kevin O'Neill was set to testify. He was the stagehand who'd shot off his mouth, claiming that Craig "was so bombed" the night of the murder "he couldn't walk ten feet." If that statement was left unchallenged, the defense could use it to prove Craig had been incapable of committing the crime. Mike and Jerry went through O'Neill's questionnaire and found O'Neill hadn't been working the night he said Craig was "so bombed." So much for O'Neill's credibility. Heffernan would have no trouble proving O'Neill didn't know what he was talking about.

During the ride down to Centre Street, O'Neill seemed to be coming apart. No more bravado. He'd tried to make himself a backstage hero, standing up for a brother stagehand. Now, Jerry thought, he'd be shown up as a loudmouth. Jerry didn't think O'Neill had realized that by giving Craig an alibi he'd make himself such a target.

Welcome to the real world, Jerry thought.

The other witness Mike and Jerry were driving downtown was Vinnie Donohue. As on the previous day, the two witnesses they drove couldn't have been less alike. Even when he was sitting, Donohue seemed to strut. He talked non-stop. He joked. He laughed. Ever since he'd first seen Donohue, Jerry had been trying to peg him. Just before they arrived at Centre Street, Jerry figured it out. Elisha Cook, Jr.

O'Neill and Donohue were the first two up.

O'Neill was on the stand just long enough to say he'd left the Met about four-thirty on the afternoon of the murder and didn't return until the next morning, when he saw Craig, "sitting in the hallway waiting to go to work like everybody else."

"Describe his appearance at that time," Heffernan asked.

So bombed he couldn't walk ten feet?

"His appearance really wasn't any different than any other day since I know him," said O'Neill, wilting, "just Craig—it was the same as all the time."

"I have no additional questions of this witness," Heffernan said.

Donohue bloomed on the stand. He described his occupation as "photographer," and didn't seem at all embarrassed when Heffernan pressed him to admit that he was currently employed at the Met as a stage carpenter.

Heffernan asked him to describe the trips he made to the locker room when Craig claimed to be in the area and the conversation he overheard between Craig and Gravina just before they went to the Atrium to be questioned. Donohue did everything but act it out.

"I was in the dark, you know . . ." Donohue said, "and . . . I heard a conversation that he"—Gravina—"was having in which he said, 'Crimmie—' Craig said, 'Yeah.' Gravina said,

'They called you down, you've got to go down.' Craig said, 'Why, what's up?' He said, 'Do you want me to say where you were in the back wagon—where—behind the projector? I'll say I saw you there.' I was hearing this conversation, and he said, 'All right. You're going down now, all right. If they call me down, you tell them that I saw you there.' "

There were half a dozen other witnesses. Mike, again. The videotape operator. Plifka. Jerry. Medina. Gross. Jerry read the confession: *I said it won't hurt, and she started to get worse. . . . That's when I took out the hammer. . . . I tried for about five minutes, and I couldn't get it in. . . .* The room was seized by an unnatural stillness, as though even the slightest motion would betray an unwholesome interest in the details. *As I was walking away, I heard her pouncing up and down, and that's when it happened. . . .*

The grand jury indicted Craig on three counts. Two counts of second-degree murder and one count of attempted rape.

Helen's family kept their grief relatively private, maintaining a decorous silence in the press, broken only by a rare article like the one in which Janis's friends said that Janis was "distressed over the delay in releasing his wife's body" and that "he looked in very bad shape."

Silence isn't good copy. The press, principally the *Daily News* and the *Post,* was forced, just to find something to write about, to focus on Craig and his family. Even if Janis had been more public in his mourning, the tabloids might have sympathized with Craig.

Craig was a regular guy with a union job, someone an average New Yorker could identify with—not like Janis, who was an artist, a bohemian-looking type with a full beard and a lion's mane, which in photographs was slicked straight back so it hung over his jacket collar. Worse, Janis was a foreigner. The press frequently described him as being "European-born," as though that could explain his un-American impulse to avoid publicity.

Helen's mother and father were also foreign. Canadian—which wasn't quite as bad as being "European-born." But they were farmers. And the *Daily News* and the *Post* were written for a city whose mayor once made fun of the rural areas of his own state.

Mike was disgusted by articles that betrayed a bias toward Craig—like the one that reported how Craig's relatives tried to visit him at Riker's Island, but, because of prison rules that divided visiting days alphabetically, had been unable to see him. Another one had been headlined: *Met Case Tight Enough? Cops Uneasy.*

"Even though prosecutors say they feel certain that Metropolitan Opera House stagehand Craig Stephen [sic] Crimmins is responsible for the brutal murder of violinist Helen Hagnes Mintiks," the piece said, "they are frankly uneasy about their circumstantial case against him. . . ."

Obviously it's a ploy, Mike thought. The defense is playing with the reporter's balls. It's an old story. The weaker the case in court, the stronger you try to make it in the press.

Papers reported that Craig offered to take a lie detector test but was turned down by the police; that "sources could not pinpoint" Craig's incriminating palm print "as coming from the roof," the murder site; that Craig "may not have been aware each time he was recorded"; and that "Crimmins, at no time, confessed to the murder."

As the truth leaked out, undercutting these assertions, the newspapers shifted their ground. Craig may have made "self-incriminating statements" that went "far beyond that fact that he merely rode in an elevator with the victim the night she was killed," but "he drank heavily" that night, "smoked marijuana for the first time in his life," and, soon after he shared an elevator with Helen, "blacked out."

"It is possible for someone to 'black out'—to commit a crime without knowing about it—because of alcohol and drugs," a newspaper claimed, reporting a statement by a University of Chicago psychiatrist who had "studied several dozen murders in which the killers were so freaked out they didn't know what they were doing."

Mike threw the newspaper across the room so hard the pages scattered. Another ploy, he thought. Craig did it, but he didn't know what he was doing.

The next day, the newspapers had a new explanation for Craig's videotaped confession. "In a psychological battle to extract a confession from Crimmins and finally pierce his alibi," Mike and Jerry—according to the article—"took turns for several hours playing 'soft guy and hard guy'—a tough interrogator and a milder one.

"Crimmins's lawyer did not deny that his client had confessed," the item went on to state. " 'If the police said that he did make a confession,' said Robert L. Ellis, 'it is one more prejudicial act that will make it harder for my client to get a fair trial.' "

That one's nice, Mike thought. The confession doesn't put him in jail; it gets him off.

Ellis "also blasted 'a systematic series of leaks' and 'perhaps most outrageous of all, the chief of detectives placing the credibility of his high office on the line by giving assurances that they have the right man.' "

That's the nut, Mike thought. If the case went down the toilet, the Chief wouldn't take the heat. That's not how it works. He and Jerry would be left holding the bag. We're going to be on trial, he thought. Not Craig.

Despite the favorable attention Craig was getting, his family was evidently dissatisfied with the way things were going. On Wednesday, the day the Grand Jury took up the case, Craig's father visited Craig at the Brooklyn House of Detention on Atlantic Avenue. Craig had been transferred there because it had a special section on the third floor for inmates who needed protective custody. Child molesters. Some homosexuals. Rapists. Guys charged with crimes that most prisoners viewed with contempt. Raping a woman and kicking her off a roof with her hands tied behind her back doesn't make you a hero. In a regular jail, Craig would have been eaten alive.

Ed Crimmins entered the Brooklyn House of Detention looking calm and left distraught.

The next day, the day before Craig was indicted, the family replaced Ellis with another lawyer, Lawrence Hochheiser. Hochheiser was known as one of the toughest defense attorneys in the city. In ten years, he had tried twenty murder cases and won them all. Mike knew a cop at the 20th Precinct who had tried to fence with Hochheiser in court and been made a fool of. Jerry knew a detective who'd had so much experience testifying that he could avoid most cross-examiners' traps and be philosophical about those into which he blundered. This man had had such a hard time on the stand with Hochheiser that the following day he landed in the hospital with an ulcer attack. When Jerry heard Craig's family had hired Hochheiser, he hummed the theme from *Jaws*.

You don't grow up on the streets of New York without plenty of practice at ranking out, making insults. Over the years, Jerry had refined this talent, sophisticated it. He was an expert at the polite needle, the grinning dig. Jerry liked to match wits, especially with someone equally sharp. He knew he'd be tempted to tangle with Hochheiser. He also knew that would be a mistake.

Jerry was wise to Hochheiser's type. They wanted to draw you out; they'd do it any way they could—by being friendly, aloof, hostile. And anything you said, either before the trial or during it, they'd eventually use against you. They were like science-fiction energy monsters: The more you attacked them, the stronger they got. With a guy like that, you couldn't win. Even if Jerry bested him in the halls, *especially* if Jerry bested him in the halls, he'd pay for it on the stand.

Jerry didn't want to do anything to jeopardize the case, so he vowed to avoid Hochheiser whenever possible and, when it wasn't possible, to limit his conversation with Hochheiser to one-word responses, preferably *yes* or *no*—which was the only way to beat him. Don't give him the nails to crucify you with.

Mike couldn't resist taking Hochheiser on. Soon after Hochheiser entered the case, he noticed Mike giving him the once-over. Apparently trying to needle Mike for staring, he said, You like this suit. I got it from my father-in-law. You won't believe it. It only cost seventy dollars.

Slowly, Mike raked his eyes from Hochheiser's collar to his cuffs and back up to his collar again.

"I believe it," he said.

Afterward, Jerry pulled Mike aside and said, "He'll get you for that. When you're on the stand, you're going to be his meat."

For the past week, they had been gathering together all the paper connected to the case: about 150 questionnaires and 850 reports, plus the raw notes from which some of the reports were made—scribbles on napkins, scraps of newspaper, matchbooks. Neither of them had ever seen or heard of a case with as much paper. Maybe the Judge Crater case, Jerry thought. The average murder might have only three or four reports. Everything had to be read—to make sure nothing was forgotten, to make sure everything had been followed up. Everyone who had ever called with a tip, even a wild tip, had to be contacted and thanked, if they hadn't already been. Medina was assigned to organize the material—filing, cross-referencing, making duplicates of key reports. Connell and an aide in the DA's office, Margaret Juliano, helped.

Mike and Jerry started making arrangements for Laura Cutler's lineup. They needed look-alikes for Craig. Guys about twenty-one years old with the right kind of hair and mustache. To find them, they went to the Police Academy. In a classroom, Jerry checked out the rookies, who gazed back at him, wide-eyed, thrilled. He remembered how impressionable he had been as a rookie twenty years earlier, how he had looked with awe at the detectives who had visited his classes. Would he make the grade? he had wondered back then. Would he ever work on an important case? Now, he was working on one of the most important cases in the entire history of the Police Department.

Hey, the rookies kidded each other. Watch out. They're going to pick you out of the lineup. You'll end up on trial.

Twenty years, Jerry thought. They could be my sons and daughters.

Two days later, the rookies who had been chosen were at the DA's office, waiting for Laura Cutler to arrive so they could go into the lineup. Outside the DA's office, also waiting for Laura's arrival, was the press. While McVeety sneaked Laura into the building through a back door, Mike and Jerry rushed a ringer, a secretary from the DA's office who'd pulled a raincoat over her head, through the front door, leading the press on a wild-goose chase.

When they got upstairs, Hochheiser had already started hassling Heffernan. He wanted two lineups, one with Craig in it, the other a dummy without Craig. Heffernan agreed—as long as Laura knew there'd be one dummy lineup.

No way, said Hochheiser. He wanted it done his way. Or there'd be no lineup.

Heffernan refused to be bullied. I'm going to exercise the prerogative of telling her one of the lineups is going to be blind, he said. Without the suspect.

Oh, for Christ sake, Hochheiser exploded. How can you be so stupid? You can't do that.

Well, Heffernan said, I think I can.

How long have you been around? Hochheiser asked.

If you're telling me no, Heffernan said, let's go to the judge.

They argued for an hour and a half, Heffernan calmly, Hochheiser abusing him. On the way to get a decision from the judge, Jerry told Heffernan, "You don't have to take that shit from him. Tell him off."

Let him do his thing now, Heffernan said. I'll do my thing during the trial.

Mike admired Hochheiser's performance. He didn't like the guy and how he had treated Heffernan. But Mike understood why Hochheiser had done what he did. Hochheiser's a sharp lawyer, Mike thought. Craig's family is getting its money's worth.

The judge was gone for the day. They'd have to get his decision the following morning. The lineup was put off.

The next day, Mike and Jerry couldn't get the same secretary to stand in for Laura. They used another secretary, who was shorter and thinner. They charged the door. The reporters and photographers ignored them.

Cute, one reporter said.

"I don't think they bought it today," said Mike.

The judge ruled that Laura would be told one of the lineups was a dummy. But Hochheiser had brought in his own guys for the lineup—including Craig's brother, who looked a lot like Craig.

"Why the hell are you letting him get away with that shit?" Jerry asked Heffernan.

He's got the right to object to certain of our people and bring in his own, Heffernan told him.

It was law by attrition: who would wear down first.

Heffernan agreed to let Hochheiser use his guys in the lineup. When the time came, everyone in the lineup looked so much alike, Laura couldn't pick anyone out.

I'm awfully sorry, she said.

It was a draw. She didn't choose Craig, but she didn't choose anyone else. Neither the prosecution nor the defense came away with a clear advantage.

"The day's not a total loss," Jerry told Mike. "I finally pegged Hochheiser."

"Who?" Mike asked.

Jerry grinned. "Ernie Kovacs."

16

ON THURSDAY, September 18, Jerry got a call from Justin Peters at the Polygraph Unit at the 13th Precinct.

They're bringing in a guy who's got something on Crimmins, Peters said.

John Sweeney seemed bright, articulate, and cold-blooded. He was not merely thin, but elongated, like a reflection in a knife blade. He sat straight backed, chin tucked in, unblinking.

About five years before, Sweeney and another guy had ripped off a junkie. The junkie put up a fight. Sweeney stabbed him dozens of times. The guy with Sweeney got twenty years to life. Sweeney got only twelve to fifteen years. He had appealed on a technicality and was set for a new trial, but the prosecution's case was stronger this time around. A new witness had surfaced. So Sweeney wanted to make a deal: his information about Craig in exchange for a reduced sentence. Eight and a third years. Including the time served.

Jerry looked at Sweeney.

Sweeney grinned.

Did Sweeney deserve twenty years to life? Probably. If it were in Jerry's power to make the deal, give him eight and a third years for the information, would he do it? Definitely.

Sweeney was brought before a judge, who lectured him, his lawyer, the assistant district attorney handling the case—and granted the plea. The lie detector verified Sweeney's story.

The Monday after Craig was indicted, Sweeney was in a Department of Correction van with Craig and a few other prisoners, who were being transported from the Brooklyn House of Detention to Manhattan Criminal Court. Craig was sitting at the back of the van, segregated from the rest of the prisoners behind a metal screen. Sweeney sat next to him on the other side of the screen. He recognized Craig and asked him for a match. Craig said he didn't have one. After a few minutes of silence, Craig said, Excuse me, do you know anything about temporary insanity pleas?

What do you want to know about them? Sweeney asked.

How hard are they to pull off? Craig said.

As far as I know, Sweeney said, they're very hard to prove. Craig looked miserable.

You all right? Sweeney asked.

I think they're going to convict me, Craig said.

From what I read in the papers, Sweeney said, the guys you work with think you're innocent.

Craig turned toward the window. If I were innocent, he said, half to himself, it would be another story completely.

On Monday, September 22, Mike got a call from a New York State trooper, Carl Summerlin, who said he had an arrest warrant for Craig's brother, Eddie, Jr.

Shit, Mike thought. If the brother gets nabbed, the press will make it look like we got a vendetta against the family.

It's a couple of years old, Summerlin said. Driving while intoxicated.

Not a major violation, Mike thought. Thank God for that.

The trooper on the case had spotted Craig's brother in a newspaper photograph.

Mike said he'd get back to Summerlin.

Two days later, during Craig's bail application, a couple of guys approached Mike in court and asked if they could talk to him in the hall for a minute.

Recognized you from your picture, one of the guys said. He introduced himself. Carl Summerlin. The trooper.

The other guy was Shelley Barsky, a senior investigator with the State Police.

Had Mike seen Craig's brother that day? they asked.

Mike said no.

Where could they find him?

Mike gave them Eddie, Jr.'s, address. But he added, "Hey, the timing's bad. It'll look like we're lowering the boom on the whole family. Do you think you could hold off for a while?"

They said they'd consider it.

Back in the courtroom, Jerry nudged Mike when Craig was brought in. Craig was shaved, washed, combed. And in a suit.

"He's got that Irish-Catholic-lad look," Jerry whispered.

"That'll get the sympathy of the do-gooders," Mike said.

The judge, Milton Williams, again denied bail. Craig went back to the Brooklyn House of Detention. The case was adjourned for nearly a month.

On the way out, Mike and Jerry avoided Craig's family.

That night, the new opera season was supposed to start at the Met, but the theater stayed closed. Two months earlier, seventeen contracts with twenty-two unions, including the American Federation of Musicians, which represented the Met orchestra, had expired. Negotiations became increasingly bitter. The management said that the unions' demands threatened the Met's financial stability. The unions said that the theater's financial stability allowed the Met to raise wages, improve the pension plan, extend vacation time, and generally enhance working conditions. The management suspended rehearsals for the new season. Mike suspected everyone, management and unions, were content to have a cooling-off time, a chance to let memories of the murder and investigation fade. When he went to the Met, he'd pass musicians playing in the vest-pocket park opposite Lincoln Center.

A strange way to picket, Mike thought.

On Friday, October 3, a detective named Tom Mansfield called Mike to tell him that a guy in jail with Craig had some information he wanted to trade.

Another Sweeney, Mike thought. The sweeter the garbage, the busier the flies.

Frederick Montero aka Salvatore Presta aka Victor Mathis swaggered into the office of the assistant district attorney handling his case and asked Mike, Well, listen, before I tell you anything, what does it mean to me?

Anything you say will be weighed, the assistant district attorney said; and, if it proves to be fact, yes, it is within the provisions of the system to bring it before the sentencing judge for consideration on your behalf. No promises. It's up to the judge.

Montero had been a bodyguard for a drug dealer in Brooklyn. He was facing a five-to-six-year sentence on a first-degree robbery charge in Manhattan and a gun charge in Brooklyn. He obviously wasn't happy to be talking to the cops; but he was very sure of himself, spoke well, and seemed smart enough for Mike to think, This guy's wasting his time being a hood. If he'd chosen the straight road, he could have done anything. Been a professional man.

While telling his story, Montero tried to control the conversation.

"Hey," Mike finally said. "I'm asking the questions. Answer what I ask you. Don't start all kinds of bullshit or we'll never get this over with. So let's cover the topic I want to talk about. Then I'll give you the floor, and you can talk about anything you want."

Montero had been in the isolation cell block at the Brooklyn House of Detention for about a week and a half when Craig was brought in.

At first, Craig kept to himself, sitting alone in the Day Room and watching television. But some of the other prisoners, including Montero, had a reliable supply of marijuana; and, after a few days, Craig came over and shared a couple of joints with them. Montero and his crowd nicknamed Craig "the Kid."

About two weeks after Craig arrived, Montero asked him, Do you think it was worth it? Was she good? Craig refused to talk about it. Another time, Montero asked, Hey, how come you smoke pot here, and the newspapers say you did not? Sure I smoke, Craig said. But I haven't done much lately. He said that he'd tried other drugs, too.

Craig never got incoherent when he smoked; he relaxed. Once when he was stoned, he said he knew the cops had been getting close. The day the fuckin' prick arrested me, he added, I had a full tank of gas and was about to go to California.

Montero noticed that when other inmates were around, Craig tended to make it sound like he was innocent. *The cops say* . . . he'd say. Or: *What they say I did.* But, when Montero was alone with Craig, Craig talked like he'd killed Helen. Montero couldn't figure out if Craig was guilty or not.

Just before the lineup for Laura Cutler, he'd asked Craig, Hey, man, man-to-man, between me and you, did you do it?

Yes, Craig said. But the only way they can really fuck me is with the girl on the elevator, and I don't think she can pick me out.

What about the confession? Montero asked.

We'll suppress that in court, Craig said.

A little later, when Montero asked Craig about bail, Craig said, if he made bail, he'd head to California.

They talked about the heavy time Craig was facing if he was convicted. Craig said he'd be happy to cop out to a five-to-fifteen-year sentence.

After the lineup, Craig was jubilant.

See, he told Montero. I told you, she couldn't pick me out. I'm going to beat this thing.

Did you have a hard-on for the girl? Montero asked Craig during another conversation. Did he know her? Think he could fuck her?

Craig said he really didn't know Helen, but whenever they passed each other he'd greet her.

When you did have the girl, Montero asked, how come you had to kill her?

It just happened, Craig said. I guess from the beer and shit.

Once when they were watching television, Burt Reynolds in *The Longest Yard*, a movie about guards and convicts playing football, Montero asked, Hey, man, at the time you had the girl, why didn't you just get some pussy instead of killing her? He evidently could understand forcing a woman to fuck, but where was the percentage in kicking her off the roof?

Craig smiled and walked away.

The other prisoners kidded Craig a lot about being so pretty, and Craig didn't seem to mind their advances. Montero thought he might be a little faggy. On the edge. He also thought Craig was a peeker. Sometimes, when they'd be watching some actress on television, Craig would say, I seen her naked. Montero couldn't figure that out. Here's someone charged with attempted rape and murder bragging about some schoolboy perving to guys who were capable of biting off their grandmothers' tits.

I seen her naked.

Mike remembered the story told by the dresser with the Berlin Ballet about seeing a guy twenty minutes before Helen vanished, hiding behind some wardrobe trunks in the hallway and trying to peek into the women's dressing room. She was startled; he was startled. Before she had a chance to say or do anything, he legged it.

Maybe, drunk and wild on wacky weed, Craig was pumping himself up all night, making himself so horny he was ready to shove his dick through a concrete wall? Craig wouldn't say anything about the kinky stuff, Mike figured, because he was ready to go down the hard way as a killer but not as a perve.

Montero mentioned one other thing.

Once, when they were smoking and Craig was really flying and trying to be just one of the guys, he said something about Helen falling down the shaft with her hands and feet sliding, banging off the walls. Montero tried to get him to say more, but Craig clammed up. That was it. Just something about the hands and feet, sliding, banging down the shaft wall. For some reason, especially the hands.

Mike promised to call Montero's girlfriend and tell her things were okay. Off and on for the next few weeks, Mike tried to get a line on Montero. He wanted to make sure that, if they put Montero on the stand, Hochheiser wouldn't be able to surprise them with anything from Montero's past—a magician reaching into his top hat and pulling out not a rabbit but a corpse.

The drug dealer Montero worked for was suspected of killing six people in a fire in Brooklyn. Mike had to find out if Montero was implicated. He called guys he knew at the 73rd and 76th precincts in Brooklyn and came up dry. He drove out to Brooklyn, poked around. After days of frustration, he turned up the arson-murder case in the 78th Precinct, Northern Flatbush, a rough area near the Brooklyn courts. The case was being handled by the Brooklyn South Task Force. The district attorney in charge told Mike that Montero was not a suspect. Now, all Mike needed to know was if Montero's story was true. He drove Montero to the 13th Precinct to check him out on the lie detector. The streets around the station house were so jammed, Mike had to double-park.

A uniformed police officer told Mike he couldn't leave his car there. Mike explained he was a detective with a prisoner in custody.

I don't care, the officer said. You can't park here.

"Look," Mike said, "I got to take him up, put him on the polygraph, and I'll be right down."

I've got my orders, the officer said. Nobody can park there.

"I'm not walking the street for two, three blocks with a guy in handcuffs," Mike said.

If you leave the car here, the officer said, I'm going to give you a summons.

"Fuck you," Mike said, walking away with Montero in tow.

Fuck you, the officer said, writing out the summons.

The polygraph confirmed Montero's story, but Mike suspected neither Montero nor Sweeney would be used in court. The only jailbirds who make good witnesses are basically straight guys who slipped once and are looking to redeem themselves. Hoods like Montero and Sweeney are too vulnerable. Since they're trading information for a consideration, the defense attorney can make their stories, no matter how true, seem self-serving, tainting the prosecution's case with something distasteful. Unless their testimony was crucial, why muddy the water?

Still, Mike thought, even if we don't use the stories, it's nice to have them.

The Met house manager, John Connonico, told Mike that on the day the grand jury indicted Craig, he and his wife were having dinner with one of the other bosses at the Met, Clem D'Alessio, and his wife, Eileen. During the meal, Eileen mentioned something odd.

A set painter who used to work at the Met had told her that three days after the murder a stagehand had identified the killer as an electrician on the fifth-floor grid named Crimmie.

A stagehand who told a set painter who told Eileen who told Connonico who told Mike . . .

Like that kid's game Telephone, Mike thought. And probably just as reliable. But it had to be checked out.

The set painter's name was Debbie Schechter. Mike left so many messages that were unreturned, he felt like subpoenaing her answering machine. He went to her union hall on Broadway near Forty-third Street and found she was working in Astoria on a movie. He even got the name of her baby-sitter. But he couldn't reach her.

Mike couldn't tell if she was avoiding him because she didn't want to get involved or if she was simply putting off calling because it didn't seem important. Probably the second, he thought.

He was continually amazed by how unaffected the performers and artists at the Met seemed to be by Helen's murder. Craig's family and friends paraded into the courtroom, but Mike hadn't noticed any of Helen's arty crowd there. He could understand—and respect—Helen's family's decision to keep a low profile, but the absence of her friends and co-workers seemed heartless, one more example of how the arty types lived in some world off on their own.

At last, on October 22, Mike interviewed Schechter.

Yes, she said, a stagehand had told her three days after the murder that he suspected Crimmie. And he said that Crimmie was creepy and hated women. And that there was more perversion backstage than you'd think. A lot of gay stuff. Guys jerking each other off.

Mike got the stagehand's name, telephone number, and address. It was one more step up the ladder; but the stagehand denied everything.

"Please hear me out," the caller told Mike over the telephone.

It was a few days after Thanksgiving. Mike had spent the past couple of weeks tying up loose ends and tracking more rumors—like the one about a maintenance worker who may have seen Helen's body before it was officially discovered and who, it turned out, had only seen her shoes on the roof after Lawrence Lennon had reported finding them to Jerry.

Much of the work was frustrating, sorting out which pieces didn't belong to the puzzle; most of it was boring. Now, to top it all off, was this guy on the phone, Ed Peterson, nervous as hell about something and running down his background—ex–City cop, now a Suffolk County cop and a PBA rep—so Mike wouldn't think he was a kook.

I'm not trying to flood you with bullshit, he said, but I happen to know this guy. He's a pretty decent guy, who's heavy into the psychic stuff.

Christ, Mike thought. Another Mandrake the Magician.

"Look," Mike said, "if he's a friend of yours and he believes in that psychic stuff, that's his thing. Just like if I believe I should get laid three times a day, that's my thing. So what? I got aunts so superstitious, they're crazy as hell."

Peterson said that a guy came to his friend, the psychic, to ask if he'd get arrested for the murder of the opera musician.

Mike spent a few days looking into the story. It turned out that the guy who went to the psychic was suspected of murdering a Met musician, but another one, a cellist who'd been killed on 110th Street, not Helen.

I didn't know music was such a dangerous profession, Mike thought.

Although the work Mike was doing was routine, the hours hadn't gotten any better. He was still living out of his locker at the 20th Precinct and sleeping in the dorm so often, one of the lower bunks became his private property. No one else used it, because they knew, if he wasn't there now, he'd probably be there later.

Boil water on the hot plate for instant coffee. Lift weights in the precinct gym. Jog around the reservoir, passing the out-of-shape puffers in their designer sweatsuits. Go back to the precinct with some take-out Chinese. Catch a little TV on the portable up on the shelf in the dorm. Go to the locker, check out the latest clippings, cartoons, and jokes the wise guys had taped up. Figure out the clothes situation for the next day. *Need to do laundry.* Slam the locker door. Go into the bunk room. Fall into bed.

Sometimes, Mike would wake long before dawn and wander out of the bunk room. He'd stand in the middle of the locker room and gaze around him.

What am I doing here? he'd think.

Lined up on the top of the lockers, laces hanging down like Fu Manchu mustaches, were pair after pair of polished shoes.

Whenever Mike had a chance to go home, usually for a day or two each week, he'd drive to some land he'd bought and walk through the woods, trying to decide which spot was best for the house he wanted to build. He'd chop wood, which always calmed his nerves, smoke a cigar, jot a note or two about the case, and soak in the autumn smells and colors.

He'd fallen so far behind in his part-time construction business, he'd given up. Until Craig's trial, everything else had to be put on hold—which didn't upset him as much as he thought it would. He didn't care how many hours he had to put into Craig's trial. It was the World Series. The Olympics. He'd never have another case as good as this one.

That was why he'd find himself at dawn in the precinct locker room, staring at shoes lined up on the top of the lockers.

17

EVER SINCE HOCHHEISER started mentioning the Wiley-Hoffert case, Jerry figured the defense would try to paint Craig as an innocent, not too bright and easily manipulated into giving a confession.

The Wiley-Hoffert case was famous, the basis of the pilot for the television series *Kojak*. In 1963, Janice Wiley, the niece of the writer Philip Wiley, and her roommate, Emily Hoffert, were murdered in their apartment. They'd been mutilated so badly that, when Jerry saw the photographs of the corpses, he winced.

The way Jerry heard the story, several months after the killings, a black kid named George Whitmore, Jr., was picked up in Brooklyn. In his wallet were pictures of two white women. One looked like Janice Wiley. Whitmore was isolated and, during a marathon interview, manipulated until he confessed.

About six months later, a junkie was arrested on the East Side for killing a drug dealer over some bad heroin. In the car on the way to night court, he told the detectives that the cops had arrested the wrong man in the Wiley-Hoffert case.

I know who killed the two broads, I'm telling you, he said. The dude came to my house that night, covered with blood, and told me, 'I just iced two girls.'

The cops were convinced by his story. They wired him, released him, and gave him drugs to entice Richard Roblas, the guy he claimed was the killer.

Roblas came to the junkie's house and got high. The junkie tried to satisfy the cops and at the same time warn his friend. As he turned the conversation to the Wiley-Hoffert murders, he pulled the hidden mike out to show Roblas the conversation was being monitored. Blind to the mike, Roblas kept talking, implicating himself. For almost four months, the cops taped Roblas. They bugged his friends' home, his girlfriend's, his mother's.

He was tried for the murders and convicted.

Whitmore was released. There was scandal, public outrage, inquiries, attacks on the police for brutalizing and manipulating a poor kid like Whitmore, who—it was claimed—was retarded and easily led. He was guiltless, sacrificed by cops who wanted to close the case.

"This is it," Mike told Jerry. "I saw it coming. Hochheiser's going to take us head-on and attack our credibility."

Given Craig's confession, this strategy was the only defense Hochheiser could mount.

Thinking of his son, who was handicapped, Jerry said, "Just let Hochheiser try that in court."

But outside of court Hochheiser's strategy seemed to be working.

Poor kid, someone said when Craig's name came up at a party Jerry attended. In the newspaper picture, he looked like a little angel. Nice girlfriend. Nice how his family stuck together.

Jerry's co-workers, only half-joking, made cracks. *Sure you got the right kid? Framing this nice boy, huh? The Italian cop getting even with the Irish.* Some of them accused Jerry of self-promotion. *Craig only wanted to talk to you, right?* If Jerry blew up, it would only lend credence to their suspicions, so he swallowed his anger and ribbed them back.

"Hey," he told one cop, "a seasoned guy like you who's been through this media bullshit time and time again—and you're swallowing everything the newspapers and TV say. You got to be kidding."

Well, the cop said defensively, we're coming to you. Give it to us firsthand.

They were fishing. They wanted to feel on the inside. Jerry wasn't giving up anything. Their cop's pride was hurt. So they went to work on Mike, telling him that Jerry was hogging the limelight.

"They want to get us going at each other again," Mike told Jerry. He was furious at the guys who were giving him the needle. A few times, he almost punched out some wiseass. Son of a bitch, he'd think. We got a damn good case. And they're looking at us, forgetting about Craig.

Even Mike's mother asked if they were sure they got the right guy. The distrust hurt, but what irked Mike and Jerry most was not how they were doubted but how Helen was forgotten.

Oh, my God, said a woman at another party Jerry attended. I feel so sorry for that kid.

"Helen?" Jerry asked.

Who's she? the woman said. I mean that poor boy. What's his name? Crimmins.

"Do you remember who was killed?" Jerry asked.

Some musician, the woman said.

"Yeah," Jerry said. "Some musician."

On Monday, December 1, after reading the minutes of the grand jury that indicted Craig, Acting Justice Milton L. Williams of the State Supreme Court in Manhattan reversed his earlier decision about releasing him.

Also, saying that "there is an enormous possibility that Assistant District Attorney Heffernan will appear as a witness" in Craig's trial since he played a role in the videotaped confession, Williams removed Heffernan from the case.

The tabloids milked Craig's release, which occurred about a week later, for pathos: The boy owed his freedom "to 25 of his Metropolitan Opera House co-workers and childhood friends who put up his $50,000 cash bail."

"It was great to be home, . . ." Craig said, "to be able to walk around free again."

His mother opened her house in New Jersey for a party.

She "cried at the reunion," Craig said. "There were a lot of tears all over the place."

"It's great to have him back!" Craig's sister said. "I missed him a lot."

Craig insisted he was a "victim of circumstances." The police sketch, Craig claimed, "did not look at all like me," even though it had been made from Laura Cutler's description of the man in the elevator with Helen, and Craig had admitted earlier he was that man. Prison was bad, Craig said, because he didn't like "being off the streets" and "not being around people." He said, "I just sat and waited, day in and day out, knowing that one day I'd be out and be able to prove my innocence." He talked as if being released on bail were a verdict of not guilty.

Mike and Jerry worried that the jurors in Craig's trial might feel the same way, might assume that the judge had released Craig because he thought the prosecution's case was weak.

One of the newspapers described how Craig spent his time watching *Superman* on Home Box Office and receiving friends and co-workers. He was like a kid home from school with a strep throat.

"I'm not angry at his release," Helen's sister said when Craig got out of jail. "We have to trust the courts." Craig's possible acquittal was "something I'll deal with in my own way," she said. "I feel very strongly about the person who killed Helen. If he is the person that did it, he may be very disturbed . . . and I would not want to see him out on the street because of what he might do to someone else. As I said, I am not angry at his release. I have a basic trust in the police, and they have a good handle on the case."

She kept clippings, but couldn't bring herself to read the details. "My sister is dead," she said, "and nothing can bring her back. My anger, frustration, grief, and sorrow are in relation to Helen's death and not the way it happened." Janis was having a rough time, she said. "We'd like him to spend the holidays with us, but I don't think he's up for it yet."

On an easel in their living room, Helen's mother and father had put a portrait of Helen playing the violin. Next to the portrait was a vase. Every morning, Helen's mother put in a fresh red rose.

Helen was dead. Craig was free.

So far, Mike thought, that about sums it up.

As for Craig's skipping town, Mike almost hoped he would. It would prove his guilt.

But what bothered Mike most was Heffernan's being removed from the case. It would take weeks to fill in the new assistant district attorney. When Mike found out who the new assistant district attorney was, he got even more depressed.

Roger Hayes was a native New Yorker; but, although he grew up partly in the Bronx, he was really Manhattan. Not a kid from the boroughs. A private-school kid. Not just private school, but a progressive one: Fieldston, from which he graduated in 1961. His father owned a small business in the garment district. His mother was a psychiatrist with a sense of mission. "I don't want to be rich," she once told Roger. "I want to be helpful."

Roger had been raised as a Humanist, a believer in the principles of the Ethical Culture Movement. He entered Cornell University wanting to change the world, to make it a decent place. He graduated in 1965, went to New York University Law School, graduated from there three years later, and joined a small firm that specialized in entertainment and labor law.

But he was restless. During college, he'd interned at the United States Attorney General's office under a lawyer named Otto Obermaier, who awed Roger with his diligence. Roger had figured the only way he'd get Obermaier's respect was to outwork him. Every morning, Obermaier was at his desk by eight o'clock. Roger made sure he was at his desk by seven forty-five.

As he became dissatisfied with labor law, Roger recalled how much he'd enjoyed working on criminal law with Obermaier. Some friends in the Manhattan district attorney's office told Roger stories of their cases. He thought he'd give it a shot. In March 1971, he joined the Manhattan district attorney's office, figuring he'd stay for four years. Eight years later, he was appointed head of the Trial Division, which dealt with street crimes—like burglary, car theft, rape, and murder. He was in charge of roughly 180 lawyers.

Roger Hayes, someone told Jerry. Holy shit!

Hayes was described as being off-the-wall, flaky, a tart guy, a prick, above-it-all, and a superstar.

That's all I need, Mike thought. Another superstar.

According to the scuttlebutt, Hayes was part of a clique of tough DA's. They kept to themselves; they drove themselves; they were committed to their work and the public good; they didn't cut corners; and they had a fierce integrity.

So far, so good, Jerry thought. As for the scuttlebutt—show me a boss, and there's going to be jealousy, Mike thought; show me a boss who gets things done, and there's going to be twice as much jealousy.

Still, there were DA's who lorded it over cops. If they told you to shit, you had to squat. Mike decided to keep his mouth shut and his eyes open. What he saw at their first meeting in Heffernan's office didn't make him happy. There was Heffernan, blond, short-haired, a major in the Army Reserves, a straight arrow. Next to him was this guy in a rumpled suit and dirty suede shoes with long hair and a beard.

Mike thought, Hayes is a beatnik.

All the principals in the case were at the meeting, Jerry, McVeety, Rosenthal. . . . But Hayes kept coming back to Mike, asking questions that Mike thought were out of line, as though he didn't trust Mike and was prying. *When was the first time you met Craig? What did you say to him?* Mike knew that, since it was his case, he'd be the natural target for Hayes's questions and that Hayes had to play devil's advocate to satisfy himself the case was strong. But he thought Hayes could have made some gesture, qualified what seemed more and more like an attack, by saying something like, "Look, I got to go at you this way."

Instead, Hayes just kept on quietly, insistently pressing. When he disagreed with something, he didn't make a fuss. He just calmly—too calmly—said, "I don't think so."

This ain't going to be easy, Mike thought. We're going to lock horns for sure.

Until the trial was over, Mike was assigned to Hayes on a permanent, twenty-four-hour basis.

"You guys worked very hard with Chuck Heffernan," Hayes had told the cops. "It's going to be a long education period. I want to know everything."

On Christmas Eve Day, Mike took Hayes to the Met for the first time.

For the previous week and a half, Mike had been going over the case with Hayes, not just the facts, but trying to give him a sense of how complicated the crime scene was.

"Not your typical crime scene: the body on the living room floor," Mike said. "She was abducted. Last seen here. Thrown from there. Found someplace else. The first time I went to the Met, I got lost."

Yeah, Hayes said. Okay.

Okay? Mike thought. What is this *okay?* The guy thinks I'm some kind of yokel for getting lost?

When they got to the Met and walked the route Helen was taken—elevator, C level, stairway, roof—with its confusing twists and turns, Mike could tell Hayes was getting bewildered. He would stop, trying to connect where they were to where they'd been and to make sure he was clear about how they got there. He'd retrace their steps, take a wrong turn, and try to find his way back to where they'd begun.

Yeah, Mike thought, echoing Hayes's words in his mind. Okay.

If Hayes asked directions, Mike would give them. If not, Mike sort of let him get lost.

After a few hours, Hayes said, I think you're going to have to take me back here again.

That night, after leaving the Met, Mike rushed around town, buying last-minute Christmas presents. Because he was putting in so much unpaid overtime on the Met case and because he hadn't been able to supplement his salary with his contracting jobs, he wasn't able to spend as much as he usually did, which depressed him.

In the windows, Christmas bulbs blinked, Santas grinned. Other shoppers, bundled up and breathing clouds, lugged boxes and shopping bags. Kids prowled, their jacket hoods tied so tightly most of their faces were hidden.

Someone's going to get ripped off, Mike thought. Merry Christmas.

He had a one-day holiday. On the drive to his in-laws in New Jersey, where he was going to meet up with his family, he thought about Hayes, about the case, about Craig and Craig's stepfather, Marty Higgins, who had appeared at the party for New York City detectives, which had been held a few days earlier in Avery Fisher Hall at Lincoln Center.

Higgins was a friend of the chief electrician for Avery Fisher Hall, who brought him in to help set up the detectives' sound equipment. Mike assumed Craig's lawyer, Hochheiser, had put Higgins up to it, so Higgins could eavesdrop on anything the detectives might say about Craig's case. Maybe Higgins was even carrying a wire.

Whatever, Mike thought. He sure ain't here to join in the celebration.

He admired Higgins's moxie, showing up like that in what for him was the enemy camp among hundreds of detectives; but since he was in charge of the party, Mike wasn't about to let him get away with it.

"I'm certainly not in a position to tell you to do anything," Mike told the Met house manager; "but we're concerned and uneasy that Mr. Higgins is here."

The house manager had Higgins ejected.

Things like that can make a man tense, Mike thought.

Mike hadn't forgotten that it was his case. If it didn't pan out, he'd be the one to take the heat. Not Hayes, not even Jerry. Only him.

But Hayes had pointed out something that turned the screw a little more.

"If this guy"—Craig—"is found not guilty," Hayes had said, "it in effect means the jury thinks you're lying."

During the late sixties and the seventies, New Yorkers had become increasingly suspicious of the police. The Knapp Commission had exposed police corruption. The Vietnam War had undermined all authority, federal to local, including the police. New Yorkers, mistaking cynicism for wisdom, trusted no one.

By the beginning of the eighties, the Police Department had made significant attempts to change its image, and public mistrust of the cops was no longer as visible as it had been during the days of the anti-war movement. Still, few people in government, particularly in the Police Department or the Attorney General's office, could tell whether there'd been a revival of public confidence in the cops.

Hayes saw the Met trial as a test case. The verdict would depend on how the jury reacted to Mike and Jerry's testimony. If the jury believed them, the Police Department would be vindicated. If the jury did not, it would be a blow to the morale of the force.

Repeatedly during the next few weeks, Mike led Hayes through the crime scene. Up the stairs once to see how tired it makes you. Up the stairs again to see how long it takes. Up the stairs a third time to see how often you run into someone. Could you walk it when you're drunk? What went through Craig's mind? What went through Helen's? Up the stairs again and again to double- and triple-check findings. Mike offered to carry Hayes piggyback.

The more Hayes learned about the facts of the case, the

more impressed he was by the quality of the investigation. "Classic detective work," he said. Not only had Mike and Jerry done what Hayes thought was "a superb, a brilliant job," Hayes found them to be "good, decent guys." They believed they had done a righteous job. They were willing to stand or fall by it. And they were being crucified by the press.

Mike and Jerry returned Hayes's respect. Although he looked like a beatnik, Hayes was a stand-up guy. If he worked them hard, he worked himself harder. He wasn't a slave driver. He'd notice when Mike was exhausted and half-crazed from going over reports and would suggest that he go to the Met to get some air. He treated detectives as peers, something not all assistant district attorneys did. Mike and Jerry never talked about it, but by the end of January 1981, they both felt that Hayes had earned not just their trust but also their loyalty.

18

FOR THE WEEK or two before the pre-trial hearing on the Met case, Jerry studied his notebook. While his family watched television in the kitchen, he retreated to the bedroom. When Kay went to bed, Jerry moved into the kitchen. He must have read the notebook at least a hundred times.

"Jerry," said Roger Hayes when they were prepping for the hearing, "you never check your notes."

"I know the case by heart," Jerry said.

"Once you say something, you can't take it back," Hayes warned him. "When you're on the stand, check your notes."

On a yellow legal pad, Jerry wrote out a guide to remind himself of what was important, first jotting key words, then putting down particulars. In his imagination, he'd go over and over the investigation, especially the marathon interview with Craig on July 16 and 17, when Craig admitted he was the man on the elevator with Helen, and the interview on August 29 and 30, when Craig confessed.

His greatest fear was that Hochheiser might say, "Detective Giorgio, take your time and tell what happened in the nine hours you and Craig talked on the sixteenth of July."

Could he possibly tell everything that happened during the sixteen hours Craig was in the Atrium? Would people believe he spoke to Craig for nine hours but couldn't remember it all in detail? So much of the conversation was general bullshit, just talking—Met gossip, sports, girlfriends, talk to put Craig at his ease. No way I took notes on that, Jerry thought.

Step by step, he went over everything he could remember. How long did it take every time they stopped for coffee, cough drops, cigarettes? How long were the pauses in the conversation? He acted out the interview, playing and timing each role —Craig, Mike, himself. He even went to the Met and with watch in hand walked through the Atrium, from office to office, desk to door. It was like a backward rehearsal: going over his part long after the show—the investigation—was over.

Everything else was neglected. Chores. Family. He fell behind and finally put aside his homework for the courses—in English, American history, collective bargaining, and the history of unionism from the 1800s on—that he was taking at Empire State Labor College.

The night before the hearing, Jerry interrupted his preparation to take a break. He sat on the railing of the deck outside the kitchen. The breeze had the sweet muddy smell of the spring thaw. Soon it would be time to get the pool ready for the weekend gatherings, put out the volleyball net.

He made himself a vow: During the hearing, he would not get into a sparring match with Hochheiser.

The pre-trial hearing on the Met case opened in State Supreme Court on Monday, March 9. It was, according to one newspaper, "likely to give New York City cops and the office of

Manhattan District Attorney Robert Morgenthau their first report card on their handling of Crimmins."

Three points would be decided. Was Craig's videotaped confession coerced? Was Laura Cutler's testimony under hypnosis admissible? Did the DA's office maneuver the case so it would be heard by Acting Justice Richard G. Denzer?

Among cops, Denzer had the reputation of being "a people's judge," not one of those liberals who—in the cop's view—favored the rights of criminals over the rights of victims. Bright, too, Jerry had heard; he'd written a chapter in the Code of Criminal Procedure Law. It was also rumored this would be Denzer's last trial. Jerry wondered how that would affect the judge's performance. Ending his career with such a major case, Denzer would be under scrutiny as much as he and Mike were.

When he met Denzer, Jerry amused himself as usual by playing the casting game. The judge was hawk-faced and hunched over with a squeaky nasal voice. Who? Arthur O'Connell? That wasn't quite right, although Denzer did have some of O'Connell's slightly bewildered air. The guy who played in that TV series with Freddy Prinze, Jerry thought. That's who Denzer looks like. Albertson? Jack Albertson.

The first day of the hearing was short. Hochheiser asked Denzer to excuse himself from the case. Saying, "Frankly, I am a bit mystified" by the issue, Denzer denied Hochheiser's motion. Then Hochheiser launched his major attack. He moved that the hearings be held in private. The public, including the press, should be excluded, Hochheiser said, because the evidence presented could contaminate potential jurors.

"This is a case, I think Mr. Hayes will concede, which has gotten a great deal of notoriety," Hochheiser said. "It's a highly celebrated case."

In fact, Hochheiser said, that very morning he'd heard a story about the case on the radio and, when he picked up the

New York *Times*, there was a long article and even a sketch of his client.

At the end of the hearing, the judge might decide that Craig's videotaped confession was not admissible in the trial; but if the press had already published the contents of the confession, the decision would be meaningless. It would be impossible to find jurors who had not read the confession in the newspapers or heard about it on radio or television.

Hayes argued that the hearing was "a matter of interest to the public" and "the public and press should be allowed to view it." For weeks, the tabloids had been arguing the case for the defense. This hearing would give the prosecution a chance to get its case into the newspapers. A decision in favor of the defense—to exclude the public and the press—would be a blow against the prosecution. Hayes pointed out that "the issue is not whether potential jurors might read something about the case, but whether what they would learn would so prejudice them" that they would be unable to decide the case only "on what they heard at the trial." He was confident that "in a county of this size" they "would be able to select a fair and impartial jury, unaffected by what goes on in these pretrial hearings." After all, he added, stories about the confession had already been published in the press. And some of these stories quoted, or were attributed to, Hochheiser or his associate. If Hochheiser was so concerned about the press—Hayes implied —why had he given those interviews?

For a good part of the session they wrangled. Hochheiser argued that his remarks to the press dealt with the legal issue of whether or not Craig's confession had been coerced, not with what Craig had said. And he complained that no matter how large the county was, if the press reported what happened in the hearing, the only potential jurors untainted by the news would be people who "don't read newspapers, don't watch television, and are unaware of the most important criminal case" of the time. This, Hochheiser said, "would leave me with a small pool of rather ignorant, unknowledgeable people or, perhaps," he added, "someone who had been on an extended sabbatical for six months in a foreign country."

"This is a very difficult proposition for me," Denzer finally said. He worried about "the virus of having the press and the public present at this hearing," because the confession "that might not be received in evidence would be known to everyone. That's a very powerful argument, in my opinion, of the defense."

Representatives from the New York *Times* and the *Daily News* urged that Denzer keep the courtroom open. Abscam and Watergate were invoked. Precedents were cited. The public's right to know was weighed and disputed.

"The accused does not have any more interest in whether or not the trial is open or closed than does the public in this matter," said the representative of the *Daily News*, Caroline Simpson.

"You say the defendant doesn't have any interest?" Denzer asked.

"No more so than the public, your honor," Simpson said.

Denzer said he would be inclined to dispute that.

The arguments and counterarguments were a jumble. Trying to pluck the just position out from the mess, Denzer was like a man playing ethical pick-up-sticks. He adjourned the hearing until the following day, Tuesday, March 10, when he ruled that "the public as well as the defendant has an interest in having court trials and proceedings kept open." He added, "It is also axiomatic that where an open pretrial hearing may constitute a genuine danger to the defendant's right to a fair trial . . . the defendant's right to exclusion must prevail." Denzer explained that the hearing "is not basically concerned with what the defendant said." The issue was whether Craig's statements—"whatever they were"—were admissible as evidence at the trial.

So, Denzer said, the trial would be open to the public and the press for arguments about the admissibility of the statements as evidence and would be closed whenever it was necessary to discuss what Craig specifically said.

Like Solomon, Denzer gave each side half of what it wanted. Unlike Solomon, what Denzer offered to split could survive the dismemberment, so the prosecution and the defense, each half-satisfied, had fought the first round to a tie.

Hochheiser was living up to his reputation. When Fred Boy testified, Hochheiser made it seem that the police composite drawing of Helen's killer could help prove Craig's innocence, not his guilt. He got Boy to admit that the sketch was of someone thirty-five to forty years old, and that Craig was only twenty-one. And he compared the beard in the composite to Craig's sparse growth.

"In your experience as a human being, as a detective, you find that some people are hairier than others?" Hochheiser asked Boy. He pointed out examples of hairiness in the courtroom. Boy could see the court reporter's stubble, couldn't he?

"Yes," Boy said.

"How about myself, sir?" Hochheiser asked. "Could you see if I let my beard somewhat grow?"

"Yes, sir," Boy said.

"And Mr. Hayes is self-explanatory," he said, drawing attention to Hayes's beard.

If Mike's first impression of Hayes was negative because of the beard, maybe Denzer's would be, too. Hochheiser was emphasizing everything that might help his case. He didn't let anything slip by.

"Mr. Crimmins," Hochheiser said, "would you step over here with the court's permission?"

Craig stood in front of Boy.

"Detective, would you look at Mr. Crimmins's face, sir," Hochheiser told Boy. "Do you see any stubble there?"

"None that I could notice," Boy said.

"Now, that sketch you had, sir," Hochheiser said. "Is that a sketch of a person who is . . . rather hairless?"

"That is a sketch with some hair on the face," Boy said.

"Some hair, sir?" Hochheiser asked.

"Yes," Boy said.

"Face seems to be covered with hair, doesn't it?" Hochheiser asked.

"Thin beard, I would say," Boy said.

Hochheiser made Boy seem as if he were engineering an almost biblical con job, substituting hairless Jacob for hairy Esau. By the time Boy left the stand, he looked whipped.

When John Bruno testified, Hochheiser unsheathed his sarcasm. He asked if the stagehands knew the cops had set up a police station in the Atrium.

The question was a Trojan horse. Ostensibly, it was about whether or not the stagehands knew something; but it smuggled in the idea that the Atrium was a police station.

Bruno answered the second part of the question: Was the Atrium a police station?

"Well," he said, "not exactly, sir."

Hochheiser responded as if Bruno had answered the first part of the question: Did the stagehands know the police were using the Atrium? "You didn't keep it a secret," Hochheiser said. "Did you?"

"No, sir," Bruno said.

Hochheiser worked this line of questioning enough for Hayes to object.

"He keeps going into the police station," he said.

The definition of the Atrium could be crucial in the trial. If it was defined as a police station, it could suggest that during Craig's marathon session he was in custody.

The judge said he didn't think calling the Atrium a police station was accurate.

"Could we have an agreement?" Hochheiser said. "If I don't call it a police station, they won't call questioning an interview."

What the talk with Craig was called could also be crucial at the trial. *Interview* suggested that Craig was not in custody.

"Let's just focus on this," the judge said. "It's not a police station."

"Well," Hochheiser said, "it was a police facility, a temporary police facility."

"The testimony is that the police used this particular area in their investigations," the judge said. "Now, I don't know, what would you like to call it?"

"Judge, a facility means a police station which they control, which they pay rent on," Hayes said. "I don't think there is a police station or a police facility in the world that looks like this"—the Atrium.

"Let's call it the investigation area," the judge said.

"The witness calls it a police facility," Hochheiser said.

"I don't think we should get into an argument," the judge said. He seemed tired of this skirmish. "It is not a police station. . . . Could you find a term which doesn't have the word police or station?"

Hochheiser suggested sarcastically, "Let's call it the *police place.*"

The judge took him up on it. He said, "All right."

"That's fine, Judge," Hayes said.

"So," Hochheiser said to Bruno, "you have this little police place at the Metropolitan Opera House."

Hochheiser may have irked Boy and Bruno, but on that first day of testimony Pat Heaney suffered the most. Hochheiser was following the strategy that led him to call the Atrium a police station and Craig's questioning an interrogation. He was trying to prove that on August 16 and 17, the night of Craig's marathon interview, Heaney had not merely asked Craig to go to the Atrium to answer some questions. He had waited until Craig could leave his backstage post and then had taken him into custody. According to Hochheiser, from the time Craig was asked to come down to the Atrium to the time he left the Met, he was unofficially, if not officially, under arrest.

Heaney had testified that one of the reasons he didn't leave a message for Craig or call, one of the reasons he went backstage to get Craig was that he wanted to see that night's performance, the Peking Ballet, which he called the Peking Opera. Hochheiser used the mistake to set a trap.

"Detective Heaney," he said, "you have an interest in the opera, I take it."

"No, sir," Heaney said.

"I'm sorry," Hochheiser said. "Ballet. Do you have an interest in ballet?"

"No, sir," Heaney said.

"You mentioned the Peking Opera," Hochheiser said. "You meant the Peking Ballet, I take it. Right?"

"Peking Ballet," Heaney repeated.

"You said that . . . one of the reasons that you went over to Mr. Crimmins was not to escort him back, but because you had an interest in seeing the opera. You said the *opera*, . . ." Hochheiser said. "Is that right?"

"Yes, sir," Heaney said.

"Did this arise out of some interest, avocation, or hobby . . . concerning either opera or ballet?" Hochheiser asked.

"No," Heaney said.

"Have you been to a ballet?"

"No."

"Have you been to an opera?"

"No."

"And, as you sit here now, do you know whether that production was a ballet or an opera?"

"No."

"So, I take it, you didn't get to see it," Hochheiser said. "Did you?"

"All of it or part of it, sir?" Heaney asked.

"Enough of it," Hochheiser said, "to know whether it was a ballet or an opera."

"No," Heaney said.

"But," Hochheiser said, "you imagine that you would be able to know whether it was a ballet or an opera if you had seen it even briefly?"

"No," Heaney said.

"Do you know what a ballet is?" Hochheiser asked.

"Basically," Heaney said, "yes."

"People dance around," Hochheiser said. "In an opera, it is where it's a play and they sing. Right?"

"A vivid description," the judge said.

"Rather fundamental, yes," Hochheiser said. "Often in Italian. Now," he asked Heaney, "as you sit here now, you don't recall seeing anything backstage of this production. Do you?"

"Yes," Heaney said.

"Did you see it?" Hochheiser asked.

"Part of it," Heaney said. "Yes."

"What did you see?"

"Dancing."

"How long did you watch it?"

"Approximately fifteen minutes."

"While you were waiting?"

"That's correct."

"Now," Hochheiser asked, "in this approximately, if I figure it correctly, six-week period" that Heaney had been working at the Met, "had you ever taken the trouble to view either an opera or ballet backstage?"

No matter what Heaney's answer was, he was trapped. If he said that during those six weeks he'd never watched an opera or ballet, Hochheiser could say, *Why now? Because he wanted to escort Craig to the Atrium.* If he said that, during those six weeks he'd on occasion watched an opera or ballet, Hochheiser could say the same thing: *Why now? Because he wanted to escort Craig to the Atrium.*

Heaney said, yes. He had taken the trouble to view either an opera or a ballet.

"So . . . it wasn't that you were going backstage because you wanted to see how one of these things looked from backstage," Hochheiser said. "Is that right? You had already experienced that?"

"Not with the Peking," Heaney said.

"Well," Hochheiser said. "You had a particular interest in the Peking?"

"No," Heaney said.

"In fact," Hochheiser said, "—not meaning to be critical—your interest was sufficiently low that you didn't know whether it was an opera or ballet, is that right?"

"I didn't know," Heaney admitted.

"So," Hochheiser said, "would it be fair to say that your primary interest in going over there had more to do perhaps with Mr. Crimmins and Mr. Gravina than it had to do with your interest in the opera or ballet?"

Heaney said, "No."

Hochheiser was good. Mean. Maybe even unfair. But good.

Jerry was the next witness. He figured he was in for a treat.

Jerry thought he might be on the stand for a day. He was on for three. On Tuesday afternoon and Wednesday morning, Hayes, trying to prove Craig had not been intimidated, coerced, or otherwise mistreated, questioned Jerry—first about the August 16–17 marathon interview.

"Do you recall how you were dressed?" Hayes asked.

"I was wearing a three-piece suit," Jerry said; "but I didn't have any jacket on."

"Do you know where your gun was?"

"On my right hip."

"Was your gun outside your vest or under your vest?"

"Under my vest."

"Did you have your badge displayed?"

"No."

"At the time Mr. Crimmins came into the conference room . . . was he under arrest?"

"No."

"Did you intend to arrest him?"

"No."

"Did you handcuff him?"

"No."

"Did you restrain him in any way while he was in that conference room?"

"I did not."

"As far as you were concerned, could Mr. Crimmins at any time . . . have gotten up and left if he wanted?"

"Yes."

"How would you describe . . . the atmosphere in that room?"

"It was cordial."

"Did you yell at Mr. Crimmins?"

"Never."

"Did you hit him . . . kick him, threaten him, scream at him, or hold him out the window?"

"Absolutely not."

"If at any time . . . Mr. Crimmins had asked to leave . . . would you have restrained him in any way?"

"No."

"Could he have left if he wanted to?" Hayes repeated.

"Yes," Jerry said.

That night, Jerry and Craig had gone to the bathroom to-gether.

"Was he handcuffed to you at that time?" Hayes asked.

"No," Jerry said.

"Were you guarding him?"

"No."

"Were you escorting him?"

"No."

"Did you or anyone in your presence yell at Craig Crimmins that evening?"

"No."

"Did anyone in your presence hit Mr. Crimmins?"

"No."

"Did they threaten him?"

"Absolutely not."

"Did they abuse him?"

"No."

"How would you describe the atmosphere during the period approximately four-forty to the conclusion of the videotape?" Hayes asked.

"Peaceful," Jerry said. "Quiet. Congenial. Cordial."

"I'm sorry," Hochheiser said, perhaps to indicate incredulity, "can I have that repeated?"

"Peaceful," Hayes said. "Quiet. Congenial. Cordial."

Jerry had testified that at one point on the night of August 16–17 Craig said that "if he . . . went home for a couple of days and thought about the answers, he might remember better and be able to clear up some of the points . . . he . . . was unclear about."

"If you feel that's what you need," Mike had said, "you can leave."

Mike—Jerry testified—had also asked Craig if he wanted an attorney.

"No," Craig had said—according to Jerry's testimony—"I'll . . . clear it up tonight."

Other than that exchange, Hayes asked Jerry, "Did Mr. Crimmins at any time and in any way indicate to you that he wanted to leave or to stop talking?"

"No," Jerry said.

"That he wanted an attorney present?"

"No."

"At any point, would you describe the questioning as grueling?" Hayes asked.

"No," Jerry said.

When Craig was picked up on August 29, the night he confessed, "was he handcuffed?" Hayes asked.

"No," Jerry said.

"Do you recall how you were dressed?"

"I was wearing a suit."

"Where did you have your badge?"

"In my left trouser pocket."

"Did you have your gun out?"

"No."

"Did Craig Crimmins in any way, shape, or form indicate to you that he did not want to go with you?"

"No."

"Did he, in any way, ask you if he could do it at a different time?"

"No."

"Did you ever tell Mr. Crimmins during this period that he was under arrest?"

"No."

The litany continued as Hayes went over the rest of the night Craig confessed.

Did anyone hit or yell at Craig? Did any detective have his

face "two inches from Mr. Crimmins's face?" When Craig confessed, did Jerry have his gun out? When Craig confessed, did Jerry hit, kick, threaten, or abuse Craig? Did Jerry scream at Craig? Did anyone else? Did Craig ask for a lawyer? Was Craig handcuffed? Was he drunk? Did anyone make an appeal to Craig's religious feelings? Did they ever say they had evidence they didn't really have?

No.

The questions, repetitious and obvious, were trying to cover every possible moment Craig was in the presence of the cops up to his arrest. The tedium of conscientiousness. But, if Hayes left even the smallest opening, Hochheiser would wriggle through it. Hayes had to make sure it was absolutely clear that Craig was not under arrest until after he had confessed.

The line, though impermeable, was thin.

Craig may not have been under arrest until after he confessed; but—Hayes asked Jerry—when Jerry went to pick Craig up the night of the confession, ". . . would you have . . . placed him under arrest if he had refused to go with you?"

Jerry said, "Yes."

This was an answer Hochheiser could use against Jerry. Within minutes after starting the cross-examination, Hochheiser was needling him.

"By the way," he said after Jerry had described Craig's questioning on the night of August 16–17, "I notice you use the word 'interview'. . . . Is there such a thing as a interrogation any more in the police department?"

Hayes objected.

The judge overruled the objection.

Jerry, cool and reasonable, said, "I usually use the word interview. When I interview someone, I interview them. Some people may interpret that as interrogation." So much for his vow not to fence with Hochheiser.

Hochheiser didn't let that go by. "Well," he said, ". . . do you see . . . a difference—perhaps subtle, perhaps not—between interview and interrogation?"

Reining in his impulse to make a witty comeback, Jerry answered simply, "Yes."

"In other words, if I went to your office, looking for a job, we might have an interview," Hochheiser said. The *we* seemed condescending. "Is that right?"

"That's correct," Jerry said. He wasn't going to get drawn in again.

"Interrogation . . . would have some added elements, no doubt," Hochheiser said. "Right?"

Jerry was dry. "No doubt," he said. "Yes."

"Now," Hochheiser said, "would it be fair to say that what you were calling an interview—let's say on August 29 and 30"—the night Craig confessed—"was what many ordinary people would call questioning?"

Jerry was wary. "The twenty-ninth and thirtieth?" he said. "Yes."

"Or," Hochheiser plowed on, "what many ordinary people would call an interrogation?"

Jerry refused to be bullied. But he was off-balance enough to skew his grammer. "I would still qualify it as question," he said. "I don't see it as an interrogation."

"Well," Hochheiser said with what seemed mock patience, "what is an interrogation in the Police Department?"

Hayes objected.

Hochheiser objected to Hayes's objection.

The judge let Hochheiser press Jerry for a few more minutes, until Hayes objected again. This time, the judge sustained Hayes's objection, saying, "I think we have had sufficient questioning in the academic phase of this." But in a short time Hochheiser had sneaked the concept of interrogation back into the cross-examination by asking with apparent innocence,

"Now, sir, on the sixteenth and seventeenth . . . what time did this interrogation take place?"

"Objection, your honor," Hayes said. "Why does he keep saying—"

"All right," the judge said. "We had some discussion about *interrogation.*" To Hochheiser, he said: "That's over now."

"But I don't have to use his word *interview,*" Hochheiser said. "Do I, your honor?"

"I'm objecting," Hayes said, "to the use of the word *interrogation.*"

"Can we say it's a conversation?" asked the judge.

"It's not exactly that, your honor," Hochheiser said. "A seventeen-hour conversation is rather unusual."

"We don't have a seventeen-hour conversation," Hayes said.

"If Mr. Hochheiser wants to refer to it as interrogation, let him," the judge said. "That's not going to influence me one way or the other."

"I object, your honor," Hayes said, because "if we reach a trial and Mr. Hochheiser then asks, 'When I asked you about an interrogation, didn't you answer such and such,' " it would imply Jerry had agreed that Craig's questioning had been an interrogation. And the word *interrogation* suggests coercion. "That's my fear." Not that the word would influence the judge, but that it might influence a jury.

"How about the word *inquiry?*" the judge asked. "Is that any better?"

"Fine," Hayes said.

"Suppose we use that," said the judge.

A few minutes later, Hochheiser was referring to the incident as "this questioning session." And later, during the cross-examination, when he asked how Craig and the detectives were arranged in the rooms on the two nights Craig made statements to the police, Hochheiser said, "Did the interrogator sit facing Mr. Crimmins and also facing the door?"

"Objection, your honor," Hayes said. "Why does he do that? We are getting into semantics here."

"Do I have to say *interviewing?*" Hochheiser asked.

"That's a fair enough word in that context," the judge told Hayes. "The man who asked the questions is the interrogator, I suppose."

"Perhaps," Hochheiser said, "I should say the host and the guest."

"Much better," Hayes said.

"Like Johnny Carson," Hochheiser said.

"Much more accurate," Hayes said.

Hochheiser trotted Jerry over the same ground he'd covered with Boy, Bruno, and Heaney. Was the Atrium a police facility? How much did Craig look like the police composite sketch? And was Craig in police custody on the nights of August 16–17 and August 29–30 when he was being interviewed-questioned-interrogated? Hochheiser drilled Jerry on whether or not Craig was kept isolated on the night of his first statement. And on whether or not, on the night of his first statement, he was a suspect. And, if Craig had been a suspect, what did that mean? Hochheiser suggested that to scare Craig into confessing to the murder, Jerry or someone else had threatened him with handcuffs and adverse publicity. Craig would be shamed in the newspapers.

"I don't know of any such conversation" with Craig, Jerry said. Jerry had the impression that Hochheiser was trying to goad him into losing his temper.

To prove that Craig could have seen Jerry's gun on the night of Craig's first statement, Hochheiser had Jerry take off his coat and pose for the court.

He's trying, Jerry thought, to make me look foolish.

And, of course, Hochheiser squeezed as much as he could out of Jerry's admission that on August 29 he was prepared to arrest Craig if Craig had not gone with him willingly. But no matter how much he squeezed, Hochheiser was still left with the dry fact that Craig did go with Jerry willingly. Jerry did not arrest him.

To build his case, Hochheiser used one ploy after another. It was a bravura performance. At one point he wanted to disclose to the public and press information—about the palm print on the roof—that he previously had asked the court to conceal. He was so theatrical, Hayes finally had to object "to the histrionics." And he continued to be sarcastic. When he asked Jerry to compare his hair with Craig's and when Jerry said it was darker than Craig's but "I have got some gray in it," Hochheiser said, "I assume your barber did that to make you look more mature."

When he asked Jerry if Craig's hair was thicker than the hair on the person Laura Cutler saw in the elevator with Helen and when Jerry said, "I would have to examine Mr. Crimmins's hair to see if it was very thick, . . ." Hochheiser said, "She didn't indicate she examined his hair like a doctor or a barber."

When he asked Jerry if Craig had a "large face" like the man Laura Cutler described and when Jerry said, "I've seen larger; I've seen smaller," Hochheiser said, "Haven't we all?"

When he asked Jerry about what happened on August 29, when Jerry met Craig outside Craig's apartment building, Hochheiser said, "When he"—Craig—"said to you, 'Is this going to take all night?' did you say to him, 'It's not only going to take all night; this may take twenty-five years' "?

And, when Jerry, thrown momentarily by the way Hochheiser had phrased a question, did the verbal equivalent of a half-gainer in order to answer the question correctly—"No, he never said that; yes, that's so; he never said that,"—Hochheiser in an aside mocked Jerry's response, saying, "Yes, we have no bananas."

Twice, Jerry betrayed anger.

Once, when Hochheiser was pressing Jerry to admit that, on the night of August 16–17, he'd used Craig's stepfather, Marty

Higgins, to coerce Craig into saying what the police wanted him to say, Jerry snapped, "Mr. Hochheiser, you know I stated over and over again that I did attempt to enlist the aid of Mr. Higgins to go in and speak to his stepson in order that we might get to the truth. And nothing else. No other version or story that I wanted to hear or that we would be satisfied with. Okay? And that's my statement!"

"And who," Hochheiser asked, using Jerry's outburst against him, "would determine whether it was the truth?"

The other time Jerry lost his temper, Hochheiser was able to exploit what Jerry said even more. Hochheiser was trying to prove that on the night of August 16–17, Jerry had purposely kept Craig and his father separated. He hammered away, until Jerry seethed.

"Mr. Hochheiser," Jerry said, "I saw an office with certain doors closed. I placed him"—Craig—"in this room, knowing that I was going to seek his father and have him speak to Craig, because that was Craig's wish. If I had seen his father sitting in an office, I would have taken Craig and said, 'Here's your father. Now, talk to him.' "

Hochheiser pounced. "So, you put him in this office," he said; "placed him in this office, as you said. . . ." *Placed him* implied that Jerry was directing Craig's movements, that Craig was not free to come and go as he pleased, that Craig was, in effect, in police custody. It was a poor choice of words, which Jerry wasn't even aware of having made.

"I didn't say *place him*," Jerry said.

"You said *place him*," Hochheiser said.

Twice, Jerry managed to bring Hochheiser up short.

Once, Hochheiser asked if the police made "any inquiries prior to the twenty-ninth of August to determine whether there was a likelihood or information as to whether Craig Crimmins knew this person"—which is how he referred to Helen—"or had any rapport with her?"

Jerry, setting Hochheiser up for the kill, asked, "Did we make any inquiries?"

"Yes," Hochheiser said.

"Mr. Hochheiser," Jerry said, his timing perfect, "we made thousands of inquiries."

The second time came when, in response to one of Jerry's answers, Hochheiser said, "Officer, I didn't ask you that."

"Then," Jerry said, "you have to make your questions clearer, sir."

Jerry left the stand feeling that he had done well. In fact, at one point during the cross-examination, when Hochheiser complained about Jerry's testimony, the judge said, "I think the witness has been sincerely attempting to answer all your questions responsively."

"Why the fuck isn't Roger calling me?" Mike kept asking.

He hated testifying as much as Jerry enjoyed it; but, since it was his case, he felt it was important for him to take the stand. Hayes thought it would be overkill.

"I don't think we're putting Mike on," he told Jerry.

"Ask him his fucking name," Jerry said, "and take him off."

If Mike wasn't used, people might misunderstand. They might think he wasn't to be trusted or didn't know his facts. And the hearing, at the least, would give Mike a trial run against Hochheiser.

"Fucko," Mike said to Hayes, "you're going to throw me to the wolves, sending me out there cold later on."

Although Mike could understand why Hayes wasn't using him, he wasn't happy about the decision.

"It's my case," Mike said, "and I'm not going to testify."

There seemed to be a contradiction in the arguments Hochheiser made during the hearing. He was claiming that probable cause didn't exist until after Craig's confession, so the arrest was illegal. He also was claiming that Craig was under arrest before the confession because he was a prime suspect, so the confession was inadmissible.

How could Craig be a prime suspect if no probable cause existed?

Somehow Hochheiser had to defuse the confession, because, as he said, "It is difficult to conceive of a potentially more damaging piece of evidence for a defendant than a videotaped confession."

Judge Milton L. Williams, who had presided over Craig's bail hearing, called the videotapes "the single most crucial piece of evidence in this case." It was "a touch-and-go situation," according to a profession who taught the law of evidence at New York University Law School. The prosecution didn't have "a strong case," he said; "but it might squeak through." A criminal-law expert said, "I can only surmise that without the results of the interrogation"—the confession—"the police did not . . . have probable cause to arrest" Craig, "and they only had it after he confessed at the police station. If so, the police took a big chance that the courts would find they committed an illegal arrest, which would lose them the confession, and probably the entire case."

Even "if all the statements in this case were suppressed," Hayes said, "we would still go to trial."

When the facts were not disputed, the hearings became a battle of words: Hayes's description of what had happened versus Hochheiser's. *Police place* or *police station. Interview* or *interrogation.* Craig's statements were like poems, texts, that Hayes and Hochheiser, literary critics, were arguing over. What did the poet mean? What was the context of the poem? The acts that the statements described began to seem secondary to

the statements themselves. The murder, like any other historical event, started to exist only in the words used to describe it.
Its reality was not lost so much as transformed—altered by the
way people spoke about it. It was no longer a private event,
something that although brutal was intimate, involving only
Helen and her killer. It had become public, changed by and
changing everyone who read about it; thought about it; used
their imagination to recreate it. Someone reading the newspaper might think, Yes, this can happen in my world; this is part
of my reality. And, having admitted the possibility of such a
murder, he or she would then think of the murder in relation to
his or her own life. The murder would take on a personal meaning. It would make a person more fearful or braver, gentler or
more violent, more religious or more of an atheist. . . . The
more people who thought about the murder, the more symbolic
the murder would become. How the case was described was
important, because how it was described would shape people's
attitudes about it.

Hayes was trying to keep Helen's death at the center of the
story. Hochheiser was trying to change the story—make it not
about Helen's death but about Craig's persecution. The public
and the jury would respond not only to which story seemed
truest to the facts but also to which story seemed truest to their
vision of the world. Which innocent victim fit best in their
own stories: Helen or Craig?

Standing in the court, trying to find the words that would
make their version of the case more convincing than any other,
the two attorneys—Hayes and Hochheiser—were like contes-
tants competing in a song contest in a Wagnerian opera, *Tann-
häuser* or *Die Meistersinger.*

On April 8, Denzer began his decision on the hearing by
complaining that Hochheiser hadn't given him the Defense

Memorandum until the day before, a week after it was due.
Both his job and Hayes's job had "not been made any easier by
defense counsel's failure to comply with a schedule agreed
upon. . . ."

As for Craig's interview on the night of August 16–17,
Denzer said, "It seems abundantly clear . . . that during that
evening neither the police nor the defendant considered the
defendant was under arrest or under any compulsion to remain
with them. . . . He was free to leave at any time he wished
and to talk to anyone whom he desired. . . . There was no
police intimidation of any sort and . . . neither the length or
the manner of the interrogation was such to create an impression of an arrest or police custody." The videotape itself de-
picted "a relaxed kind of interview and atmosphere. . . ."

On the night of August 29–30, however, the interrogation
"was custodial. Despite the fact that the defendant apparently
did not believe . . . he was under arrest, . . . the officers testified that they would not have released him had he asked or
tried to leave. . . . So far as they were concerned, he was under arrest." But, Denzer added, the police had probable cause
to hold Craig, so "the custody or arrest was perfectly legal."

As for the confession: Denzer dismissed the question of coercion and focused on the claim that "by deception and trickery,
the police sealed off the most likely avenues by which assistance
of counsel could reach the defendant. . . . The main defense
argument is that" Craig's confession was "inadmissible because
. . . the police . . . prevented members of the defendant's
family . . . from seeing and talking to" Craig "on the evening
of August 29," so they couldn't convince Craig to get a lawyer
before answering any questions. "There was a great deal of
evidence upon this subject," Denzer said, "much of it conflict-
ing.

"Testimony of the defendant's stepfather and mother de-
picted them as making vigorous efforts to see, communicate

with the defendant during the hours immediately before and during his interrogation, being frustrated by failure of the police to give correct information and by a kind of passive stonewalling that kept them at bay. This was supplemented by other testimony concerning an asserted family plan agreed upon after the August 16 interrogation of the defendant that, if he were ever again approached by the authorities for questioning, he was to have a lawyer for the occasion.

"The police witnesses on the other hand disclaimed any action, attempt or plan on their part to keep members of the defendant's family away from him. Declared that the defendant never asked to see any of them and asserted that much of the defense testimony on this subject is shaded or untrue."

Denzer continued, "I will not attempt to resolve all of those credibility issues here." But, he pointed out, even if the police had stonewalled the family, Craig still was "fully advised of his Miranda rights." He had declared that he fully understood them and was willing to answer questions without an attorney present. And he didn't ask to see any members of his family. So, Denzer concluded, "I fail to observe any violation of the defendant's rights. . . ."

There might have been a problem if a lawyer had been hired; but, despite the "considerable defense testimony about a family plan of retaining" a lawyer, "if the need should arise, no attorney had been hired by August 29."

The only circumstances under which the defense claim—that the confession was inadmissible because the police prevented the family from urging Craig to get a lawyer—would be valid was if the defendant "had . . . been a callow youth of fifteen, sixteen, or seventeen years, living under the guardianship of his parents, or . . . feeble-minded. Under such circumstances, he would surely be deemed incompetent to waive his rights" and statements obtained from him would be inadmissible.

Craig, Denzer said, "does not belong in that category."

"Despite his mother's testimony that he had been slow in school and required special attention," Denzer said, Craig got "through the tenth grade." When he confessed, he was twenty-one years old, held a job as a Met stagehand "at a good salary, well in excess of the earnings of most people in his age group." Although he lived with his father, he paid rent. He had his own bank account. And he was "generally independent in his own life style."

"He was," Denzer added, "more than merely self-supporting. He owned and drove an automobile and a motorcycle and . . . spent time with his peers at ski resorts and other places of entertainment." He was obviously able "to make decisions and to understand conscious waver of his right to counsel."

Craig's videotaped confession was admissible.

The district attorney's office, Mike and Jerry had their first report card on their handling of the case. They got an A.

19

Soon after the hearing ended, Jerry heard a radio newscaster report that Hochheiser had said about Jerry's testimony, "Detective Giorgio is going to choke on his words."

"Pal," Jerry said to the radio, "I ain't going to choke."

Since it was Jerry who had taken Craig's initial confession, he would be Hochheiser's primary target in the trial.

Hochheiser thinks he's good, Jerry thought. Goddamn it, I know I'm good.

The trial was shaping up as a battle of egos.

"You'll get your chance at bat in the trial," Jerry told Mike.

Mike was as glum as Jerry was elated. Other detectives would come up to him and say things like, Hey, didn't you work on that case with Giorgio? Mike knew they were jealous and wanted to pit him against Jerry. Still, it hurt. Jerry was getting all the glory. All Mike's old suspicions of Jerry nagged. Jerry would come out of the case a superstar. Mike had heard plenty of stories like the one about Sonny Grasso, the French Connection detective, who had parlayed a major investigation into a career in the movies and television. The very qualities that apparently separated a cop from the world of the arts could be a way into that world. Mike pictured Jerry being toasted by show-biz big shots, the same kind of people who ran places like the Met, while he was forgotten.

Mike cared more about the recognition of his peers. He was a cop; they were cops. Fuck the show-biz big shots, he thought. While having a drink at the Metropolitan Improvement Company, the cops' bar near 1 Police Plaza, he glanced at the wall of photographs, the Hall of Fame. If he got aced out of major testimony at the trial, would they hang his picture? Or only Jerry's?

Then he dismissed the question. He told himself, First, let's win the case.

After another two-day hearing, Denzer ruled that Laura Cutler's "hypnotic session and inquiry were conducted by a qualified and experienced professional in the field; that great care was used during the interrogation to avoid suggestiveness; that the basic conversations, both before and during hypnosis, were faithfully recorded, by audio- if not by videotape; and that there were no factors, of either a personal or physical nature, which tainted the inquiry."

Denzer also pointed out that when Laura was hypnotized and questioned, "no defendant or specific perpetrator had been unearthed, identified or was even suspected, much less arrested, charged, or indicted. In other words, the investigation was, at the time, barren of a named target—this defendant or anyone else—and, therefore, presented no possible opportunity for suggestive interrogation aimed at this defendant even had the police been so inclined."

The description Laura gave under hypnosis of what happened at and in the elevator the night Helen was killed was more detailed than her unhypnotized version, but similar enough to rule out any taint. And, Denzer said, Laura's statement under hypnosis was "corroborated by other evidence much more damaging to the defendant than anything said by Miss Cutler"—like Craig's admission that the night of the murder he'd met Helen at the elevator.

The statement Laura gave under hypnosis was admissible.

The prosecution was going into the trial with all its ammunition intact.

During the weeks before the trial started, Mike and Jerry finished tying up loose ends. Who was on each floor at the Met at the time of the murder? Were all the reports in order? Where were the phones Craig's stepfather might have used to call home the night of August 16–17? What calls were made from the Met? What time did the *Daily News* with the story about the Met murder suspect hit the streets on August 29?

Roger Hayes reinterviewed each possible defense witness. Half of them were getting nervous about testifying. Some had shady pasts they didn't want exposed: former arrests and convictions, treatment at mental hospitals, erratic, violent, or deviant behavior. Others were still living secret lives they wanted to keep hidden: booze, drugs, girlfriends their wives didn't know about. A few simply didn't want to get involved: The word backstage at the Met was that Craig was innocent and anyone who helped convict him was a traitor.

Mike and Jerry began getting as paranoid as some of the backstage crew. What if one of the witnesses changed his story or suffered a sudden lapse of memory on the stand? Could the defense get to any of their witnesses? Would any of Craig's supporters use a witness's private life to shut him up? Could the prosecution's phone be tapped? Would the defense fish for information? A detective who was a friend of someone who worked for Hochheiser sought Jerry out one day and asked, How's the case going? You got a strong case?

Paranoia.

"We have an excellent case," Jerry said.

By the time Sandy Hacker, one of the Met bosses, told Jerry he was sure Craig was innocent and that one of the Germans had killed Helen, Jerry was out of patience. He cut him off with, "Sandy, what can I tell you?"

But their worst fear was that they'd never find out who belonged to the fingertip prints found on Helen's skirt. As long as those prints were unidentified, the defense could exploit them for reasonable doubt. The prints were Craig's key out of jail.

On April 10, ten days before jury selection was set to start, Billy Plifka matched the prints to someone who had touched the sensitized paper used to lift the prints from cloth.

The prints had never been on the skirt.

Hayes was confident Mike and Jerry would be good witnesses. Their strengths complemented each other. Jerry came across as genial. He was well dressed without being too sharp: no gold bracelets or thousand-dollar watches. Professional. He seemed to take a courtroom into his confidence. Mike came across as direct, no-nonsense, tough.

"He fills out a Van Heusen," Hayes said.

Both were honest. Both knew their stuff.

Hayes told them: Don't anticipate Hochheiser's questions; don't be a wiseass; and make sure you call Craig "Mr. Crimmins." For days, wherever they went, together or separately,

Mike and Jerry, as though surrendering to a mutual obsession, muttered, "Mr. Crimmins. Mr. Crimmins."

The bulldozer was parked next to the house. Mike sat on it smoking a cigar in the twilight. In the kitchen, lights were on. Through the windows, Mike caught glimpses of Marion and Stacy. In neighboring homes, kitchen lights were also on. Mike saw people moving back and forth, cooking, setting tables, families coming to dinner. Kids shouted, their voices in the half-dark as thin as balloon strings. Screen doors slammed. Dogs barked. All the typical suburban sound effects. It was peaceful.

"Ma," Jerry said when he talked to his mother, "don't forget, when you go to church, light another candle."

She was praying at Our Lady of Pompeii on Bleecker Street in the Village that the prosecution would win the case and Jerry would be vindicated.

The jury was chosen. When Jerry was asked what he thought of the selection, he said he could live with it, but, he added, "I would have preferred twelve cops."

The night before the trial began, Jerry dreamed Denzer threw out Craig's confession. Jerry knew that was impossible; the confession could be thrown out only in the hearing. He knew he was having a nightmare, but he couldn't force himself awake. He was being called to the stand. He had to testify about the thrown-out confession, which would be like trying to take a test without knowing the questions. Hochheiser was raising or had raised some crazy technicality.

Jerry sat up in bed, sweating. Beside him, Kay slept soundly. He went into the kitchen and made a cup of coffee. He knew he wouldn't be able to go back to sleep.

Whatever the outcome of the trial, things would never be

the same as they'd been. He and Mike would end up heroes or pariahs. He realized that on the day they'd arrested Craig, they had crossed some shadow line in their lives just as surely as Craig had.

PART THREE

20

A CRIMINAL JURY TRIAL is like a novel with ten chapters.

On the morning of Monday, April 27, Denzer explained to the jurors in the Met murder case what happens in each chapter.

Chapter One is the selection of the jury—which, Denzer said, "we have now completed."

Chapter Two is the judge's opening remarks.

"As you can see," Denzer said, "that is where we are now."

Chapter Three is the prosecutor's opening remarks.

Chapter Four is the defense's opening remarks—an optional chapter, excluded or included depending upon the judgment of the defense attorney. In a novel, this would be an avant-garde touch; in a trial, it is practical.

Chapter Five is testimony and the introduction of other evidence. This chapter is organized antiphonally.

The prosecutor, who must prove the defendant's guilt, starts. He calls his witnesses and asks them questions.

"This is called direct examination," Denzer said.

The defense attorney then gets a chance to question the witnesses.

"This is called cross-examination," Denzer said.

Often cross-examination is used to try to discredit the witness's testimony.

After the cross-examination, the prosecutor can again question the witness—but only about things brought up in the cross-examination.

"This is called redirect examination," Denzer said.

After the redirect, the defense attorney can again question the witness—but only about things brought up in the redirect.

This is called the recross-examination.

It's a bit like playing mumblety-peg: The field of contest keeps shrinking.

Once the prosecutor has called his witnesses, and they have gone through the direct examination, the cross-examination, the redirect, and the recross, the defense attorney can, if he wishes, call witnesses—who then go through the same process: direct examination, cross-examination, redirect, and recross. Except the attorneys reverse roles, the defense attorney doing the direct and redirect and the prosecutor doing the cross and recross.

The prosecutor can then offer a rebuttal, calling witnesses who are questioned in the same way: direct, cross, redirect, and recross.

And the defense attorney can offer his rebuttal of the rebuttal—called the surrebuttal—calling witnesses who go through the direct-cross-redirect-recross rigamarole.

The form—

> prosecutor
> defense attorney
> prosecutor
> defense attorney

> defense attorney
> prosecutor
> defense attorney
> prosecutor

—is poetic, the Elegiac Stanza. If the trial were a novel, this chapter would be in verse.

Chapter Six is the defense attorney's summation: his closing argument.

Chapter Seven is the prosecutor's summation.

Chapter Eight is the court's charge to the jury.

"There," Denzer told the jurors, "I am required to instruct you upon the alleged crimes or charges before you, to advise you what has to be proved, to establish . . . and to explain the legal principles which apply to and control this case."

The jury writes the last two chapters.

Chapter Nine is the deliberation of the jurors.

Chapter Ten is the announcement in court of the verdict.

Like Ahab in *Moby Dick,* Jerry and Mike were introduced into the story long before they made their appearance. In his opening statement, Hayes referred to them, although not by name. He called them *the police,* as though they were an impersonal collective force, like the Fates. *The Police:* the Spirit of Law Enforcement. Hochheiser, in his opening statement, implied that Jerry and Mike were more fallible than Hayes had suggested. He started by arguing so strongly that the police had been motivated only by good intentions that the jury could have been led to suspect the opposite.

If he were a juror, Hochheiser said, "I would resist the idea [that] in a free society where we are supposed to be in control of our civil servants, . . . anyone like a policeman . . . would intentionally do something so wrong, which in itself could be

. . . characterized in many ways as worse than the underlying crime.

"What I hope to show you, what I hope you will understand is that a miscarriage such as we are going to see presented during this trial is not done by evil men who seek to frame someone who is entirely innocent of a murder, of attempted rape, in order to get to their own ends. Not at all.

"What you are going to see is these policemen were well-meaning men."

Well-meaning men, who—Hochheiser had already argued—were under pressure "both from superiors in the Police Department and perhaps the public" to solve the case and who would, if they did solve it, "get those benefits" that flow from a well-done job.

Well-meaning men. Honorable men. Hochheiser was playing Mark Antony.

But within a few minutes, Hochheiser had dropped the mask of courtesy. Instead of calling the police "well-meaning men," he was characterizing them as liars. Hochheiser said that "this policeman"—it was unclear whether he was speaking of Jerry or Mike—"may . . . try to sell you on the idea that Craig Crimmins somehow lost weight from the time they originally had seen him." *Somehow*—as though losing weight were a difficult and mysterious art. "That is not so, . . ." he said; Craig did not lose weight. If Jerry or Mike said he did—Hochheiser claimed—they were lying.

Hochheiser mined the court so half of what Jerry and Mike would testify to was already labeled lies. He claimed Jerry—he finally named him—used "subtle methods" to keep Marty Higgins from calling Craig's mother on the night of August 16–17. He ridiculed Jerry and the other cops.

"These officers seem like nice fellows," he said. "They wear their suits with vests and tie[s], and they all look respectful.

. . . Always trust the policeman. See the man in blue, he'll cross you across the street."

He made them seem insensitive monsters. When he described how Craig's mother would testify that she spent all night trying to locate Craig, Hochheiser said the cops "will just laugh at her and say no such things happened. . . ."

And he asserted that Jerry created Craig's confession.

"Everyone," Hochheiser said, "has to concede that he created it at least in some respect."

Not content to smear Jerry and Mike, Hochheiser went after Boy, who—he said—"will testify otherwise" than what his "true feelings" were.

He also went after Heffernan, who—he said—on the night of August 16–17 wanted "to put everybody," Craig, his father, and his stepfather, "at ease, keep them off balance, and keep them pliable," and who on the night of the confession "chooses not to be" around the room where Jerry and Craig are talking, so "he doesn't see anything, he doesn't hear anything, and he can't say anything about what happened. . . ."

Hochheiser even hinted that Hayes was lying. He described how Hayes, in his opening statement, "turned and he looked at Craig Crimmins and he . . . was about to characterize the statement"—Craig's confession—"and eventually the word *voluntary* came out. I wonder," Hochheiser said, "if you remember how he did that. I think that you are going to see that all of the witnesses in this case who had anything to do with that statement are going to virtually choke over that word"— *voluntary.* "If they are able to get it out at all."

For over an hour and a half, Hochheiser spoke; and his opening statement was so argumentative, it sounded like a closing statement. At last, Hayes objected. "I have remained mute up to this point, your honor—"

"I know," Denzer said. "This is a summation." Denzer told Hochheiser, "I don't want any more argumentation."

But a few minutes later, Hochheiser again was stopped by the judge.

"This is purely argumentative," Denzer said. "That's for summation, Mr. Hochheiser. Will you please confine yourself to what the evidence will be."

And soon after that Denzer once more interrupted.

"Again, you are being very argumentative," he said. ". . . Will you please confine yourself to what the evidence is."

Hochheiser ended his statement by pointing out that "although I have no burden to prove anything, I am confident that you will walk out of here and not only say that you had a reasonable doubt, but that you had a reasonable doubt for a very simple reason. And that was that this young man is entirely innocent."

Hochheiser was even better than he had been in the hearings.

21

PROSECUTION WITNESSES.

Ronald Antonnucci, the police cartographer, described the layout of the Met. Julia Kocick, who had been the Met stage manager on the night of the murder, gave that night's performance schedule. Janis identified Helen's shoes and pen, told about the last time he spoke to his wife and how he waited for her outside the Met. Alice Montoya told about leaving the orchestra pit with Helen. Suzanne Ornstein, the violinist who sat behind Helen, told about searching for her. Jesse Levine, another musician, told about calling the 20th Precinct to see if any accident had been reported that might explain Helen's absence. Donald MacCourt, the subcontractor for the orchestra, told about calling Helen's apartment. Antonia Sunderland, the assistant house manager, told about reporting Helen's disappearance to the police. The testimony of all these witnesses was straightforward; indisputable facts. What the building looked like. When Helen vanished. What the musicians did. Nothing controversial.

James Devlin, the Met engineer, described the moan or groan he heard on C level. Lawrence Lennon, the maintenance mechanic, described finding Helen's shoes on the fan roof. Elliot Gross, the Chief Medical Examiner, described the autopsy findings. "There was blood present about her nostrils and her mouth," he said. "There was blood adjacent to the head. The body was bound with the binding in back. . . ." The contrast between the clinical language and the awful details was disturbing—like a room painted white, walls, ceiling, and floor, and empty except for a single muddy footprint. "There were some hemorrhages in the left eye. There was blood coming from the ears. . . ."

John Sineno, a New York City fireman who moonlighted at the Met, described the dirty napkins that usually lay around the sixth floor near the fan roof. Frederick Collay, Jr., Craig's supervisor the night of the murder, told of missing Craig about the time Helen vanished and described various knots used by Met stagehands. When he was asked if a clove hitch, which had bound Helen, was secure, he said, "I wouldn't tie it around my head."

Most of the witnesses testified with proper solemnity; but a couple acted as if they thought they were on the *Tonight Show*, as if a public appearance demanded a comic pose.

"Approximately how many times did you go to your locker room that evening?" Hayes asked Vincent Donohue, the Met stagehand. Hayes was using Donohue's testimony to destroy part of the alibi Craig had given on the night of August 16–17: He was drinking beer at his locker when Helen was being molested and murdered.

"Four or five times," Donohue said.

"And what was the purpose in going there?" Hayes asked.

"Well, as it turned out, I had some cocaine in my locker,"

Donohue said. *As it turned out.* "So I was going down to in-
dulge in a little of that."

"On the times that you went down to your locker room,"
Hayes asked, "was anyone else there?"

"No," Donohue said.

"Did you check to make sure that no one else was there?"
Hayes asked.

"Yeah," Donohue said. He paused. "From experience I do
check."

Hayes finished.

Hochheiser crossed-examined Donohue. He apparently expected to use the issue of drugs to discredit Donohue's testimony. In fact, it was crucial for the defense to discredit Donohue. He had testified about overhearing Tommy Gravina tell
Craig he would lie about where Craig was when Helen was
killed. And he had testified about how Craig had taught him to
express the Met elevators, the technique of making an elevator
skip stops, which causes an elevator door to flutter the way the
door did on the elevator Helen had shared with her killer.

Hochheiser began with a snide reference to the elevator
trick.

"May I correctly assume," he said, "that after having had
the opportunity to take in such a valuable piece of information,
. . . that you didn't kill anybody?"

He was trying to prove that knowing how to express an elevator wasn't a sign of guilt. But instead of cowing Donohue, it
riled him.

"I resent you asking me that, you know," Donohue said.

"The question assumed you did not," Hochheiser said.

"Well," Donohue said. "I still resent you asking me that."

It seemed Hochheiser had misjudged the witness. Donohue
wasn't someone to take head-on. Still, head-on was how
Hochheiser took him.

"Well," Hochheiser said, "you say that you used cocaine on July 23 when you went downstairs?"

"That's one of the occasions that I had used cocaine," Donohue said. "Sure."

One of the occasions. A perfect opening for proving Donohue was a habitual drug user and therefore an untrustworthy witness.

"I'm a little confused," Hochheiser said. "Is it that you used cocaine on July 23 one time and that one time is one of many occasions, or is it that you used cocaine on July 23 more than one time?"

"Both," Donohue said. "Both are true."

"Okay," Hochheiser said. "Around July 23, how often did you use cocaine?"

"While I was in the opera house?"

"Yes."

"Approximately four. Possibly five times."

"Is this on July 23?"

"On July 23," Donohue said.

"It was during this period of time that you made the observations that are so clear in your mind today?" Hochheiser asked.

He was moving toward the question: How could Donohue be clear about something that happened while he was under the influence of drugs? But Donohue derailed him.

"What observations are you talking about?" Donohue asked.

"You testified about going down and looking around, you know, in the lounge area," Hochheiser said.

"Oh, sure," Donohue said, "yeah, definitely."

"Have you—" Hochheiser began and then interrupted himself. "I didn't mean to pick on you."

"You are more than welcome to, you know," Donohue said.

"Okay," Hochheiser said. "You understand that the question I asked you before about . . . that elevator thing—I didn't mean to indicate you did anything wrong. I didn't mean to jump on you for that."

"You can lock horns with me any time," Donohue said.

"Okay," Hochheiser said, going in for the kill. "I would just like to know, if I may, if you exercised your discretion in favor of cocaine this morning?"

"This morning?" Donohue asked.

"This very morning," Hochheiser said.

Donohue admitted he had.

"Actually," he said, "I did it on purpose."

"I see," Hochheiser said.

"If that gives you an edge," Donohue said, "I'm glad."

Hochheiser pointed out that Donohue claimed he didn't want anyone to see him snorting cocaine on the night Helen was killed. "But," he said, "you're sitting here in the middle of the whole criminal justice system announcing that you're on cocaine now. That does not seem to bother you?"

"It doesn't," Donohue said. "I think it is irrelevant."

When Hochheiser started on his next question, Donohue interrupted him to invoke "Sigmund Freud and the rest of them" to help defend cocaine use. It was unclear who "the rest of them" were, although they seemed to be as respectable as Freud. And Donohue used them—with Freud—as though they were the four-out-of-five dentists who approved of sugarless gum. It was not just advertising logic, but celebrity logic: If someone famous endorses a product or behavior, it had to be all right.

Donohue said Hochheiser's question about cocaine use "was light-years away of understanding, you know, you know. . . . What can I—cocaine is—I don't think, you know. . . ." As though his statement were a maze from which he finally emerged, Donohue ended with, "I don't think you know enough about the drug. I don't think you know enough about it to make an intelligent judgment like that."

Hochheiser said that Donohue seemed to think "I have suggested . . . cocaine might have a negative effect on your ability to recall and observe." Before Donohue could respond, Hochheiser added, "Do you feel that is not so? Does it have a neutral effect rather than a positive effect on you?"

Donohue was a little confused by the way Hochheiser had phrased his question: *Do you feel that is not so?*—the yes-we-have-no-bananas structure Hochheiser had ridiculed Jerry for using in the hearing.

"What are you saying?" Donohue asked. "Does it lose your memory? Sharpen your memory? What?"

"Do you feel your memory is better and more accurate here in court today as a result of having used cocaine?" Hochheiser asked.

Cocaine didn't affect his memory, Donohue said.

"If I was smoking marijuana, it would be a different story," he continued. "That would have a tendency to cloud my memory. . . . I have shot heroin. I have taken LSD, you know. I have been around the world. I have been in India. [Used] Peyote. So you can judge my character for what it is. But, as an observer and as a person, I am not one who suffers delusions, you know." Donohue knew what he saw in the locker room. Or rather what he didn't see. And he didn't see Craig. "I am a visual person, you know," he said. "Photographer."

After a few more questions and answers, so filled with mutual misunderstanding and non sequiturs they sounded like dialogue from a Marx Brothers' movie, the judge finally intervened, trying to get Donohue to reply simply and directly.

"All right," Denzer said, "the answer [to the last question] is—"

"What do you mean, 'The answer is . . . ,'" Donohue said. "I am trying to tell you. If it is too many words, then it is too many words; but I am trying to tell you what happened."

"All right," Denzer said.

"You know," Donohue started, "this man—" referring to Hochheiser.

"All right," Denzer cut Donohue off. "You have answered the question."

"Okay," Donohue said. "Good. It is easier for me that way."

"I have had enough," Hochheiser said, ending the cross-examination. "I give up."

The press loved Donohue, who—Jerry had heard—said, If I'd known there'd be this much publicity, I'd have confessed for the movie rights.

Steve Diaz, Jr., testified about searching for Craig. Laura Cutler testified about seeing a man at the elevator with Helen. Mike Murray testified about going to the electricians' lounge at the time Craig had claimed to be asleep there and finding the room empty. Jimmy Magnifico. Jimmy Jordan. Robert Shaler. Tommy Gravina.

What happened at the Met the night of the murder? Were there any traces of semen on Helen's corpse? What happened on the afternoon and evening of Craig's first marathon interview with the police?

Winnie Klotz, the assistant photographer who worked on the Met's second floor, part of the route Helen and her killer may have taken. Robert C. Westerman, the assistant chief engineer of the Central Mechanical Plant at Lincoln Center, whose job included checking the Met's sixth-floor fan roof. Joseph Ferraro, the detective in the Crime Scene Unit, who testified about the palm print that was lifted from the pipe on the sixth-floor fan roof. William Plifka, the Police Department fingerprint technician who identified the palm print as Craig's. Fred Boy, the first detective to interview Craig. John Bruno, the detective who took down the answers Craig gave for the questionnaire. Witnesses passed like boxcars on a freight train. At times it seemed like an endless procession.

Hochheiser indulged in occasional sarcasms. In describing his understanding of what happened on the night Craig confessed, he said the cops told Ed Crimmins, "You wait in this room and the polygraph operator"—who Ed Crimmins thought was going to give him a lie-detector test—"is going to arrive from Long Island or Neptune. . . ." In discussing the potential impartiality of a juror who turned out to know a prosecutor, he said, "Maybe she just loves all prosecutors and can't wait to give the prosecutor"—in this case, Hayes—"his verdict." In an argument about how to handle certain photographs, when Hayes asked, "Where do you want me to carry them, Mr. Hochheiser?" Hochheiser almost told Hayes to shove it: "Do you want me to tell you where to put them?" And, frustrated by one witness's inattentive responses, he said, "I feel like I am in someone else's dream."

Hayes occasionally lost his temper. Annoyed at Hochheiser's imperious attitude during a discussion with the judge, Hayes said, "I am sure Mr. Hochheiser would like to try my case. . . ." When Hochheiser demanded that Hayes tip him off about who the next day's prosecution witnesses would be so he'd have a chance to comb through the Rosario material—1,200 pages of documents (such as police notes) that the prosecutor's office had given to the defense—Hayes snapped, "Your honor, this isn't an awesome amount of work. . . . If Mr. Hochheiser [had] worked from nine in the morning until nine at night"—over the previous weekend—"the way I did, then there would be no problem. . . ."

They were well-matched adversaries, whose professional antagonism gave the trial shape—like arm-wrestlers of equal strength who have clasped hands to create a contest that is interesting only as long as neither one wins.

During the hearing, Jerry had testified for four days. For the trial, he figured he'd go at least that long. Once, during a trial for parking-meter burglaries, Hochheiser had kept the investigating detective on the stand for five days. That wasn't even a grand-larceny case. Five days for petty larceny!

Jerry had been following the trial in the press. On the first day, a newspaper reported that "Mr. Hochheiser has asserted that the police used 'psychological threats' to induce his client to confess. . . ." The confession "is not a reading by Craig Crimmins, even," another newspaper quoted Hochheiser as saying. "Why, in this supposedly powerful videotape, does Craig Crimmins never render the facts himself?" *The Camera Doesn't Lie—Or Does It?* asked the headline of another item. Hochheiser was hinting it wasn't just the camera that lied. "There . . . [was] nobody in that room but Detective Giorgio" when Craig confessed, Hochheiser said in another article. One clipping stated that Hochheiser had claimed Jerry and the other detectives "told Crimmins he would 'see a doctor' instead of going to prison if he told the truth" and that they " 'made a racial, sexual threat . . . as to the jail alternative' if Crimmins refused to cooperate." *Met Defense: Confession Was A Trick,* said another headline. "Mr. Hochheiser repeated his contention that detectives had put words into Mr. Crimmins's mouth," said an article. Craig—Hochheiser was quoted as saying—"couldn't have told Detective Giorgio anything . . . because he didn't know anything." Photographs of Craig were run by the press—family snapshots: Craig with his mother, Craig with his brother, Craig with his girlfriend, Craig's mother and her cousin, Craig eating a hot dog at a Sabrette's cart.

In the witness waiting room, Jerry leafed through the newspapers. In the evening before driving home, he'd call Kay to make sure she'd watch the six-o'clock television news. In the car, he'd listen to the radio.

Every day, Jerry would make out his own morning line on the reporters. The newscaster on WMCA was favorable. Irene Cornell on WCBS: favorable. Heather Bernard on Channel 4: favorable; she called Jerry "the Smiling Detective." E. R. Shipp of the New York *Times* did the most thorough and balanced coverage. Chris Borgan of Channel 2 was also even-handed, although he continually tried to crack Jerry up on camera. Once when Borgan filmed Jerry leaving court, he whispered, Your fly is open. But Jerry resisted the temptation to glance or reach down to check.

Although the New York *Daily News* occasionally zapped the cops, usually their coverage passed Jerry's muster. But the New York *Post* kept up a drumbeat: anti-cop, pro-Craig. Cynthia Fagen, one of the *Post*'s two principal reporters on the case, had a reputation as a "way-out liberal," which to Jerry meant she'd automatically favor the defense.

Once—before the Met case—Mike saw her sitting in the squad room at the 20th Precinct. He thought she was a complainant. For half an hour, she watched and listened. Finally, Mike turned to another detective and asked, "Who is she?"

"I thought she was with you," the other detective said.

"Oh?" Mike said. "I thought she was with you." Mike asked her, "Who are you?"

She told him.

"What do you want?" Mike asked.

Apparently, she was just fishing for news.

Shortly after Helen was killed, Fagen appeared in the Atrium. When she was challenged, she said Mike had invited her.

"At least," Mike later told Jerry, "that's what the cop told me she said. She can use a ruse as well as any detective. She doesn't sit on her hands. I got to admit she's one moxie broad."

During Craig's trial, when Hochheiser would make a point, Fagen would run out to the phone to call the paper. Half the times Mike and Jerry saw her, she was in a corner, talking to Craig's family and friends.

"The minute I spotted her byline"—on pieces about the Met case—Mike told Jerry, "I knew we'd have to watch her."

Jerry didn't like Mike Pearl, the other principal *Post* reporter on the case, any better. As Jerry went in to testify, Pearl said, Hochheiser's going to eat you alive.

22

ON TUESDAY, May 5, at twelve-sixteen in the afternoon, Jerry entered the courtroom.

Be seated. State your name, shield number, and assignment. . . . How long have you been a police officer? How long have you been a detective? Are you married? Do you have any children? Were you working on the early morning hours of July 24, 1980?

Jerry was confident. A question arose about what was the correct voucher number of Helen's gag and the binding from her feet. Hayes said, "I'll have to check my paperwork." Jerry said, "If I may, your honor. . . ." And he gave the number.

So many items had been introduced as evidence that when Hayes brought out seven color photographs, the judge said, "We're getting overloaded with exhibits here." Hayes said he thought it "would be easier" to deal with photographs than with the items photographed, like the rope that had bound Helen, because the blood staining it "really smells."

When Hayes offered a photograph of the tampon found on C level as evidence, Hochheiser, while objecting, betrayed his belief that Craig was innocent and Helen was on trial. Twice he called Helen the defendant.

Just before the end of the day's session, Jerry went through the same litany he'd gone through in the hearing. No, Craig was never hit, kicked, physically abused, screamed at, or threatened.

"I told him," Jerry said, " 'I want you to tell me the truth. . . . Just tell me the truth. . . .' "

A strong ending to the day's testimony. Jerry left the courtroom feeling good. When he reached home, he took a shower, went over his notes, and, after watching the eleven-o'clock news, slept.

The next day, Hayes began by backtracking—like the narrator of a serial. *In the last episode.* He also brought in a photograph of Helen's corpse to remind the jury of what the case was all about. He asked questions about the bindings on Helen's ankles and wrists and about how Jerry brought Craig down to the 13th Precinct on the evening of August 29. Halfway through the morning, Hayes had Jerry read Craig's confession. This was the first time it was made public. The courtroom was hushed. Jerry read the statement in a matter-of-fact voice.

I seen her at the back elevator. . . . When she smacked me on the elevator, she said something snooty and loud. . . . We went to either C or B level, and I sort of talked her into fooling around. I said, 'It won't hurt.' And she started to get worse. . . . That's when I took out the hammer. . . . When she saw the hammer, she started taking off her clothes. She took them all off, and I saw her take out the rag. . . . I told her to lay down, and I tried to put it in. It wouldn't go in. I tried for about five minutes, and I couldn't get it in. . . . We went to the roof.

. . . She was trying to make conversation. . . . I tied her right there, because I was going to leave her there. . . . I didn't have anything to do with her sexually after the first time on C deck. . . . I came on C deck. I was just rubbing against her and came on her. . . . I left her there. . . . I saw her with her feet undone. . . . I ran after her, jumped over the pipe, caught her. . . . I tied her feet. . . . I picked her up and carried her in my arms. . . . She was talking to me, trying to be nice. I decided to gag her and laid her flat on her stomach. . . . I thought she might get away again, so I decided to take her clothes off. . . . I had my knife in the case on my belt. . . . I was just sitting there thinking. . . . I decided to leave. . . . That's when it happened. I went back and kicked her off.

"At that point the interview ended," Jerry said. "I asked Mr. Crimmins to sign it, which he did. I have the date. Eight, thirty, meaning August 30. And I have zero-zero-zero-five hours —which would be five minutes after twelve. I have my signature and my shield number."

This was the pivot of the trial.

In his cross-examination, Hochheiser's job was to prove Jerry was lying.

"Detective Giorgio, could you tell the ladies and gentlemen of the jury whether, other than yourself, if there's any person in this whole world, be he detective, an assistant district attorney, or anyone else that you observed hear my client utter these words that you say resulted in the answers that you say are written down on these pieces of paper?"

That was Hochheiser's first question to Jerry.

"That I observed?" Jerry asked.

"Yes," Hochheiser said.

"No," Jerry said.

"We will take a recess for twenty minutes, ladies and gentle-men," the judge said.

A recess underlines the last thing said. *Did Jerry observe any-one else listening to Craig's answers? No.* It was not the best way to end.

When the trial continued, Hochheiser resurrected the issue of *interview* versus *interrogation.*

"When was the last time you conducted an interrogation?" he asked.

"If I were to check my notebook," Jerry said, "I could tell you. . . . Might be 1979."

Hochheiser asked if Jerry and the other detectives referred to Craig as "the kid"? *Kid* suggests a minor or someone incapable of making his own decisions.

Jerry kept eye contact with Hochheiser and always called him *Mister,* not *Counselor.* He didn't want to dignify Hochheiser.

Just before lunch, Hochheiser asked Jerry what time, on the night of August 29, he was told Ed Crimmins was in the 13th Precinct.

Jerry said it was about five after twelve.

Hochheiser said that at about eleven forty-five Detective Boy told Craig's mother that Ed Crimmins had already left.

"So . . . either Ed Crimmins was at the precinct up until five after twelve and that information to Mrs. Higgins was in-correct," Hochheiser said, "or that information to Mrs. Higgins was correct and your previous testimony—that you were first told that Mr. Ed Crimmins was present at five after twelve—is an error."

Hochheiser's question sounded triumphant—as if he be-lieved the apparent contradiction between Jerry's testimony and Boy's proved one of them was lying.

Jerry explained Hochheiser had simply caught him in a mistake.

"I know now that his father was not there," Jerry said. "When I told Craig that at five after twelve, it was my belief that he was there."

Jerry figured he won that round on points.

After lunch, Hochheiser hammered away at Jerry about the conditions under which Craig confessed. Except for Jerry, there were no witnesses in the room. Craig only answered questions. He didn't offer a narrative of what happened.

He also pointed out Jerry had promised the crew that "anything they said to you about goofing off on the job, getting drunk, snorting cocaine, snorting diet pills" would "be confidential."

"Is that right?" Hochheiser asked.

Jerry said, "Yes."

"And there were some fears these things might become known," Hochheiser said. "Is that right?"

"Yes," Jerry said.

"In fact," Hochheiser said, ". . . all of this has been made public, hasn't it?"

"Yes," Jerry said, "it has."

A few minutes later, Hochheiser pressed his point that Jerry wasn't to be trusted.

"By the way," he said, "you told Mr. Gravina" his admission that he really hadn't seen Craig asleep on the rear wagon "would be privately held also, right?"

"I told Mr. Gravina that we would not divulge where we obtained whatever information we obtained," Jerry said.

"But all of that has become public anyway," Hochheiser said. "Is that correct?"

"That's correct," Jerry said.

And—what Jerry thought was even more unfair—
Hochheiser said, "Now, by the way, your colleague, Mr. Bruno,
Detective Bruno, is head of security at the Metropolitan Opera
House. Is that right?"

"Yes," Jerry said. "He is."

"You don't have any plans to work at the Met," Hochheiser
asked. "Do you?"

"I have no such aspirations, Mr. Hochheiser," he said.

"Have you ever had any conversation or discussion about
that subject?" Hochheiser asked.

"Regarding my working at the Met?" Jerry asked.

"Yes," Hochheiser said.

"Mr. Bruno said if I ever wished to retire and work at the
Met, he might consider me," Jerry said. "And I said, 'I don't
wish to work at the Met,' but I thanked him anyway."

Every time Hochheiser needled him, Jerry reminded himself
to keep cool. At one point, Jerry was so furious that he took
advantage of a sidebar discussion between the judge and the
two attorneys to go into a back alcove, light a cigarette, and
straighten his jacket and tie.

I can't let the son of a bitch get to me like that, he thought.
I'm playing right into his hands.

"By the way," Hochheiser said, "you have a memo book?"

It was a third of the way through the afternoon session.

He thinks he's got me, Jerry thought. I love it.

"A stenographer's notepad," Jerry said.

"That stenographer's pad is more or less like one hundred
pages of notes?" Hochheiser asked.

"Does it have one hundred pages of notes regarding this
case?" Jerry asked.

"Yes," Hochheiser said.

"It has a lot of pages," Jerry said. "I never took the time to count it."

"These notes are neatly printed by hand," Hochheiser said. "Is that right?"

"Yes," Jerry said.

Hochheiser said, "In those many pages, which I characterize as seventy-five to one hundred pages—but I realize you have not counted them—[in] all of those pages of handwritten notes is there anything in there . . . scratched out or written over?"

"Maybe," Jerry said.

"Aren't these notes virtually, from beginning to end, letter-perfect?" Hochheiser asked. "With hardly an erasure, a mistake, a second thought?"

"Do you want me to go through it, Mr. Hochheiser?" Jerry asked.

"Just take a look," Hochheiser said.

"There are two corrections here on some letters," Jerry said. He was deliberately being over-precise.

"Let me see that," Hochheiser said.

"*A* and *B*," Jerry said. "I believe I started *1* and *2*."

Hochheiser seized Jerry's answer.

"Is that because you were copying from something?" he asked.

"Yes," Jerry said.

"As a matter of fact," Hochheiser said, "isn't this entire notebook a recopy of that notebook," the original notebook? Hochheiser was implying that in the transcription something may have been added, left out, or altered. "Have you seen the notebooks of the other policemen in this case?" he asked.

"Yes," Jerry said.

"Have you seen the notebook[s] of, for example, Rosenthal and Boy and Struk?"

"I have."

"Bruno?"

"Yes."

"Have you seen any notebook that goes page after page, letter-perfect? No mistakes. No corrections of the day-to-day activities?" Hochheiser asked.

"I have not examined them that closely," Jerry said, enjoying himself. The more Hochheiser hinted at something improper about the transcription of the notes, the better Jerry would come out looking. He had the original notebook in his attaché case and a comparison would show that nothing had been changed.

"I had a stenographer's pad with a number of pages available," Jerry explained. "I ran out of pages and rather than carry two pads—there were thirty or forty pages in the other book—copied in this one and continued with this one to have a complete chronology of the case."

Hochheiser tried to drop the issue; but Jerry wouldn't let it go.

"Shall I continue to look through my book for changes?" he asked.

"No," Hochheiser said. "You already told us it is a rewrite."

"There may be [more] corrections in here," Jerry said.

"No," Hochheiser said, "that will be all right, Detective Giorgio."

"Okay," Jerry said.

Jerry thought this incident had damaged Hochheiser's whole attack. It proved that Hochheiser could find the appearance of impropriety and be wrong.

For another day and a half, they fought, Hochheiser hacking away, rarely getting past Jerry's defense; Jerry dodging Hochheiser's blows and hoping Hochheiser would injure himself with his own attacks.

". . . Did Mr. Heffernan ever say to my client in front of

the camera, in words or substance, 'Mr. Crimmins, tell me in your own words how could a thing like this have happened?' " he asked.

"No," Jerry said.

"Did he ever say, 'Mr. Crimmins, tell me in your own words what made a nice boy like you do a thing like this?' " Hochheiser asked.

"He did not," Jerry said.

"Did he ever say, 'Mr. Crimmins, tell me in your own words what happened?' "

"He never said that," Jerry said.

Repeating the question was like rubbing a thumb against skin: Eventually, the spot gets sore.

"Sir," Hochheiser asked, "have you ever been involved in a case where there has been a videotape confession before?"

"Yes," Jerry said.

"How many times?"

"Maybe a dozen."

"A dozen?"

"Dozens. Plural."

"Are you not taught, sir, as a police investigator, to always try to get a narrative and always try to capture the person's own words to the extent possible?" Hochheiser asked.

"Yes," Jerry said.

"And in the dozens of videotaped confessions you have witnessed," Hochheiser said, "you have never seen one done in this fashion"—the way it was done in Craig's case—"have you?"

"Videotaped," Jerry said; "no."

Hochheiser asked if Jerry could explain why—in the videotape—Craig never tells his own story.

"Well," Jerry said, "there is a reason for it."

"Yes," Hochheiser said.

"Which I stated on my direct, I believe," Jerry said.

"You did," Hochheiser said.

"The defendant, Craig Crimmins, wished it to be done that way," Jerry said.

"That is the reason that you have stated," Hochheiser said. "Is that right?"

"That's the truth," Jerry said.

"Yes," Hochheiser said, the word barbed enough to hook in a juror's memory and fester there.

Although most of the time Hochheiser used the confession to claim Jerry had put words in Craig's mouth, sometimes he used it to claim Craig didn't know enough to be guilty. He pointed out that Craig referred to "a bucket . . . with a whole shitful of rags in it" on the roof. In fact there was not a bucket, but a crate. He also pointed out that in the confession Craig said he cut off Helen's clothes with his knife. The police laboratory said the clothes had been cut off with scissors.

But, if Craig's story didn't match the facts, then Jerry couldn't have put words in his mouth. If Jerry had fed Craig the confession, why did he have Craig say *bucket* instead of *crate,* and *knife* instead of *scissors*—when the difference might hurt the prosecution's case?

On the last day of Jerry's testimony, both Jerry and Hochheiser were edgy. When Hochheiser kept pressing the question of *knife* versus *scissors,* Jerry exploded, "Mr. Hochheiser, I stated earlier that I never suggested to Mr. Crimmins anything about tools, anything like that. . . . I never made any such suggestion to him."

Coolly, Hochheiser said, "I just asked you if you asked him if he had a scissor."

When Hochheiser cross-examined Jerry about what happened on the night of August 16–17, he couldn't resist insinuating that Jerry acted differently in private, alone with Craig, than he did in public with him.

He quoted a section of the videotape transcript.

"Did that occur?" he asked.

"Yes," Jerry said. "It did."

"And you were on your best behavior in the videotape," Hochheiser said. "Weren't you?"

Hayes objected.

The judge sustained the objection.

"You know that is improper, Mr. Hochheiser," the judge said. "Will you please not repeat anything of that nature."

A little later, when Jerry described a statement Craig had made to the police about being on the fan roof, Hochheiser said sarcastically, "Yeah. And then you straightened that out, didn't you?"

"I asked him to clarify it," Jerry said. "Yes."

Hochheiser saw Jerry's questions to Craig as cues. Jerry saw them as simply questions.

When Jerry noted that the report about how the clothing was cut had been made by "Sergeant Yander, who since has been promoted to lieutenant," Hochheiser said, "For his good work?"

"No," Jerry said. "It's an examination you have to take."

"For his intelligence," Hochheiser said.

"Yes," Jerry said.

"I'm being facetious," Hochheiser said. And he added a snide aside, "He passed the examination. That shows something, I guess."

But Jerry thought Hochheiser was at his most vicious in the last question of the cross-examination.

"In connection with this case, sir," he asked, "did you ever make any application for or receive any awards or commendations?"

The subtext was *Did the department think you did a good job?*

"I did not," Jerry said.

"Okay," Hochheiser said. "Thank you."

23

HOCHHEISER'S HAD HIS SHOT at Jerry and didn't shake him, Mike thought, so now he's got to go at me with everything he's got. Jerry's the Three-Piece Suit. Hochheiser's going to make me the Goon.

For days, Mike had been psyching himself up to testify and crashing when he wasn't called. It's like being nine months pregnant, Mike thought. Waiting every day for the baby. Or like getting ready for surgery that keeps getting put off. What made it worse was that everyone was saying Jerry did so well.

Mike was tired of being the poor relation. Jerry was getting all the press—star witness this, star witness that. "The detective, Gennaro Giorgio, was one of the first officers to spot the battered body. . . ." "The breakthrough came after Giorgio picked up Crimmins near his home. . . ." "Giorgio was also the detective to whom . . . Crimmins broke down. . . ." "Giorgio gave a blow-by-blow account of the breakthrough interview. . . ." "Detective Gennaro Giorgio read a graphic, six-page admission in which Craig . . ." Every newspaper Mike picked up had Jerry's picture.

When an item acknowledged that Jerry was not the only one working on the case, it usually referred to unnamed "other detectives." In the articles that were more specific, Jerry still had the lead—as in the piece that talked about "Detective Giorgio, who was accompanied by Detective Michael Struk . . ."

But it was still Mike's case; and, if Craig went free, Mike would still be the one to answer for it.

Jerry tried to help. He couldn't discuss any testimony, but he did say, "Mike, it's going to be a piece of cake. You know your shit." But the encouragement irked Mike. It seemed condescending.

When he took the stand, Mike thought the court officer was looking at him as if he were thinking, Now it's your turn, chump.

The first three rows of the visitors' seating was packed with reporters and court artists.

It's like being in a play, Mike thought. Except there was no script. And instead of reviews there would be a verdict.

All Hochheiser needed to do was discredit one significant statement of Mike's to shake the jury's faith in him.

Just one.

How long have you . . . ? Are you . . . ? Do you have any . . . ?

During the direct, Mike sketched in his credentials and personal history. Hayes then asked him about the night of Craig's confession.

"Did you read to him from what is known as a Miranda card or Miranda warnings?"

"Yes, I did."

"After you read it to him, did there come a time when he signed it?"

"Yes."

"Who . . . was present in the room?"

"Myself, Detective Giorgio, Detective Rosenthal, and Mr. Crimmins."

"Did there come a time when everyone except Detective Giorgio and Craig Crimmins left Captain Burke's office?"

"Yes."

"What caused you and the other detectives to leave the room?"

"Mr. Crimmins had asked Detective Giorgio if he could speak to him alone."

"When you left the room . . . what did you do?"

"I crouched down near the door. The lower part of the door had louvers, and I overheard a conversation."

I crouched down. . . . As Mike said it, he realized that would be the statement Hochheiser would use to try to make a monkey out of him.

"Hello, Detective Struk," Hochheiser said at the start of the cross-examination.

Mike was restrained. "Mr. Hochheiser." He was going to make short answers. One word, if possible. *Yes. No.* He didn't want to give Hochheiser any ammunition.

"Now, did you keep a notebook in this case?" Hochheiser asked.

"Yes," Mike said. "I did."

"And do you have that notebook with you?"

"Yes, I do."

"Could I see the notebook for a moment?" Hochheiser asked.

"Yes," Mike said. He handed it to Hochheiser.

"Do you have any idea how many pages of notes you have in your notebook?" Hochheiser said.

"No, sir," Mike said. "I don't."

"But it is a stenographic notebook, essentially filled with notes of this case. Is that right?"

"Yes, sir."

"Back and front of the pages?" Hochheiser asked.

"On some pages," Mike said.

Hochheiser flipped to a reproduction of the composite of the man Laura Cutler had described.

"It even has a little picture of our old friend here," he said. Hochheiser was taking his time, building toward his point. "You took detailed notes of things that you did in this investigation?" he asked.

"Yes," Mike said.

"Little notes on a day-to-day basis of what you wanted to remind yourself to do?"

"That's possible."

"Check on this porter or see if that porter showed up for work. . . . Right?"

"Yes."

"Name the people . . . you want interview[ed]?"

"Yes, sir."

"Details about what people said, what you hear[d] them say. Is that right?"

"Yes."

"Would it be fair to say there's a lot of details in this notebook?"

"Yes."

"And a lot of the details in this notebook turned out not to be important. Is that right?"

"It's possible. Yes."

"And certainly that which you believed to be important at the time you made note of it. Is that right?"

"Most of which. Yes."

"Could you think of anything that you thought was important that you didn't write down in your notebook?"

"Off-hand, no."

"Where's the part about listening at the door?" Hochheiser asked. "Maybe I missed it. Could you show me in your . . . notebook, where you wrote down all the details about this case, . . . where you listened at the door and . . . heard the critical piece of evidence, which constituted a major break in this case?"

"I didn't write that," Mike said.

"I'm sorry," Hochheiser said, "maybe you wrote it somewhere else. Maybe in an official report . . . later. . . . Perhaps in a DD-5?"

"No," Mike said.

"Before testifying to the grand jury about the events of August 29 and 30, did you tell Mr. Heffernan that you had listened at the door?"

"At that particular preparation?"

"Yes."

"I don't know if it came up at that time."

"He certainly didn't ask you the question in the grand jury, did he?"

"Not according to what I read."

"And, since he didn't ask you that question, you certainly never gave that information to the grand jury, did you?"

"Not to the grand jury."

"So," Hochheiser said, "we don't have it in your notebook."

"No," Mike said.

"We don't have it to Mr. Heffernan just before the grand jury session. Right?"

"Probably not at that time."

"And you filed numerous DD-5's—that's official reports—in this case?"

"Yes, I did."

"But am I correct that there's no mention in this official Police Department report of having heard through the door or in any other fashion what was said to Detective Giorgio?"

"I did not write it. That's correct."

"I see," Hochheiser said. "What did you do?"

"I made Mr. Heffernan aware of it that night, that night I overheard it," Mike said.

Hochheiser was suggesting that Mike never listened at the door when Craig first confessed to Jerry—an extravagant claim. To be true, it would mean that not only were Mike and Jerry lying, but so were the detectives who saw Mike at the door. And so was Heffernan, since Mike told him what had happened right after the event.

If Hochheiser's version of what happened the night Craig confessed were true, it would mean there had been a conspiracy to frame Craig involving so many people and so unwieldy it would not have been worth the risk. But it was the best strategy the defense could use to discredit the confession.

"What are the louvers like on that door?" Hochheiser asked.

"It's in the lower half of the door," Mike said. "They run horizontal."

"In other words, if we can divide the door in two parts, the top half would be plain steel—"

"I believe it's a full door."

"—and the bottom half would be the louver part you're talking about."

"That's right."

"So that [would] be like a normal seven-foot door—or whatever height doors are?"

"That would be correct."

"So in order to listen at the louver, you would have to bend down like this." Hochheiser demonstrated. "Is that it?"

"It depends on how tall you are," Mike said.

"How tall are you?" Hochheiser asked.

"Six foot two."

"Okay. Did you have to put your knees on the floor to listen?"

"No."

"So you could just bend down without putting your knees on the floor. Right?"

"No."

"Well, how did you do it?" Hochheiser asked.

Here it comes, Mike thought. Monkey-on-a-string time.

"Would you show us how you did it?" Hochheiser said. "With the court's permission, would you indicate to us what position you took to listen at the door?"

Mike hunkered down.

"I was squatting like this," he said.

"Your honor," Hochheiser interrupted Mike's performance, "could the witness come in front of the jury so we can all see him describing it."

So we can all see him.

Mike left the witness stand and stood facing the jury box.

"The louvers would have been here," Mike said, pointing about knee-level. "And I was squatting—" Mike squatted. "—like that."

I hate this, Mike thought.

"Squatting like that," Hochheiser said. "And the louvers would be approximately near your ear?"

Mike straightened up.

"That's right," he said.

"Could we describe it for the record, your honor?" Hayes asked. "The officer or Mr. Hochheiser?"

"Why don't you describe it," Hochheiser said to Hayes.

"Officer," Hayes said, "would you get back to the position you were in?"

Give me a break, Roger, Mike thought.

"Yes," he said.

"The officer has one knee completely bent," Hayes said. "His other knee is bent. He is—"

"He is on the flat of his right foot," Hochheiser interjected, "and he is on the toe of his left foot."

"I would state the lowest portion of his anatomy is approximately a foot from the floor, your honor," Hayes said. To Mike, he said, "Can you show us how your head was at the louvers, officer?"

Mike had kept his head up so he wouldn't look too foolish. Now, he ducked.

"Approximately like this," he said.

"Approximately—would you say eight inches to a foot above the height of the jury rail, Mr. Hochheiser?" Hayes asked. "Is that accurate?"

Hayes and Hochheiser discussed how high Mike's head was, how high the jury rail was. Mike crouched.

"May I stand up?" Mike asked.

"Yes," Hochheiser said.

Mike returned to the witness stand. He had never had a more unpleasant time testifying, but he had maintained his dignity.

In the midst of questioning Mike about how he had eavesdropped on Jerry and Craig, Hochheiser took a detour that led to the turning point in Mike's testimony.

"There comes a time, does there not, after a person is arrested that he is brought to court?" Hochheiser asked.

"Yes," Mike said. "There is."

"All right. Now, when you come into court, you sign and swear to a statement, . . . called a complaint?"

"Yes."

"Now, in the complaint that you signed, you swore, did you not, that you were informed by a person known to the district attorney and yourself that Craig Crimmins committed the murder? Isn't that what you said?"

"Are you talking about the terminology on the complaint?"

"Yeah. I'm talking about the statement that you swore to under oath when you first brought . . . [Craig] to court. I ask you to look at that"—Hochheiser gave Mike a copy of the complaint—"and see if you did not swear that you were charging him with murder based upon the following information: that you are informed by a person known to the district attorney and to yourself that Craig Crimmins committed the crime?"

"Yes," Mike said.

"Okay," Hochheiser said. "Now, who is that person?"

"Craig Crimmins," Mike said.

Hochheiser picked at Mike's answer.

How many times had Mike signed complaints? Usually, when a case is based on a confession, doesn't the complaint say that? Why the coy wording in this instance? Hochheiser was trying to prove that Craig had been arrested not because of his confession, but because of Laura Cutler's composite, which he believed didn't look anything like Craig.

The moment was comparable to when Hochheiser had questioned Jerry about the copy of his notebook. He apparently thought he had Mike mousetrapped.

"If the message that you were trying to convey to the judge —that you swore to in that complaint—was that you wished to charge this person in that complaint based on his own statement, wouldn't you simply say so?" Hochheiser asked.

Mike's answer was as effective as Jerry's had been. "That is not my wording, Mr. Hochheiser." The complaint had been written—Mike believed—by Heffernan, which was a customary procedure. Complaints—Mike explained—were "usually prepared by a DA and . . . signed by the arresting officer."

Hochheiser had been attacking Mike for something Mike had not done.

The language of the complaint. The language of the confession. During the trial Hochheiser returned again and again to the matter of language. Were there words and phrases in the confession Craig wouldn't use, but Jerry—if he had manufactured the confession—would?

Craig had said, "I seen her at the back elevator, number 12."

When Hochheiser had questioned Jerry, he'd asked if Jerry knew the elevator's identifying number.

"Yes," Jerry had said.

"Did you ever meet any stagehand that knew the numbers of the elevators?" Hochheiser had asked.

"I am fairly certain some of them do," Jerry had said.

"But as a matter of fact, sir," Hochheiser had said, didn't the stagehands refer to elevators not by number but by location? Upstage, downstage. Left, right.

"Yes," Jerry had said.

The confession says *C deck*. Didn't the stagehands usually refer to the floor at the Met as *levels?* Wasn't it the cops who usually refer to the floor at the precinct as *decks?*

In Mike's notes of the August 29–30 interview, he'd written that when Craig heard Helen asking "another woman" directions, Craig said, "he put his two cents in."

"You don't hear young people using that expression anymore," Hochheiser said to Mike.

"What kind of expression?" Mike asked.

"Put your two cents in," Hochheiser said.

"I can't answer that," Mike said.

"It's kind of from our generation," Hochheiser said.

"How old are you?" Mike asked.

"Thirty-nine," Hochheiser said. "And I don't use it."

About halfway through Mike's testimony, Hochheiser said, "Detective Struk, I think you told us some of the words you heard"—through the louvers in the door to Captain Burke's office—"at the end of the confession. Right?"

"Yes," Mike said.

"What were the words?" Hochheiser asked. "Do you remember?"

"Detective Giorgio said, 'What . . . [did] you decide to do then?' So Crimmins said, 'I decided to leave her. As I was walking away, I heard her pouncing up and down, and that is when it happened. I kicked her off the roof. I kicked her off.' "

"Pouncing?"

"Pouncing."

"Pouncing?"

"Yes."

"It wasn't bouncing up and down, was it?"

"I think it was pouncing."

"Pouncing?" Hochheiser repeated.

"Yes," Mike said.

Hochheiser asserted that Mike never heard *pouncing*, because Craig never said *pouncing*. *Pouncing* was—Hochheiser said—in Jerry's transcription of the confession. Jerry had written the *b* incorrectly, so it looked like a *p*. That's how Mike came up with *pouncing*. He'd read it.

Which proved—according to Hochheiser—that Mike was lying when he said he overheard Craig confessing.

"You never heard anybody say *pouncing*," Hochheiser said. "You never heard anybody say *pouncing*, and you never heard anybody say *bouncing*, did you?"

"I heard a word that sounded very similar to that," Mike said.

"So, that . . . statement, which was said in the most audible and clearest manner of all—the statement itself was not very clear. Was it?"

"I know the flavor of the statement, yes."

"The flavor?"

"Yes," Mike said.

"The flavor," Hochheiser said. "The aroma?"

Hochheiser was saying: This testimony stinks!

But the inappropriateness of the word *pouncing* could just as easily prove Craig really said it. It was only Hochheiser's assertion that Jerry miswrote a *p* for a *b*. If the *p* was in fact what it looked like and the word really was *pouncing*, why would Jerry, if he were inventing the confession, use such an odd word?

And in the throes of confession, Craig may have fused his memory of having pounced on Helen with a memory of her bucking up and down, trying to escape.

Where did the language of the confession come from? Did it betray undue influence? Did it prove coercion? Why didn't Craig ever give what Hochheiser kept calling a narration of the events of the night of the murder?

Like the hearing, the trial was about words.

At the beginning of the investigation, Mike and Jerry believed their professional world was different from the world of the Met: the world of the street versus the world of art.

By the end of their testimony, it was clear that what they had done to solve the case was not that different from what someone does in creating a work of art: They selected relevant details; put them in an order that made sense; and tested their creation against the truth.

24

Dark World Behind Met's Gold Curtain?

The newspapers reveled in the stories of drunk and drugged stagehands.

"When the gold curtain rises on the stage of the Metropolitan Opera House, the audience applauds enthusiastically and the dancers whirl into a world of fantasy," one article said. "Everything is beautiful at the ballet. But the gold doesn't glitter on the other side of the curtain—the side the audience doesn't see. It is a backstage world of rope and pulleys and 600-pound pieces of scenery; a world of burly, sweaty men who work hard and talk rough, and stick together. And, as the trial of former stagehand Craig Crimmins in the slaying of violinist Helen Hagnes Mintiks enters its third week today, the ranks are closing. The stagehands' frustration about publicity from the trial has created a backlash of suspicion, anxiety and resentment."

The press portrayed the Met as though it were the world of

Fritz Lang's *Metropolis* or the future in H. G. Wells's *The Time Machine,* in which an effete overclass lives in an Eden made possible by the work of a brutal underclass. The gods and goddesses drift from their limousines to their seats in the audience while backstage the crew keeps the machinery of paradise running.

But, unlike Lang's and Wells's fantasies, the Met had a middle class, the performers and musicians, who shared artistic values with the audience and the job of putting on the show with the crew. Shared values make better ties than shared work.

There was little the artists could agree on with the stagehands.

One person's refreshment may be another's drunkenness.

"We have to lift thirty-to-forty-foot wings," one stagehand said. "You can't be drunk to do that."

"Sometimes you can smell it on their breath," said a dancer.

One person's heavy schedule may be another's goofing-off.

"We work long hours—from nine A.M. to whenever the show's over at night, fifty hours a week," said another stagehand.

The dancer said crew members "tend to lurk around. Some seem to have a lot of time on their hands." Especially during ballet season, which is so easy compared to opera that it was nicknamed heaven.

And one's flirtation is another's assault.

A wolf whistle or a pat on the fanny might seem a compliment to the stagehand doing it, but could scare the woman receiving it into being " 'more cautious' about the way she dresses and more wary about wandering in the Met's labyrinth of backstage corridors and elevators," as one article said about one of the performers.

The mutual misunderstanding between the artists and the crew was so complete that some crew members didn't believe there was even a conflict.

"Don't go looking for angles that aren't there," one said.

Since many of the performers and musicians came from the working class and aspired to rise into the leisure class, they tended to treat the stagehands—who could have been their fathers, uncles, and brothers and who represented the life they were trying to escape—with contempt or indifference.

No one likes to be treated badly or ignored. The stagehands resented the performers and musicians. And, if this resentment turned savage, it could lead to the kind of viciousness that ended Helen's life. Helen's murder wasn't just a sex crime. It was a class crime as well.

The press couldn't have resisted milking the trial for sensation and pathos. It was a legal soap opera, filled with comedy, rancor, and sentimentality. There was the moment when Hochheiser asked Juan Medina if he had discussed the trial with any of the other detectives, something he was forbidden by law to do. Medina replied that the cops all "said one thing." That Hochheiser was "a good lawyer."

"I knew if I asked long enough, I'd get . . . a compliment like that," Hochheiser said.

When Hochheiser asked Heffernan if he made a note of Mike's saying that he had eavesdropped on Craig's confession, Heffernan said he had made a mental note.

"Where is it?" Hochheiser asked.

"I assumed it is in my head, Mr. Hochheiser," Heffernan said.

Perhaps because Hochheiser was responsible for Heffernan's being taken off the case, Hochheiser and Heffernan didn't get along. They clashed so often, to the delight of the press, that at last the judge told Hochheiser, "There is no need to be rude." Not long after, the judge was forced to say, "Will you stop arguing." But Hochheiser continued to bait Heffernan. Finally the judge told Hochheiser, "Will you please refrain from remarks like that."

"I'm sorry, your honor," Hochheiser said.

"I don't think you're sorry," the judge said. "You keep doing it."

But the high point of the courtroom soap opera came when Hayes argued that the prosecution had shown its case was so strong there was a risk Craig would bolt. The judge decided to revoke Craig's bail.

Hochheiser patted his client on the back.

"Take it easy," he said. "Don't worry."

Craig's girlfriend, Mary Ann Fennell, started to cry. Craig gave his wallet, watch, keys, and loose change to his mother's cousin. He asked Mary Ann, "Do you have any cigarettes?" When she held out a pack, a guard intercepted it, examined it, and passed it on to Craig, who was taken in custody to Riker's Island.

After Craig left the courtroom, Mary Ann said tearfully, "I didn't expect this. I didn't even get a chance to talk to him."

"What he was concerned about most," Hochheiser told the press, "was he wanted to get home in time to see the fight" between Jerry Cooney and Ken Norton.

Every day after the trial recessed, Mike or Jerry would tell Hayes, "We got 'im."

Hayes would answer, "Yeah, we got 'im."

This was their only comment on what they were all going through, a ritual to keep their spirits up.

One day, toward the end of the trial, after one of these exchanges, Jerry told Hayes, "You know, you're not sounding convincing, you son of a bitch."

During the defense case, when Craig's father was claiming that he was brought to the 13th Precinct under false pretenses and isolated from his son, and when Craig's mother was claiming that the cops didn't tell her the truth about Craig's plight, Hayes looked grim.

The only time Hayes left the courtroom looking pleased was after he had cross-examined one of the two psychologists the defense had called. They had testified that Craig suffered from minimal brain dysfunction, which caused him to have a short attention span and a poor memory. He frequently became confused. He couldn't understand certain words or think deeply. Under pressure, he readily agreed with what other people told him. And he suffered blackouts when he drank too much. At least, this was what the defense psychologists claimed.

Because of Craig's mental makeup, the videotaped confession—Hochheiser had said outside the court one evening— "was worth about as much as a tape of an American prisoner of war of the Viet Cong or the Iranians, confessing he is a spy."

But when Hayes questioned one of the defense psychologists, she admitted that Craig had average powers of concentration and recall. Hayes also pointed out that in one of the psychological tests Craig had taken, he described sexual activity as *fooling around*, the same words used in the confession to describe the attempted rape.

Just as Hochheiser could try to prove that the language of the confession was Jerry's, Hayes could try to prove it was Craig's.

And Hayes had reminded the psychologist that in her notes of the tests she had given Craig, she had written, "I feel a bit manipulated. He"—Craig—"may think he is smarter than others, as a defense." That didn't sound like someone who was dependent, passive, and pliable.

A psychiatrist Hayes called during the rebuttal said that Craig exhibited "no irregularity in his thinking," and that there was nothing in the tests he took that would indicate he was extraordinarily suggestible.

Hayes had been in a state of gloom so long that Jerry had begun to worry. When he finally came out of the courtroom smiling, Jerry thought, Thank God!

With a few exceptions, the press continued to tilt toward Craig. *Met Suspect's Devoted Mom Prays For Her 'Innocent Boy,'* one headline said. The article, written by Cynthia Fagen of the New York *Post,* began, "For 14 hellish days Dolores Higgins, the mother of accused Met Opera murderer Craig Crimmins, has paced alone outside the ninth-floor courtroom and prayed that soon she will be able to embrace him without the cold shadow of prison bars." Fagen quoted Craig's mother as saying, "I'll never believe my son is guilty of this crime. I'm his mother and I know my son." She talked about how Craig enjoyed "simple things like playing stickball and collecting miniature cars," how it broke her heart to see what a slow learner he was, and how he always remembered to get birthday and Mother's Day cards. "Mrs. Higgins carries rosary beads in her handbag," the article continued. "For her, the hard part is having to endure the damaging testimony relatives relay to her during frequent breaks in the trial." Fagen ended the article with Mrs. Higgins clutching her coffee cup and "pulling nervously on a cigarette."

Even Heather Bernard of Channel 4, who Jerry thought had been giving him favorable coverage, seemed to turn on him.

"Your friend Heather," a co-worker said to Jerry after Heffernan's testimony. "The one who calls you 'The Smiling Detective.' She really fucked you. Stuck it right up your ass."

Jerry was told she had reported that the confession was given in a question-and-answer format because Jerry, not Craig, had wanted to do it that way.

The next day, when Jerry entered the hallway outside the courtroom, Heather Bernard got off the windowsill where she had been sitting and started to approach. Jerry froze her in her tracks. The Smiling Detective had stopped smiling.

In his charge to the jury, the judge said, "Consider only the testimony—both on direct and cross-examination, any stipulations agreed upon, and the exhibits received in evidence. You are to determine whether and to what extent you believe or do not believe each of the witnesses. There are various guidelines to help you in making these credibility determinations, although your best weapon is probably common sense. You should consider the conduct, appearance, and demeanor of each witness on the witness stand, meaning, of course, his or her frankness or lack of frankness, inconsistencies, if any, between his testimony and any previous statements he may have made, his character as indicated by his past history and conduct, any possible motive or lack of motive he may have had for testifying the way he did, any interest or lack of interest he may have in the outcome of the trial, any relationship with or feeling for or against the defendant which he may have, the factual probability or improbability of his testimony, and his opportunity for observation or acquisition of information with respect to the matters about which he testified.

"Some of the witnesses as you know were police officers and are police officers. You use the same yardstick in measuring the credibility of a police officer as that of any other witness. His testimony must not be arbitrarily accepted nor arbitrarily rejected merely because he is a member of the police force. Assess it as you would that of any other witness.

"Is he telling the truth?"

Denzer reminded the jury that Craig was innocent "until, if the time comes, you are convinced beyond a reasonable doubt that he is guilty."

Of the three counts Craig was charged with, Denzer submit-

ted to the jury only two: the first count, murder in the second
degree, intentional murder, and the second count, murder
while committing a felony.

Felony murder was also a form of second-degree murder, but
unlike the crime in the first count, the killing was not neces-
sarily intentional.

He threw out the third count: the rape charge.

"The fact that I am not submitting the third count to you is
of no significance," Denzer said. "This omission provides no
basis whatever for speculation that it implies some failure of
proof or defect in the two charges before you." Helen had been
killed, but there was no evidence she had been raped.

The two counts, murder in the second degree and murder
while committing a felony, had to be considered separately. For
Craig to be guilty of the first count, the jury had to believe
beyond a reasonable doubt that on the night of July 23 Helen
was killed in a fall from the Met roof, that Craig caused the
fall, and that Craig intended to kill her. For Craig to be guilty
of the second count, the jury had to believe beyond a reasonable doubt that Helen was killed in the fall, that Craig had *tried*
to rape Helen, and that, whether or not he meant to kill her, he
caused her to fall as he was trying to escape from the scene of
the rape.

Craig could be guilty of one and not the other. Guilty of
both. Or not guilty of both.

It worried Mike and Jerry that Denzer had thrown out the
rape charge. The judge had been quoted as saying that, if the
jury found Craig not guilty on the first count, he didn't think
they would find him guilty on the second count.

"Why didn't you argue more?" Jerry asked Hayes.

"Can we sit in the court for the verdict?" Mike asked.

Absolutely not, Hayes said. You wait in the witness room.

Jerry smoked cigarettes. Mike smoked cigars. They drank coffee. Although, now that the jury had been charged, they could talk about the trial, they didn't. By the end of the day, after deliberating for five and a half hours, the jury had not come to a verdict. The next day, June 4, at two fifty-four in the afternoon, after deliberating for three and a half hours, the jurors reentered the courtroom. They took their seats in the jury box.

Hochheiser had told Craig's family to stay calm, "no matter what happens."

The forewoman stood and read the verdict.

On the first count, intentional murder, the jury found Craig Crimmins not guilty.

"Oh, my God," Craig's mother cried.

On the second count, felony murder, the jury found Craig Crimmins guilty.

The swinging doors of the witness room flew open, booming against the wall. Reporters rushed in. Everyone was shouting. Mike and Jerry kept repeating, "No comment. No comment." They couldn't figure out what the verdict was.

One of the female reporters who had been most hostile to Mike during the trial threw her arms around his neck, said, "Great job," and kissed him.

Hayes appeared, caught Mike and Jerry's attention, and, grinning, said, "We got 'im."

Craig faced a minimum sentence of fifteen years to life.

"They're wrong," Mary Ann Fennell sobbed. "He didn't do it."

In the car, on her way home, she fainted and had to be taken to Beekman Downtown Hospital.

"I feel very bad," Marty Higgins said. "There's nothing more I can say. It's like we lost a kid. We did everything possible. We had a good lawyer, but twelve people didn't believe him." He added that they would stand by Craig "for the rest of our lives."

Craig's mother wept.

When he heard the news, a spokesman for Helen's parents said, "I hope he never gets out."

Helen's sister said, "Oh, wow. That's great. I guess I'm relieved that the justice system has carried through and that it is at an end now. I don't know if I can ever get over Helen's death. It's a hard and frightening thing to deal with."

Janis heard the news on the radio.

"Everything is over," he said.

In the hallway outside the court, Heather Bernard of Channel 4 was trying to reach Jerry for a statement. Jerry noticed her asking people to step aside, as she worked her way through the crowd with her cameraman. Just as she was about to shoot, Irene Cornell of WCBS came over.

I'd like to talk to the detective, she said.

No, no, Heather Bernard said. The whole crew is ready. Would you step out of the way?

No, Irene Cornell said. I won't step out of the way. Detective Giorgio, do you want to do the film footage first?

Jerry thought Irene Cornell had been giving him favorable coverage. And he remembered how Heather Bernard had said that *he* had wanted the question-and-answer format for the confession.

Jerry turned to Irene Cornell. "I want to talk to you."

The verdict—Hayes told the press—vindicated the police.

"This will end once and for all any questions about police conduct in this case," Hayes said.

When Craig first heard the verdict, he had turned to his family and furrowed his brow.

"He doesn't really demonstrate a lot of outward emotion," Hochheiser later said to the press. "Obviously, he felt awful about it."

"I think he was in shock from beginning to end," Ed Crimmins said.

When he was taken to Riker's Island, Craig cried in his cell.

"Oh, he's pretty shaken up," Ed Crimmins said, after talking to him on the telephone. "He was pretty bad."

Craig hadn't cried since he was a baby, Craig's father said.

Craig hated the prison food. He bought fifteen pounds of potato chips.

"I think that's what he's living on," his father said.

He was put in the prison infirmary, where he was placed on a suicide watch. His only companion was Mark David Chapman, the man who had murdered John Lennon. Although Craig helped shave Chapman's head, they didn't get along. Craig complained that Chapman spent all his time reading *Catcher in the Rye* and listening to Lennon's records. He called Chapman "a nut case." Chapman complained about Craig's chain-smoking and finally went berserk. They were separated. Chapman was transferred to Ossining Correctional Facility.

Two days after the verdict had been handed down, the press turned on Craig. He was now "the baby-faced killer," who would have been "nailed . . . faster" if the prosecution had used some "blistering evidence" it had chosen not to bring into court.

Craig was sentenced on September 2, 1981.

About three hundred spectators crowded into the courtroom. On one side, three rows were filled with Craig's family and friends. On the other, Mike, Jerry, and the detectives who had worked on the case sat in one row. Neither Helen's family nor friends were there.

Craig rubbed his eyes and, when Hayes was describing Helen, tapped his left foot. When he had a chance to address the court, Craig said, "I'd like to thank my parents, my girlfriend Mary Ann, my family, friends, and my lawyers for their help and support, and I hope to return home soon some day to repay them."

Jerry passed Mike a note with his guess about the sentence: fifteen years to life. Mike's guess was twenty-two years.

After talking a little about the nearly one hundred letters Craig's supporters had written, pleading for the minimum sentence, Denzer said, "This homicide was a most unusual one, unusual with respect to the place of its commission and the manner of its commission and the people involved. It may be characterized as bizarre, and many, I am sure, would use the adjective 'horrifying.' "

He described what Craig had done to Helen: how he had attacked her, made her undress, tried to rape her, walked her around the Met, and finally killed her to eliminate the only witness to his crime.

"Throughout this case," he said, "I could not help but sense an unusually strong undercurrent of public anger, perhaps rage or fury would be a more appropriate word, over this crime. I have been trying to pinpoint the cause of this community anger, not entirely successfully. Undoubtedly, it stems in part from the underlying facts I have just mentioned, relating to the nature of and the motive for the killing. Also, I think the character of the victim has something to do with it."

Helen—he said—was gifted, attractive, and amiable.

But, as he said, "Law and justice do not gauge the serious-ness of a homicide by the caliber of the deceased victim. A dissolute victim has just as much a right to live as an honorable person of fine reputation. The punishment for homicide is not imposed in accordance with such distinctions."

Craig's mother chewed on her left forefinger.

Denzer said he would not sentence Craig to the maximum term of twenty-five years to life. That penalty should be re-served for killers who had a brutal history.

Denzer also did not sentence Craig to the minimum: fifteen years to life.

He sentenced Craig to twenty years to life. Craig would have to serve twenty years before being eligible for parole. It was the stiffest sentence anyone could recall Denzer ever giving.

When Mike and Jerry went to the Metropolitan Improve-ment Company to celebrate, the bartender asked them for a photograph. They chose one that included them both, equally prominent. And, when they brought it in, it was put up on the wall, the Hall of Fame.

Months after Craig was sentenced, Mike and Jerry returned to the Met. The backstage, which once had baffled them with its complicated twists and crossovers, now seemed as familiar as some childhood haunt—and as distant, part of their past. They walked through the corridor to elevator 12, ascended to the second floor, went along the hall, down the stairs to C level, and up to the roof, the route Craig had taken Helen; but the intensity that used to heighten their visits to the Met was miss-ing. They were just on a tour of a building.

For almost two years, they had been bound to Craig and Helen and each other in a public drama. But that show was over. What they all had in common, the investigation and trial, no longer connected them. They were like actors in a long-running celebrated play that had ended. They felt a little let down, deprived of something that had temporarily given their lives shape and consequence. Both Mike and Jerry understood that they might never again work on as important a case. The murder at the Met could be the high point of their careers.

They left the Met. In the vest-pocket park across from Lincoln Center, the statue of Dante, green as a dollar bill, loomed over some kids who were hanging around, their boom-boxes rapping out music. Across the street, limousines glided up the ramp to Lincoln Center and discharged passengers. Mike and Jerry stopped for a moment in the park. On the statue's pedestal, someone had spray-painted an obscenity.